Women in Nazi Germany

Women in Nazi Germany

Jill Stephenson

An imprint of **Pearson Education**

Harlow, England · London · New York · Reading, Massachusetts · San Francisco · Toronto · Don Mills, Ontario · Sydney
Tokyo · Singapore · Hong Kong · Seoul · Taipei · Cape Town · Madrid · Mexico City · Amsterdam · Munich · Paris · Milan

Pearson Education Limited

Head Office:
Edinburgh Gate
Harlow CM20 2JE
Tel: +44 (0)1279 623623
Fax: +44 (0)1279 431059

London Office:
128 Long Acre
London WC2E 9AN
Tel: +44 (0)20 7447 2000
Fax: +44 (0)20 7240 5771
Website: www.history-minds.com

First published in Great Britain in 2001

ISBN 0 582 41836 4

British Library Cataloguing in Publication Data
A CIP catalogue record for this book can be obtained from the British Library

10 9 8 7 6 5 4 3 2 1

Typeset in 9.5/15pt Sabon Roman by Graphicraft Limited, Hong Kong
Printed and bound in Great Britain by

The Publishers' policy is to use paper manufactured from sustainable forests.

Esmonde M. Robertson
In memoriam

Contents

List of tables   x
List of maps   x
Author's acknowledgements   xi
Publisher's acknowledgements   xii
Chronology   xiii
Maps   xviii

PART ONE: INTRODUCTION   1

1   German women and National Socialism   3

    Introduction   3
    The Nazis' inheritance   6
    Who were 'women in Nazi Germany'?   11
    Nazi ideology and its limitations   16

PART TWO: WOMEN IN THE RACIAL STATE   21

2   Reproduction, family, sexuality   23

    Reproduction as racial policy   23
    Marriage and motherhood in 'valuable' families   27
    Motherhood in 'hereditarily unhealthy' and 'asocial'
    families   33
    Birth control: contraception and abortion   37
    'Sexual deviants': single mothers, lesbians, prostitutes   40
    Wartime marriages and wartime liaisons   46

3   Women at work   50

    Patterns of employment from depression to war   50
    The employment question in wartime   55
    The modern economy: industry   58

The modern economy: white-collar and clerical work   61
The modern economy: the professions   63
The traditional economy: domestic service   65
The traditional economy: small-scale farming   67

4 Education, socialization, organization   70

Education and opportunity   70
Youth organizations   75
Service schemes   79
Non-Nazi women's organizations   82
Nazi women's organizations: growth and 'co-ordination'   83
Nazi 'women's work', 1934–39   88

5 The crisis of war   94

War on the home front   94
Bombing of towns   96
Consumers and the 'black market'   97
Migrants, evacuees and refugees   100
Nazi women at war   103
The last days of the war   106

6 Opponents, perpetrators and the persecuted   109

Opposition and reprisals   109
Perpetrators: warders, professionals, denunciators   112
The persecuted: non-'Aryan' women   116
The persecuted: inmates of prisons and the camps   118
The persecuted: non-German women workers   121
Can women be classed as either victims or
perpetrators?   124

PART THREE: ASSESSMENT   129

7 Three issues: class, empowerment and
international comparisons   131

The salience of class in Nazi Germany   131
Was there anything 'emancipatory' about the Nazi
women's organizations?   133

Were women in Nazi Germany discriminated against
to a greater extent than women elsewhere?   136

PART FOUR: DOCUMENTS   139

Glossary   181
Who's who   184
References   186
Guide to further reading   195
Index   199

List of tables

1.1 Infant mortality, 1905, 1913, 1930 and 1933–40   7

1.2 Women's marital status in 1933   11

1.3 Religious affiliation of Germans in 1933   11

2.1 Marriages and live and illegitimate births, 1900, 1905, 1910 and 1913–41   24

3.1 Employment in 1932   51

3.2 The number of women working in industry, 1933–38   53

3.3 The number of employed married women, 1925, 1933 and 1939   54

4.1 Numbers in the women's Labour Service in selected months in 1934   80

4.2 Number of girls starting their *Pflichtjahr* in 1940   81

4.3 The number of NSF functionaries *c.* 1939 (in the *Altreich*)   84

List of maps

1 Germany by its borders of 1937 – the *Altreich*   xviii

2 Greater Germany in August 1939   xix

3 The Greater German Reich at its height, 1942   xx

Author's acknowledgements

When I began research on women in Nazi Germany in the mid-1960s, the subject looked insufficiently substantial for a PhD thesis. This time, given the amount of work that has been done in the intervening decades, it has been extremely difficult to condense the subject into a small book. The many debts which I have incurred over thirty-five years have also expanded. I would particularly like to thank the Librarian of the German Historical Institute, London, for her efficient and friendly assistance. Additionally, the University of Edinburgh's library staff have willingly met my requests.

Various colleagues have encouraged me over the years, especially at the start of my research and then in later periods of self-doubt. I would like to mention particularly John Fout, Mary Fulbrook, Liz Harvey, Michael Kater, Ian Kershaw, Victor Kiernan, Arthur Marwick, the late Tim Mason, Beate Meyer, Robert Moeller, Tony Nicholls, Richard Overy, Cornelie Usborne. To all of them, I am grateful. I owe a special debt to Liz Harvey and Jim McMillan for reading parts of the text in draft and offering helpful comments. The errors and shortcomings that remain are entirely my responsibility.

My husband, Steve, has been remarkably patient when I have been in intolerant (and intolerable) writing mode.

My greatest debt is to the late Esmonde Robertson. He suggested to me, in 1966, that I should take this subject for my PhD thesis, at a time when most historians of modern Germany were concerned with political and diplomatic history. Without his inspiration, I would never have thought of the subject; without his encouragement, I would not have had the confidence to pursue it. This book is dedicated to his memory.

Publisher's acknowledgements

We are grateful to the following for permission to reproduce copyright material:

Centaurus Verlags GmbH & Co KG for an extract from *Verrat für die Volksgemeinschaft. Denunziantinnen im Dritten Reich* by R. Wolters; Institut für Zeitgeschichte Archiv (Munich) for extracts from a letter to Field Marshal Keitel from Himmler, MA 468 ('Labour Development in Wartime') and MA 441/6 ('The Position in German Universities in the Summer Semester of 1942'); Rowohlt Taschenbuch Verlag GmbH for extracts from *Alltag unterm Hakenkreuz* by Harald Focke and Uwe Reimer, © 1979 by Rowohlt Taschenbuch Verlag GmbH, Reinbek bei Hamburg; Silberburg-Verlag Titus Haussermann GmbH for extracts from *Die Hitlerfahn' muss weg! Zwanzig dramatische Stationen in einer schwäbischen Kleinstadt* by U. Rothfuss and *Als Krankenschwester in KZ Theresienstadt. Erinnerungen einer Ulmer Judin* by R. Weglein; and the Stuttgart Kulturamt-Stadarchiv for extracts from *Chronik der Stadt Stuttgart 1933–1945* edited by Kurt Leipner.

Tables 1.2, 1.3 and 4.1 from *Statistisches Reichsamt: Statistisches Jahrbuch für das Deutsche Reich, 1935* and Table 4.2 from *Statistisches Reichsamt: Statistisches Jahrbuch für das Deutsche Reich, 1941/42* reprinted by permission of Statistisches Bundesamt.

In some cases we have been unable to trace the owners of copyright material and we would appreciate any information that would enable us to do so.

Chronology

1919

9 January
Founding of the *Deutsche Arbeiterpartei* (German Workers' Party) (from February 1920, the NSDAP) in Munich.

28 June
German delegation signs the Versailles Treaty in Paris.

1920

24 February
NSDAP's 25-point programme published.

1921

January
NSDAP resolves to bar women from political life.

1926

May
Reform of the 1871 Criminal Code's provisions on abortion.

1928

January
Elsbeth Zander's *Deutscher Frauenorden* affiliates to the NSDAP.

1929

October
US stock market crash unleashes the great depression.

1930

15 September
Reichstag election gives the NSDAP 6.4 million votes, 107 seats.

1931

1 October
Founding of the *NS-Frauenschaft* as the Nazi women's group.

1932

30 May
Law permits the dismissal of married women public employees.

July	BDM assigned a monopoly of Nazi girls' organization.
31 July	*Reichstag* election gives the NSDAP 13.75 million votes, 230 seats.
6 November	*Reichstag* election gives the NSDAP 11.74 million votes, 192 seats.

1933

30 January	Hitler appointed Chancellor of Germany.
27 February	*Reichstag* building set on fire.
28 February	Law for the Protection of the People and the State suspends some civil rights.
5 March	*Reichstag* election gives the NSDAP 17.28 million votes, 288 seats.
1 April	First official boycott of Jewish-owned shops and businesses.
7 April	Law for the Restoration of the Professional Civil Service discriminates against non-'Aryans' and political opponents.
25 April	Law to Combat the Surplus in German Schools and Colleges discriminates against Jews.
15 May	*Bund deutscher Frauenvereine* dissolves itself.
1 June	Law to Reduce Unemployment introduces marriage loans.
20 June	Order decrees the cancellation of one quarter of a marriage loan on the birth of a child.
30 June	Law discriminates against women in the public service.
14 July	The one-party state declared; law permits compulsory sterilization.
20 July	Concordat between Hitler's regime and the Vatican formally signed.
5 December	Decree orders doctors to report candidates for sterilization.
28 December	Decree restricts women to 10 percent of student body. This is not enforced.

1934

24 February	Gertrud Scholtz-Klink becomes leader of the NSF and DFW.

May	National Mothers' Service of the DFW created.
November	Honour cards for mothers of large families introduced; Gertrud Scholtz-Klink appointed *Reichsfrauenführerin*.

1935

16 March	Decree introduces military conscription for men.
15 September	Nuremberg Laws deprive Jews of German citizenship and civil rights.
18 October	Marriage Health Law enacted.

1936

March	Decree excludes Jewish large families from receiving family allowances.
August	Hitler rules that women lawyers may not become judges or barristers.
September	Four Year Plan for the economy announced.
1 December	Law on the Hitler Youth assigns to it the organization of all German young people.

1937

May	Order that single women can choose to be addressed as 'Frau' (Mrs) rather than 'Fräulein' (Miss).
July	Hitler decrees that, other than exceptionally, only men should be appointed to the highest administrative posts.
3 November	Change in the Marriage Loan law – the wife must be in, and remain in, employment.
December	The first Honour Books of the German Family awarded to RdK members.

1938

29 January	New senior schools' curriculum published.
15 February	Göring announces a compulsory year of service (*Pflichtjahr*) in domestic or agricultural work for all women under the age of 25.
13 March	*Anschluss* – the annexation of Austria, making it part of Greater Germany.
6 July	New marriage and divorce law issued.

1 October	The Sudetenland annexed under the Munich Agreement.
9/10 November	*Kristallnacht* – massive official pogrom against Jews in Germany.
November	*Jüdischer Frauenbund* ordered to dissolve itself.
December	The Honour Cross of the German Mother announced.

1939

January	Decree admitting girls with homecraft qualifications to universities, after passing an exam in academic subjects.
25 March	Hitler Youth and BDM membership becomes compulsory.
August	Decree admitting girls with homecraft qualifications only to universities, from Easter 1941.
24 August	Molotov–Ribbentrop non-aggression pact between the USSR and Germany signed.
27 August	Food rationing of some items introduced.
1 September	German armed forces attack Poland.
3 September	Britain and France declare war on Germany.
4 September	Order decreeing compulsory Labour Service for all women aged 17–25. This is not fully enforced.
December	Hess announces the NSDAP's assumption of guardianship of illegitimate children whose fathers perish in the war.

1940

18 June	France surrenders to German forces.

1941

January	The Himmler Ordinance prohibits the production and distribution of contraceptives (but the condom is exempted for the *Wehrmacht*).
22 June	*Wehrmacht* attacks the USSR.
29 July	Decree that female Labour Service conscripts must serve a further six months' Auxiliary War Service.
November	'Postmortem marriage' introduced for fiancées of men killed in military action.
December	The first deportations of German Jews 'to the east'.

1942

28 March	Area bombing starts – Lübeck is attacked.
17 May	Law for the Protection of Mothers in Gainful Employment issued.

1943

24 January	Roosevelt and Churchill issue a declaration demanding the 'unconditional surrender' of German forces.
27 January	Labour conscription for women aged 17–45 introduced.
2 February	German forces surrender at Stalingrad.
9 March	Death penalty introduced for abortionists.
March	Decree that a soldier's adulterous widow may have her pension cancelled as a result of a 'postmortem divorce'.
24 July–2 August	'Operation Gomorrha' – the intensive bombing of Hamburg.
Autumn	Auxiliary War Service women brought into work with the *Wehrmacht*.

1944

20 July	Plot to kill Hitler at Rastenburg fails.
21 October	US army takes Aachen – start of the invasion of western Germany.
22 October	Red Army takes Nemmersdorf, East Prussia – start of the invasion of eastern Germany.

1945

February	Bormann devises a scheme for a 'women's battalion' of the army.
30 April	Hitler commits suicide in his Berlin bunker.
8 May	Surrender of German armed forces to the Allies.

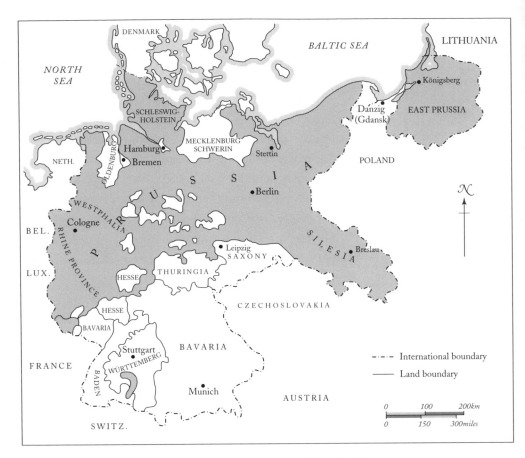

Map 1 Germany by its borders of 1937 – the *Altreich*

Map 2 Greater Germany in August 1939

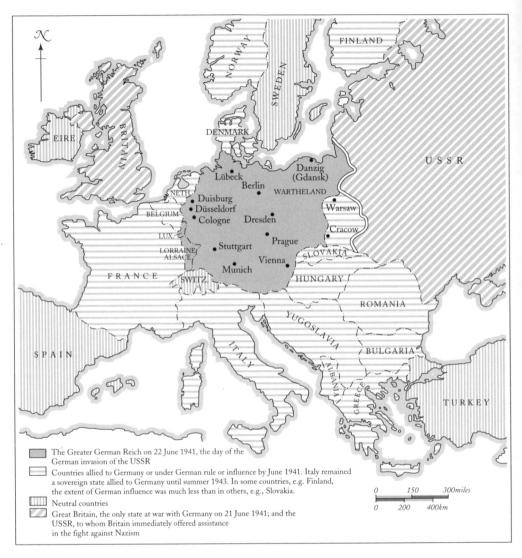

N

FINLAND

NORWAY

SWEDEN

EIRE

BRITAIN

DENMARK

USSR

Lübeck
Berlin
Danzig
(Gdansk)
WARTHELAND
NETH.
Duisburg
Düsseldorf
Cologne
Dresden
Warsaw
BELGIUM
LUX.
Cracow
LORRAINE
ALSACE
Stuttgart
Prague
SLOVAKIA
FRANCE
SWITZ.
Munich
Vienna
HUNGARY
ROMANIA
YUGOSLAVIA
ITALY
SPAIN
BULGARIA
ALBANIA
GREECE
TURKEY

The Greater German Reich on 22 June 1941, the day of the German invasion of the USSR

Countries allied to Germany or under German rule or influence by June 1941. Italy remained a sovereign state allied to Germany until summer 1943. In some countries, e.g. Finland, the extent of German influence was much less than in others, e.g., Slovakia.

Neutral countries

Great Britain, the only state at war with Germany on 21 June 1941; and the USSR, to whom Britain immediately offered assistance in the fight against Nazism

0   150   300miles
0   200   400km

Map 3   The Greater German Reich at its height, 1942

PART ONE

INTRODUCTION

1

German women and National Socialism

Introduction

The explosion of interest in the history of women and gender, triggered in the 1960s, has produced theories about how women's status and opportunities have been determined in recent centuries. The way in which men have accumulated and exercised political, economic and social power, in Judæo-Christian society in particular, has been called 'patriarchy'. In patriarchal society, women are subordinate to men in virtually all areas of both public and private life. This has not merely been an informal arrangement; rather, it has been entrenched in a wide variety of societies by legislation and custom. Religious institutions, including the Christian churches with their male clergy, have sanctified it and contributed to a social system in which the dominance of men and the subordination of women have been enforced by the discipline of a community's acceptance or disapproval of individuals' conduct. There has been no doubt about who has held power, in society and in individual households: men's greater physical strength has been the implicit, and at times the explicit, guarantee of their authority.

Under this cultural code, the normative division of labour between men and women in urban, industrial society has, until recently, been that of men acting as breadwinners and women as homemakers. Where a woman worked in a family concern like a small farm or trade, as in pre-industrial society, she remained responsible for the conduct of the household and for child-rearing. She would normally be excluded from associational, public or political life, arenas reserved for men, although she might belong to gender-segregated groups, mostly those associated with her church. Some historians have viewed these 'separate spheres' – the 'public' and the 'private' spheres – as arenas in which each gender could realize its potential. Where women have largely been confined to the 'private sphere' of the home, and excluded from the 'public sphere' of employment and political and public affairs, they are, some believe, able to construct distinctive centres of power and influence, especially in specifically women's social and organizational life. This has empowered them, as agents responsible for their own destiny, rather than waiting passively as subjects or victims of men wielding power.

These ideas have particular relevance for the study of women in Nazi Germany. Questions have been asked about whether women can be considered accomplices of the Nazis if they supported the NSDAP as voters and/or participated in Nazi women's organizations. Again, economic recovery, with the expansion of the armed forces and heavy industry in the 1930s, followed by war from 1939 to 1945, brought more women into multifarious activities outside the home – into the public sphere. This has provoked claims that the Nazi regime – albeit unintentionally – provided more rather than fewer opportunities for women beyond the private sphere of the home. Further, it has been suggested that, by insisting on gender-segregated organizational life, the Nazis afforded women 'space' to empower themselves and to liberate themselves from traditional constraints. Conversely, it has been argued that women willingly retreated into their traditional domestic space, so that German wives and mothers, by providing a comfortable home for men committing racist atrocities, were themselves guilty of colluding in heinous crimes. By contrast, some have argued that women were particularly and peculiarly victims of the National Socialist system.

These questions of entrenched male dominance, or patriarchy, separate spheres, female agency, and whether women were 'perpetrators or victims' in the Third Reich remain, in varying degrees, controversial. They should be tested against an empirical reconstruction of the past, particularly because during and since the 1930s myths and misinformation have distorted representations of women's position in Nazi Germany. Although some historians have exploded these myths, they persist as the common currency of even educated opinion about the Third Reich, perhaps because the distortion is more sensational than prosaic reality. Suffice it to say that, while National Socialism was an evil creed that brought misery and death to millions of both sexes, we should not assume that in the Third Reich all women were reduced to the status of serfs. Some women – like some men – were treated with appalling and often calculated cruelty, but the majority were not. Women as a gender were discriminated against in various ways in Nazi Germany, but often this reflected the experience of women in other industrially-advanced, patriarchal societies, where lower wages, a marriage bar and extreme underrepresentation in the higher reaches of management, the professions and public life obtained. Where women's experience under Nazism was unusual, indeed unique, was in the realm of reproduction, where woman's function as mother of the species made her distinctively the focus of attention, pressure and, in some cases, both physical and mental cruelty.

This justifies treating 'women in Nazi Germany' as a category, even when 'women's history' is being superseded by 'gender history'. Further, we should confront Eve Rosenhaft's astute challenge that 'women *are* invisible unless we are looking straight at them' (1992: 160, her emphasis). This book, then, looks straight at women, reviewing the roles, functions and room for manoeuvre of women in the Third Reich against how these were conceived and controlled by the Nazi leadership. Nevertheless, women's experience must be assessed in comparison with men's. For example, if 'women' had no political power in Nazi Germany, neither did 'men', in a one-party dictatorship. Even if the only people wielding political power were men, the vast majority of men were politically impotent. Further, given the way in which gender-segregated organizations developed, some women were able to wield within them – and within only them – authority of a kind inaccessible to most men. Yet while there is merit in assessing women's roles and opportunities separately, 'women' should be integrated into history, particularly social history, and should not be 'ghettoized' as they have been, either with an obligatory separate chapter or chapters on 'women' in anthologies or else – even in books by some of the best historians – confined to a couple of paragraphs or pages.

Provided that this does not result in renewed invisibility for women in history, it should be the aim.

The Nazis' inheritance

Like any aspect of the past, 'women in Nazi Germany' should be viewed within its historical context. This does not mean minimizing the extent and wickedness of Nazi atrocities, or 'relativizing' National Socialism by comparing it with other political systems. Simply, whatever programmatic ideas Nazi leaders had, they did not start from scratch. Firstly, they were partly constrained by the German, and European, socio-economic context. The evolution of German society, from being predominantly agrarian *c.* 1870 to being predominantly urban in the 1920s, had profound effects on women's roles and on both sexes' perceptions of them. Nevertheless, traditional attitudes remained entrenched in most sectors of society, and in the views of the highly-influential Christian churches in particular. In the 1933 census, 95 percent of Germans claimed membership of either the Evangelical (Protestant) or Roman Catholic churches – in a ratio of two to one (*Statistisches Jahrbuch*, 1935: 14) – which favoured a domestic, maternal role for women and deplored both increasing resort to contraception to limit family size and the employment of married women outside the home.

Further, Germany did not exist in a vacuum: developments in other countries coloured attitudes and influenced Germans. The example of 'Bolshevism' in the USSR, bringing radical changes in women's status after the October Revolution in 1917, was for some Germans an inspiration but for most an outrage, while the permeation of Germany, like other advanced countries, by American cultural influences in cinema and popular music was, similarly, embraced by some and deplored by others. Traditional opinion, dominant within the urban middle classes and among rural dwellers, found a scapegoat for Germany's ills in the quixotic amalgam of Bolshevik radicalism and licence with American consumerism. The removal of traditional restraints that both symbolized was epitomized by the image of the 'new woman', the 'cigarette-smoking, motorbike-riding, silk-stockinged or tennis-skirted young women out on the streets, in bars or on the sports field' (Harvey, 1997: 281).

In Germany, as in other industrially-advanced countries, fundamental changes had affected women's lives and expectations. In particular, a dramatic reduction in rates of perinatal maternal mortality – death of mothers in childbirth – from *c*. 1900 decisively altered the balance of life expectancy: thus, in the twentieth century women could, on average, expect to live longer than men. Further, medical advances meant fewer women spending years as invalids after some mishap in childbirth. Significantly, also, a consistent decline in infant mortality meant that achieving a desired family size was increasingly predictable, especially with the increasing availability of fairly reliable contraceptives, along with safer abortion techniques. These developments had enormous implications for women's health and aspirations. The possibility of achieving control over their fertility – although for many this was only imperfectly realized – enabled many more women to develop ambitions in the public sphere beyond the realm of home and family.

Table 1.1 Infant mortality, 1905, 1913, 1930 and 1933–40, per 100 live births

1905	1913	1930	1933	1934	1935	1936	1937	1938	1939	1940
20.5	15.1	8.5	7.7	6.6	6.9	6.6	6.4	6.0	6.1	6.3

(*Statistisches Jahrbuch des Deutschen Reiches*: 1914: 33; 1934: 48; 1938: 66; 1941/42: 21*)

The growth of large-scale industry enabled women, like men, to find regular paid work outside the home, with physical strength no longer vital in many mechanized occupations. Further, the invention of the telephone and typewriter in the later nineteenth century created employment opportunities for women – who, allegedly, not only had nimble fingers well-suited to work with a keyboard or switchboard, but also were mentally and psychologically fitted for repetitive tasks. If it was obvious that women and men were physiologically different, in both reproductive functions and physical strength, it seemed to many equally clear that women were psychologically and intellectually different from – and, generally, inferior to – men. Nevertheless, although some university professors claimed that academic study 'is not suitable for the feminine nature' because women were 'always more intuitive and irrational', women students' numbers increased steadily during and after the First World

War, while a few women entered professions for which a university degree was required (Stephenson, 1975a: 42–43). Yet the Civil Code of 1900 gave fathers sole authority in determining the nature and duration of their children's education; therefore even girls showing academic promise might be denied an academic education because it would be 'wasted' when they married. The Weimar Constitution's pledge of equal opportunity for the sexes in education did not override that.

While there are spinsters and widows in any society, adult single women were unusually evident in Germany in the 1920s and 1930s, after the wartime slaughter of around two million men, of whom some 85 percent were aged between 18 and 34, and almost 70 percent were unmarried (Bessel, 1993: 6–10). This 'surplus of women' (Daniel, 1997: 288), as it was inelegantly termed, was therefore prominent among women in their thirties, forties and fifties during the 1930s. Many had never married, but some were young widows of the slain. Further, after 1918 the incidence of divorce was more than double its prewar rate, and it continued rising into the 1930s (Stephenson, 1975: 38, 52). Women who remained or became single during and after the war had to support themselves and perhaps also dependants, and therefore required paid employment, whether they were middle-class or working-class. Only in wealthy homes which escaped impoverishment by the inflation crisis of the early 1920s and the depression from 1929 could an unmarried woman enjoy a life of leisure. The spectacle of substantial numbers of independent single women both at work and pursuing an active social life created anxiety in conservative and church circles, and convinced many that the institution of the family was in crisis, particularly as 'the family' now had fewer children than in the prewar years.

Yet the traditional ideal persisted: a young woman's education would prepare and socialize her for her presumed future as a wife and mother; she would take paid work until she married – as she undoubtedly hoped to, with 'old maid' still a pejorative term (Bergen, 1996: 122) – when she would retire to devote herself to unwaged work for husband, home and family. This was the expectation not merely in the middle classes but also in better-off urban working-class circles. In these families, daughters and sons were nurtured distinctively differently, to accord with the differing futures envisaged for them. Nevertheless, many working-class wives worked from home – perhaps as seamstresses – while a minority would, through poverty, need to work outside the home, possibly in a factory. In families with a small business, like a shop or an artisanal trade, the women – wife, daughters and perhaps sisters – were expected to assist as and when the male proprietor required, without receiving a formal wage. Similarly, in farming families, women worked on the farm. Women working in a family business were considered appendages to their male head of household, and were classed as 'assisting family members' in censuses. In 1925, over four million women, in a total female employed population of 11.5 million, met this description (Winkler, 1977: 195).

Catastrophic depression from 1929 acutely affected women's socio-economic position. With jobs increasingly scarce, there was resentment when women – and especially married women – were employed; they were, allegedly, stealing men's jobs. This was only partly plausible: many women worked in traditionally gender-specific occupations like nursing, childcare, sewing. Cold facts, however, did not appease those who believed that an 'emancipation of women' had occurred in the 1920s, to the detriment of men and at the expense of population growth. If this had some substance, the sadder truth was that employers might dismiss male employees in order to employ women, whose wage rates were lower.

The depression sharpened antagonisms throughout German society, especially between those campaigning for enhanced rights and opportunities for women and those determined to prevent further erosion of traditional gender norms and relations. The economic crisis both disposed more Germans to suspect feminists and put feminists of various kinds on the defensive. The long-standing divisions in their ranks would make it easy for the National Socialists, in government, to suppress their organizations and victimize their leaders, most of whom were middle-aged or elderly single women who met neither society's nor the NSDAP's ideal standard. Those who had always suspected feminists seemed, in the depression, vindicated in their view that the place of a married woman, and, especially, a mother, was in the home.

The image of a married woman's life as that of full-time housewife and mother reflected not only entrenched tradition but also the realities of early twentieth-century life in societies where the traditional division of labour obtained. Certainly, industry mass-produced various consumer goods, but not the 'consumer durables' that revolutionized housekeeping later in the century. Thus running a home in an advanced European country in the 1930s consumed much time and energy. In poorer homes where a wife needed to take paid employment outside, the 'double burden' of work and housework drained her and aged her – like the small farmer's wife – prematurely. The political parties of the left upheld the status quo, if only by default, while those on the centre and right positively defended it against any perceived attack on traditional values.

Thus a husband was proud that his middle-class wife or thrifty working-class wife did not 'go out to work', demonstrating his ability to support her and confirming his status as breadwinner and head of the family. In Germany, his authority was enshrined in the Civil Code, effective from 1900. Certainly, Article 119 of the Weimar Constitution of 1919 declared that, for example, 'marriage is based on the equality of the sexes'. But the Civil Code, the law of the land, stated that a wife was 'entitled and obliged to conduct the family household' and to work in her husband's business 'if this was customary in their social position', while a husband could prevent his wife from working for another (Stephenson, 1975: 17, 13). The Civil Code's clauses detailing a husband's authority and a wife's duties remained effective beyond 1945. Without legislation to amend them, Article 119, and others in the Weimar Constitution declaring equal status and equal rights for women and men, remained aspirations.

This entire social system was undoubtedly both paternalistic and patriarchal; some have argued that it legitimized an 'oppression of women within marriage' (Abrams/Harvey, 1996a: 3). Certainly, the law denied women free choice and subjected them to the will of a father or husband. Where he frustrated a wife's or daughter's aspirations, this was indeed oppressive. But, between the wars, many women were unwilling to work outside the home and regarded marriage and family life as a welcome alternative, whatever its restrictions, repetitive routine and limited horizons. Further, there were marriages, particularly in the urban working class, in which – whatever the law said – the wife was the dominant partner. Nevertheless, men were *formally* invested with power over wives and daughters: how 'oppressive' that was in practice depended on how far they exercised that power. Therefore, partly because it was entrenched in legislation

and custom, and partly because its enforcement depended on unpredictable variables – both the ability and the will of the family's patriarch – the
patriarchal system which the Nazis inherited was intrinsically oppressive.

Who were 'women in Nazi Germany'?

As Claudia Koonz says, commentators 'have grouped women – like members of a religious or ethnic minority – in a single category and viewed
them as a single "problem"' (1976: 663). Yet it cannot be assumed that
the female half of the population has overwhelmingly common interests
in any polity, including Nazi Germany. According to the 1933 census, in
a population of 65,218,461, women accounted for 51.4 percent of the
total, divided according to marital status (Table 1.2). There were various
additional differences: religion; regional loyalty; habitat; employment
status; class. Table 1.3 lists religious affiliation in 1933, per thousand of
the population: few Germans had none. Evangelicals were in a large
minority in southern Germany; there were pockets of Catholics in the
north and east. Germans also had strong regional loyalties, with major

Table 1.2 Women's marital status in 1933

Marital status	Absolute numbers	Percentage of total
Unmarried	15,878,191	47.4
Married	14,316,709	42.7
Widowed	3,026,477	9.0
Divorced	311,522	0.9
Total	33,532,899	100.0

(*Statistisches Reichsamt: Statistisches Jahrbuch für das Deutsche Reich*, 1935: 11)

Table 1.3 Religious affiliation of Germans in 1933

Evangelicals (Protestants)	626.6	(mostly in the north and east)
Roman Catholics	324.6	(mostly in the south and west)
Other Christians	0.5	
Religious Jews	7.7	(overwhelmingly in urban areas)
Others (no religion)	40.6	(overwhelmingly in urban areas)

(*Statistisches Reichsamt: Statistisches Jahrbuch für das Deutsche Reich*, 1935: 14) differences – not to say animosities – between north Germans in Prussia and south Germans in Baden, Bavaria and Württemberg. Small farmers in the south and the Rhineland had little in common with estate owners of the east in Pomerania, Silesia and East Prussia. None of these had much in common with the denizens of towns and cities, the largest of which were Berlin and Hamburg [Map 1].

Most married women were not employed outside the home, but many worked in a family concern – a farm, a small shop, perhaps – as 'assisting family members', as did some single women. But most single women worked outside the home. Employment did not necessarily define a woman's social position as it tended to define a man's. A young woman clerical worker might come from a conservative middle-class home; or, if her father was a skilled manual worker, she might belong to the Social Democratic Party (SPD) milieu. If a lower middle-class shorthand-typist married her businessman or professional boss, her status would rise accordingly. The domestic servant from a rural background might seek a factory job, but she would not have the working-class affiliations of those nurtured in an SPD or KPD (Communist Party) milieu. To what class did a lawyer, like Hilde Benjamin, a KPD activist, belong? She might have said 'to the working class', but to many she was a middle-class professional.

To Nazi leaders, agonizing about class was not irrelevant, but it was entirely subordinate to their preoccupation with 'race'. Humankind, they believed, was divided into different races with varying degrees of value, and they supported pseudo-scientific theories of racial development which were fashionable from *c.* 1900. The 'Aryan race', to which, they believed, most ethnic Germans as well as 'nordic' peoples like the Dutch and Scandinavians belonged, was utterly 'superior', but, equally, it was 'threatened' by 'inferior' races like Slavs and, particularly, Jews. As with men, there were, in their view, 'valuable' women and 'worthless' women. The 'valuable' were of 'Aryan' stock, with no alleged hereditary blemishes through 'Aryan' antecedents marrying and reproducing with people from other races. They also conformed to the Nazi regime's political and social norms. The 'worthless' included not only Jews and Slavs but also Roma and Sinti 'Gypsies', as well as others considered 'inferior' to the 'Aryan race', including Blacks like African-Americans.

Jews were particularly earmarked for discriminatory, degrading and brutal treatment which first marginalized and dispossessed them, and ultimately attempted to exterminate them. The Holocaust, in which six million European Jews were murdered during the Second World War, was a unique atrocity. But 'Aryans', too, could be designated 'worthless' if they were 'asocial' or 'hereditarily unhealthy'. The latter might be profoundly deaf or have poor eyesight, or they might have an acute physical or mental disability requiring institutional care. The 'asocial' might be alcoholics or prostitutes or the 'workshy'; they might be lesbian or gay; 'asocial' women might be single mothers, or they might not order their home and family as Nazi social workers prescribed. Both men and women who were categorized as 'worthless' faced an increasingly bleak future, as laws and other restrictions segregated them from 'valuable' citizens, denied them all state assistance, and prevented them from reproducing. Many would be consigned to a concentration camp, and some would miserably end their days there through starvation, disease, brutality, or else face outright murder in an extermination camp.

Then there were the 'politically unreliable', activists in organizations either associated with the SPD or the KPD, or with pacifist or feminist groups. Feminists of all colours were particular targets of Nazi contempt. But, apart from SPD and KPD leaders and activists, who were brutally persecuted, members of political parties and other groups which had been either doubtful about or hostile to National Socialism before 1933 could, Nazi leaders hoped, be won over, once the leaders who had 'misled' them had either fled abroad or been incarcerated or killed. Treating all who were 'Aryan' and 'hereditarily healthy', and who were not 'asocial', as potentially 'valuable' won the Nazis the enthusiasm of a few and the uncommitted acquiescence of most of the rest – in peacetime, at least. There remained those who could not be reconciled to National Socialism and those whom it alienated with policies which oppressed either them or others with whose plight they identified. Small numbers maintained ties with opposition groups outside and secret networks within Germany, but the ease with which the *Gestapo* (secret state police) uncovered and ruthlessly punished dissidents was a major deterrent. The more prudent turned to 'inner emigration', keeping the faith – whether it was political, religious or simply principled – but outwardly conforming as necessary.

Initial success in the Second World War allowed Nazi leaders to bring newcomers into Germany, including ethnic Germans whose antecedents had for long lived in eastern Europe. After the Molotov–Ribbentrop Pact of August 1939 sealed Poland's fate, these ethnic Germans were 'brought home' from the Baltic States, Romania or Poland to what, to them, was a foreign country, where their women were trained by the Nazi women's organizations to become capable German housewives. Some western Europeans, too, in annexed areas like Alsace, Lorraine and Luxembourg, were regarded as ethnically German. To them also the benefits of citizenship in the Greater German Reich [Map 3] were extended, whether they liked it or not. By contrast, among the millions of foreign workers who were enticed or, increasingly, seized and forced to work in Germany in wartime, a substantial minority were women. Some came from western Europe, but the great majority were from Poland and the USSR [Plate 7]. These new and unprivileged workers in German industry and agriculture were not German women, but they were women in Nazi Germany. Those from eastern Europe, in particular, were often treated with a complete disregard for their health and well-being.

The distinctions drawn between different racial and ethnic groups, between victors and vanquished, between 'responsible' and 'asocial', between 'hereditarily healthy' and 'hereditarily diseased', cut across conventional class barriers. Jewish doctors, lawyers and business proprietors were no less vulnerable than Jewish proletarians. A 'hereditary disease' could affect any family. There were lesbians and gays in all strata of society. Money and connections could perhaps mitigate dangers and penalties in individual cases, but they did not guarantee immunity from harassment. Where class had relevance was in categorizing some 'asocials'. For example, working-class prostitutes and single mothers were more likely to be branded as 'asocial' than their better-off sisters. Many 'asocials' were identified by (middle-class) state social workers – who were often women – who came into contact with people receiving welfare benefits or in foster care; these were more likely to be working-class.

German women in one class did not necessarily – and perhaps did not often – feel solidarity with German women in another class, and did not necessarily feel solidarity with women in their own class but from different circumstances. The part played by female social workers, nurses, teachers and members of the Nazi women's organizations and other party affiliates in marginalizing and persecuting both women and men from anathematized groups in different classes confirms that. There were, then, women who worked within the Nazi system for the Nazi leadership's nefarious goals. Many were perfectly aware of what they were doing, and believed in it wholeheartedly. This included in particular young women who were educated and socialized during the Third Reich.

Nevertheless, this says little about how far women in general supported National Socialism. Certainly, before 1933 millions of women voted for the NSDAP in elections at local, *Land* (regional) and national level, as did millions of men. Voting patterns were fluid during the depression, and some individuals' allegiances changed from one election to another. Women were generally slower to support both the KPD and the NSDAP, as radical parties with a violent public profile. Roman Catholic women often preferred the Catholic parties, the Centre or the Bavarian People's Party, while Protestant middle-class and rural women often supported conservative parties or local peasant parties, respectively. Proletarian women from an SPD or KPD milieu would mostly support the SPD or the KPD, respectively. Nevertheless, in the national elections of July and November 1932, women supported the NSDAP virtually proportionately. As Helen Boak says, 'because of the preponderance of women in the electorate, the NSDAP received more votes from women than from men in some areas before 1932 and throughout the Reich in 1932' (1989: 303).

The reasons for this are various: for both women and men, a vote for the NSDAP was a vote for the charismatic leader, Hitler, or for new solutions to the depression's intractable problems, or for a reassertion of Germany's power after a lost war. Often, people voted NSDAP *against* other parties, in particular the KPD and the SPD, at a time when organized conservative opposition to 'Marxism' seemed in disarray and liberalism had collapsed. For them, Soviet domestic policy from the 1917 Revolution through the first Five Year Plan served as an awful portent of what the left in power might bring. Again, some voters' main motive may have been antisemitic or antifeminist sentiment, or support for policies of 'social hygiene'. Many were voting to destroy the Republic which seemed to have brought only crisis and despair. These considerations, in varying degrees and permutations, prompted both men and women to vote for the NSDAP, and were undoubtedly stronger in motivating most women than any 'gender interest' or distinctive 'women's issues'. That women were, in the end, neither more nor less likely to vote for the NSDAP than men confirms that.

Nazi ideology and its limitations

Was there a National Socialist view of women's nature and role? Given the varieties of Nazi ideology espoused by NSDAP notables, by 1933 there was remarkable unanimity among Nazi leaders about women's nature and role, whatever is said about the 'widely divergent views . . . [of] Nazi writers' (Rupp, 1978: 15). This was perhaps because the primacy of racist population policy in Nazi ideology determined women's place in it: the 'Aryan', 'hereditarily healthy' woman who had not compromised her 'value' by becoming 'asocial' was to marry an equally 'valuable' man and produce several 'valuable' children, to combat Germany's numerical disadvantage compared with its perceived enemies. The Nazi message to women was: be a mother, first, foremost and always, preferably a married mother of several children [Doc. 1a] [Plate 1]. All other aspects of a 'valuable Aryan' woman's life had to accommodate that core value; 'worth-less' women were to be prevented from reproducing [Doc. 3].

Other views were expressed within the NSDAP before 1933, and ardent female Nazi supporters tried, especially in 1933–34, to argue for a less restrictive attitude to enable talented women to progress in a career and even in public life. But these views were doomed in a system based on the *Führerprinzip* (leadership principle), where the views of the NSDAP's supreme leader, the *Führer*, Adolf Hitler, carried incontestable weight. Hitler believed unswervingly that women had no place in public or political life, although, he claimed, that did not mean that women were inferior to men. It was simply, he said, that women and men had un-alterably different natures which determined their differing and com-plementary functions. This was not merely a matter of physiological difference and biological destiny, with woman the bearer and nurturer of the young of the 'race'. In psychological and emotional terms, women were, he said, completely different from men [Doc. 1b]. Many conser-vative Germans could comfortably identify with these views.

Also influential in conditioning Nazi leaders' attitudes to women was the NSDAP's explicitly male chauvinist character which derived partly from the experience of some early members and leaders in the emphatically masculine environment of the armed forces during 1914–18. In the grim years of instability and upheaval after 1918, they recalled with misplaced nostalgia the male bonding of the 'comradeship of the trenches'. For these men, the home front, with women a substantial part of it, had stabbed combatants like themselves in the back. After the – in their view – humiliating peace treaty in 1919, they faced civilian life where politics was democratized and women enfranchised, with some women sitting as representatives in the *Reichstag* (parliament), and a few working as senior bureaucrats or junior ministers at national or *Land* level for the first time.

Before 1933, the NSDAP's public profile was most prominent in its *Reichstag* delegation, numbering 230 at its height between elections in July and November 1932, and in its paramilitary wing, the SA (Storm Troopers). These bodies were exclusively male, because 'actual political campaigning is a man's task. . . . Women are not to be accepted as candidates' in elections (Source 1). While women could join the NSDAP, in true patriarchal fashion they were excluded from leading positions within it, as a matter of principle, in January 1921; their membership remained small, in 1925–32 sinking from eight to five percent of the total (Kater, 1983: 206). But those with a husband, father or brother in the party often worked for their local NSDAP branch without joining. They sewed and cooked for male party activists, nursed the sick or injured among them, and made collections of clothes and other essentials for distribution to needy local people.

This conformed with Hitler's conception of the division of labour, with women permitted some 'womanly' activity outside the family [Plate 2]. It also accorded with Alfred Rosenberg's opaque ideas about the 'polarity' of the sexes as a productive force [Doc. 2]. For some Nazi leaders – the 'blood and soil' agrarian romantics – 'womanly work' included not only caring for men and children but also working in agriculture. Industrialization, urbanization and mechanization had, they said, created a dirty, dangerous, soul-destroying working environment into which women, particularly young single women, had been lured by the prospect of earning a wage [Doc. 4]. Women were more likely to thrive in fresh country air, following the natural rhythms of work on a farm. This view, shared in varying degrees by Rosenberg, Darré and Himmler, among others, ignored the squalor and drudgery of life on many small farms, and contradicted the Nazis' own anxiety about the rigours of life for rural women and their effects on the health of children in rural areas [Doc. 11]. Hitler had some sympathy with these unrealistic views, and they remained influential, even when, from the mid-1930s, economic realities contradicted them.

The views of leading Nazis differed more in detail and emphasis than in substance. The ideal remained the married woman who bore several children and worked contentedly at maintaining a clean and orderly home, shopping thriftily and making limited demands as a consumer, educating her children to be both conscious of their racial identity and eager to engage in a life of service to the 'Aryan' community. The woman who devoted herself unstintingly to these tasks yet still found time to serve her community, through participation in a Nazi women's organiza- tion, could be satisfied that she was both 'conscious of her responsibility' (*verantwortungsbewusst*) to her nation and 'ready to make sacrifices' (*opferbereit*) to further its interests. The idea of a woman's self-sacrifice, devoting herself to others, recurred like a mantra in Nazi leaders' speeches and writings about women. Young unmarried women, especially, were expected to demonstrate their devotion to the community by engaging in service projects of various kinds. In prescribing this life of selflessness and service for 'Aryan' women, Nazi leaders dismissed concepts like 'women's emancipation' and 'feminism' as abhorrent [Doc. 2].

Nazi thinkers rightly claimed that 'emancipation' and 'feminism' were issues which became prominent where liberalism flourished; for them, 'liberal individualism' meant not the enlightened self-determination of each person's identity but the selfish pursuit of a person's or a family's aspirations, regardless of its effect on the community as a whole [Docs 2 and 4]. By contrast with liberals, Nazis – like communists – favoured a collectivist approach, advocating, as Point 24 of the NSDAP's programme of 1920 put it, 'the common interest before self-interest' (Noakes/Pridham, 1983: 16). This really meant: 'what we decide is good for German "Aryans" collectively, at the expense of the rights of the individual, particularly the non-"Aryan" individual'. Yet the ostensible selflessness of their creed attracted many, both before and after 1933, and had particular appeal for some younger Germans who grew to adolescence and adulthood conscious of no other political form than National Socialism. After the hedonism of the 1920s – in cities like Berlin, at least – and the grim desperation of the depression, where it was everyone for him/herself, many young people were fired by a genuine, if woefully misplaced, idealism involving the submission of individual desires to what was, allegedly, the good of the community. Like other Nazi devotees, they embraced the notion of an 'ethnic community' (*Volksgemeinschaft*) whose whole transcended the sum of its parts [Doc. 24]. But this *Volksgemeinschaft* was exclusive as well as inclusive: service to it explicitly involved degradation and cruelty for those who did not meet its distorted criteria.

Despite their explicitly male chauvinist outlook, Nazi leaders argued that 'valuable' women and 'valuable' men were of equal worth – that they were 'equivalent but different' (*gleichwertig aber nicht gleichartig*). The 'difference' lay in both their contrasting natures and their complementary functions [Doc. 1b]. In essence, this affirmed the traditional division of labour, with men dominating the public sphere and women controlling the private sphere, although, as we have seen, the Civil Code gave a husband or father formal authority in the private sphere of home and family. Other potential contradictions became apparent: a mother was 'the first educator of the new generation' (Stephenson, 1975: 45), yet the Nazi intention was to mould a child's primary loyalty through the youth organizations of the NSDAP, even if that involved conflict with the home. And in the Third Reich 'valuable' women would not be restricted to home and family: increasingly, they were expected to demonstrate their politicization by participating in the Nazi women's organizations and in other institutions of the Nazi state, like the Labour Service and the National Socialist People's Welfare organization (NSV) [Docs 20 and 24]. This, rather than participation in a pluralist political system, was the definition of 'active citizen'. In this specious way, it was claimed that women participated in political life in Nazi Germany. In reality, women, like men, were to serve their 'ethnic community' in the manner decreed by their political masters, for goals over which only these masters had jurisdiction.

However high a 'value' Nazi leaders placed on women and however much they flattered them, the intention was to deny them free choice and self-determination. Yet even if their system seems like the ultimate in patriarchal social engineering, it was also true that most men had little in the way of rights; increasingly, by invading the private sphere, it was the state rather than individual patriarchs who determined women's activities and duties, although the Nazi system left wide-ranging discretionary power in the hands of men. All of this applied to 'valuable' women and men, the only ones whom Nazi leaders directly addressed. Those who were regarded as 'worthless' were ignored and excluded from both the obligations and the benefits of membership of the 'people's community' of the 'master race'. This was an integral part of the policy of marginalizing the non-'Aryan', the 'hereditarily unhealthy' and the 'asocial' from Nazified German society, a process which for many would lead to Auschwitz and other sites of human extermination [Plate 11].

PART TWO

WOMEN IN THE RACIAL STATE

2

Reproduction, family, sexuality

Reproduction as racial policy

Since the 1930s, there has been particular interest in Nazi reproductive policies. Contemporary commentators agreed that Nazi policy towards women derived from the belief that women's place was in the home, with a family of several children, and that the public sphere should be reserved for men. Observers emphasized the revocation and denial of the kind of rights which advanced western countries (including Weimar Germany) had extended to women, and the Nazi use of encouragement or even compulsion to remove women from the public sphere and confine them to the private, domestic sphere. When, from the 1960s, historians surveyed Nazi society, they contested these ideas, arguing that, while the pronatalist motive was dominant in Nazi policy towards women, strenuous efforts did not persuade Germans to revert to high pre-1914 levels of fecundity (Table 2.1). The influence of the Cold War shaped the differing views of Marxist and non-Marxist historians. Marxists saw working-class German women as the particular victims of the regime and its capitalist-friendly policies. Non-Marxists identified a mismatch between propaganda and reality, seeing the development of a war economy as crucial in determining Nazi policies towards women. They all accepted the Holocaust as historical fact, and that racial prejudice was inherent in National Socialism. But non-Marxists overwhelmingly considered the majority of 'Aryan', 'politically reliable' and socially-conformist German

Table 2.1   Marriages and live and illegitimate births, 1900, 1905, 1910 and 1913–41

| Year | Per 1,000 of the population | | Live births per 1,000 women of childbearing age | Illegitimate births per 1,000 births |
	Marriages	Live births		
1900	8.5	35.6	*	8.7
1905	8.1	32.9	*	8.5
1910	7.7	29.8	128.0†	9.1
1913	7.7	27.5	*	9.7
1914	6.8	26.8	*	9.8
1915	4.1	20.4	*	11.2
1916	4.1	15.2	*	11.1
1917	4.7	13.9	*	11.5
1918	5.4	14.3	*	13.1
1919	13.4	20.0	*	11.2
1920	14.5	25.9	*	11.4
1921	11.9	25.3	*	10.7
1922	11.2	23.0	90.0	10.7
1923	9.4	21.2	82.3	10.4
1924	7.1	20.6	79.8	10.5
1925	7.7	20.8	80.2	11.9
1926	7.7	19.6	75.4	12.5
1927	8.5	18.4	70.6	12.3
1928	9.2	18.6	71.3	12.3
1929	9.2	18.0	68.7	12.1
1930	8.8	17.6	67.3	12.0
1931	8.0	16.0	62.0	11.8
1932	7.9	15.1	59.5	11.6
1933	9.7	14.7	58.9	10.7
1934	11.1	18.0	73.3	8.6
1935	9.7	18.9	77.2	7.8
1936	9.1	19.0	77.6	7.8
1937	9.1	18.8	77.1	7.7
1938	9.4	19.6	80.9	7.7
1939	11.2	20.4	84.8	7.8
1940	8.8	20.0	84.2	*
1941	7.2	18.6	*	*
1942	7.4	14.9	*	*
1943	7.3	16.0	*	*

* not recorded † for 1910/11

(*Statistisches Jahrbuch des Deutschen Reiches*: 1938: 47; 1941/42: 77; 1952: 36)

women, while most Marxists saw Nazism as an integral part of transnational fascism, bent on suppressing the working class, its organizations and its alleged champion, the USSR.

A change of emphasis in the 1980s placed race and racial policy at the centre of the study of Nazism. This led to subtler nuances, with 'racial persecution' comprehending not only murderous antisemitism but also punitive antipathy towards people of other racial groups and people regarded as 'degenerate', as polluting the collective healthy 'Aryan' body. Thus the Third Reich was not merely 'fascist' and 'antisemitic': it was *The Racial State*, as Burleigh and Wippermann entitled their influential book in 1991. Further, concentration on race fused with the feminist convictions of many women historians. Women were 'the second sex in the Third Reich' (Koonz, 1987: 175–219), with their fate determined by their reproductive capability. The Third Reich was *When Biology Became Destiny*, the title of an anthology published in 1984, in which Gisela Bock's essay, 'Racism and Sexism in Nazi Germany', was fundamental in setting a new agenda:

> most historians seem to agree that . . . women counted merely as mothers who should bear and rear as many children as possible, and that Nazi antifeminism tended to promote, protect and even finance women as childbearers, housewives, and mothers. It seems necessary to challenge various aspects of this . . . , but particularly its neglect of racism. . . . [T]he Nazis were by no means simply interested in raising the number of childbearing women. They were just as bent on excluding many women from bearing and rearing children – and men from begetting them – with sterilization as their principal deterrent. (1984: 273)

Racism and sexism, therefore, were inextricably linked, with implications for every German, and particularly, Bock believes, for every German woman.

Certainly, issues of fertility and reproduction were fundamentally important in Nazi Germany. Selectively interpreting early twentieth-century ideas in biology, eugenics and anthropology, Nazi leaders believed that only a genetically pure 'racial body' would prosper. Thus, state intervention should ensure that only 'valuable' and 'Aryan' Germans married and reproduced, while others should be prevented from reproducing. A battery of legislation tried to identify the 'valuable' and impose procedures to ensure that they, and only they, produced future generations of Germans. Miscegenation – racial mixing through marriage and/or sexual intercourse – was therefore anathema to Nazis. Anyone with parents belonging to different races was regarded as a mongrel fully belonging to neither. For those with some 'Aryan' antecedents, but also either one or two Jewish grandparents, the term *'Mischling'* indicated that s/he was a 'half-caste'.

While the single-mindedness, ruthlessness and inhumanity with which Nazi leaders held these views, and pursued policies based on them entrenching discrimination and persecution, was unique, they were not alone in their concern about population policy, in both qualitative and quantitative terms. In the early twentieth century, eugenics – the science of 'race' improvement – was fashionable, gaining support across the political spectrum in many European countries, including Britain, and in the USA. Eugenists believed that distressing heritable diseases could be eliminated by preventing their carriers from reproducing; some extrapolated from that to suggest that certain *social* characteristics were 'hereditary', and that these could, and should, be eliminated, by a policy of selective sterilization. In 1932, a bill permitting the *voluntary* sterilization of 'hereditarily ill' individuals was drafted but not enacted in Prussia, the largest *Land*. Nazi leaders were not alone in claiming that only the 'valuable' should be permitted to reproduce, and that the 'worthless' should be either persuaded, or even forced, to refrain from reproducing and therefore from contributing to the continuing 'degeneration' of the 'Aryan race': doctors interested in 'social hygiene' agreed. But, although 'social hygiene' was discussed as an integral part of population policy, there was no legislation on it before 1933. Then, Hitler's government hastened to enact legislation entrenching a policy of 'racial hygiene', which included the concerns of 'social hygienists' but stressed the decisiveness of 'race' as an individual's fundamental characteristic.

The aim of selective breeding exacerbated another perceived problem in population policy. In Germany – as in other industrialized countries – the birth rate had, after an initial upsurge, markedly declined. In depression-wracked 1933, there were far fewer births than twenty years earlier (Table 2.1). Many, including liberals and Social Democrats as well as conservatives, were concerned about this sharp demographic decline.

Although it was mitigated by declining infant mortality rates (Table 2.1), exaggerated claims were made about 'the nation dying out' (Stephenson, 1979: 350). In response, Nazi policy aimed to achieve the high levels of fecundity evident before 1914. Therefore, quite apart from the misery inflicted on many individuals, Nazi racial policy hamstrung the regime, because it aimed to increase births while excluding the anathematized from contributing. That is, a smaller pool of potential parents was exhorted to produce a globally larger number of offspring. This explains the urgency with which motherhood in 'valuable' families was promoted.

Marriage and motherhood in 'valuable' families

Government intervention in individuals' reproductive life, along with efforts to monitor and order individuals' conduct, profoundly affected the family. As both Lisa Pine and Elizabeth Heineman argue, the division between the 'public' and 'private' spheres became blurred as a result of 'the Nazis' politicization of and incursions into the family' (Heineman, 1999: 73). With their obsession with 'race', reproduction and selective population growth, with the deployment of social workers to monitor families' conduct [Doc. 7], and with attempts to indoctrinate and control young people especially, the privacy of the 'private sphere' was challenged. How far this succeeded is difficult to estimate, but 'Aryan' families which conformed, or appeared to conform, to Nazi norms probably retained considerable cohesion and privacy. It was particularly difficult – although not impossible – to breach the solidarity of families which were economic units, on farms and in other small businesses, especially in scattered villages. Nevertheless, the establishment of public health offices even in some smaller communities ensured that families, like individuals, which contravened Nazi norms – whether consciously or involuntarily – were subjected to scrutiny and supervision.

With the overwhelming majority of German children born within wedlock (Table 2.1), regulating marriage seemed vital for controlling the 'quality' of reproduction. Essentially, marriage between the 'hereditarily valuable' was to be facilitated while marriages where one or both partners were considered 'unfit' to reproduce, according to the regime's 'race and heredity' criteria, were to be prevented. Thus whether a marriage was 'desirable' or not was a matter of state policy, with individuals' interests subordinate. As a Nazi Women's Group (*NS-Frauenschaft* – NSF) functionary said, 'marriage is not merely a private matter, but one which directly affects the fate of a nation at its very roots' (Stephenson, 1975: 40). Clifford Kirkpatrick was more pungent: 'National Socialism reiterates with crushing conviction that the task of the family is reproduction. For companionate marriage it has nothing but scorn' (1939: 94).

While Nazi conceptions of 'desirable' marriage were already explicit [Doc. 3], the state's position was formally declared in the 'Law for the Protection of the Hereditary Health of the German People' (Marriage Health Law) (18 October 1935). Thereafter, in theory, intending spouses had to obtain a 'Certificate of Suitability for Marriage' signed by a doctor; this was denied to those with serious infectious diseases or 'hereditary illnesses'. Then, to try to prevent miscegenation between 'Aryans' and non-'Aryans', the Nuremberg Laws of 15 September 1935 and subsequent addenda were issued (Noakes/Pridham, 1986: 535–37). A line of demarcation was therefore drawn between those whose marriage was regarded as beneficial to the community and those who had to be prevented from reproducing, but not necessarily from marrying if they could be guaranteed to remain childless [Doc. 8]. On both sides of the line, there was regulation and scrutiny of marriage and divorce, to the extent that Gabriele Czarnowski has written of 'the supervised couple' (1991).

Encouragement to the 'valuable' to marry began with the 'Law to Reduce Unemployment' (1 June 1933) which offered an interest-free loan to couples, provided that both were 'of Aryan descent' and that the woman had a job which she would relinquish on marriage (Noakes/ Pridham, 1986: 451). Reversing the marriage rate's decline was a priority (Table 2.1), and enticing women from employment would, it was hoped, release jobs for unemployed men. Later in June 1933, another law prescribed the cancellation of one quarter of the loan for each child born, with a moratorium on repayments for a year after the birth. Loan-aided couples were therefore encouraged to reproduce, in popular parlance to 'baby off' (*'abkindern'*) the loan, with four children in quick succession cancelling repayments altogether (Mason, 1976, I: 111). Some exploited this, concluding, with one Berlin woman, 'now I just need another baby and I shan't have to pay back any more' (Stephenson, 1975: 46). In later

1933, 37 percent of marriages involved loan-aided couples. The figures fell in 1934–37, probably because requiring women to leave work was a deterrent: in rural Bavaria, for example, lower loan applications reflected a farmer's wife's status as an 'assisting family member'. The *dis*advantage in a farmer's replacing his unwaged wife with a paid labourer was too great. After the revocation, in November 1937, of the requirement that the wife leave work, 1939 saw by far the highest level of loan-aided marriages, in a year with an abnormally high marriage rate (Table 2.1).

One reason for 1939's high marriage rate was that paragraph 55 of the 1938 marriage law introduced 'irretrievable breakdown' as grounds for divorce, whereas previously one partner had to be found 'guilty' of adultery, cruelty or desertion, with the stigma that that implied. Paragraph 55 facilitated the formal ending, without blame, of a marriage whose partners had lived apart for three years. In addition, the new law enshrined growing court practice: divorce was granted for refusal to procreate or resort to illegal means (i.e., abortion) to prevent a birth; and divorce was obtainable on grounds of premature infertility, unless the couple already had 'hereditarily healthy' children. Barely one percent of divorces were sought on these grounds between 1938/39 and 1941. Divorce trial judges began cautiously, mostly reflecting 'the traditional conservative view of marriage' and granting a divorce on grounds of 'guilt'; barely seven percent of divorces in these years were granted for 'irretrievable breakdown', mostly with the husband as petitioner (Czarnowski, 1996: 107–08). The increase in marriages in 1939 was probably partly because partners from these dissolved marriages regularized existing relationships. This accorded with official policy, because these relationships might produce offspring, whereas failed marriages would not. After 1941 more divorces were granted under paragraph 55, probably because of the stresses of war on marriages [Doc. 25]. One NSDAP local branch leader, however, obtained a divorce in 1942 because his wife of four years 'stubbornly refused to join the [Nazi women's organization]' (Staff, 1964: 182–83).

Tim Mason justifiably describes Nazi policy towards 'valuable' mothers as 'multiple exploitation and simultaneous repressive protection' (1976, I: 76). Mothers of 'valuable' families were flattered by propaganda and encouraged by financial and symbolic incentives to boost the birth rate. 'Valuable' young Germans were encouraged to marry and establish a sizable family. This has, however, led to misunderstanding. For example, saying that 'Nazi policy rested on the right of the nation to force women to bear children' (Koonz, 1987: 197) implies that women were forced to bear children. Using the terms 'compulsory motherhood' and 'mother-hood as forced labour' (Bock, 1984: 277, 279; Schupetta, 1981: 314), when they are qualified only obliquely in the context, runs a similar risk. The images evoked are inappropriate to a system in which the 'valuable' were tiresomely persuaded and cajoled in reproductive matters, but not coerced in the way that the 'worthless' routinely were.

The 'repressive protection' involved state supervision of 'valuable' preg-nant women and mothers who were monitored by social workers and midwives. The 'Mother and Child' section of the NSV offered practical advice and assistance [Doc. 5]. For example, in the southwestern town of Lahr (Baden) in 1935, it 'provided over two thousand marks' worth of food and clothing to families . . . [and] also brought to Lahr some 363 children from other parts of Germany and sent 225 Lahr children and twenty mothers on vacation' (Rinderle/Norling, 1993: 163). The Nazi women's organizations ran courses in modern childcare, which young women were strongly encouraged to attend [Doc. 4]. By March 1939, over 1.7 million women had attended such courses, out of an adult female population of about 30 million (Stephenson, 1981: 164–65).

As for incentives, the marriage loan was particularly attractive to poorer couples, the majority of applicants for it, although the discounts persuaded few to incur the long-term cost of several children. The government's reluctance to finance its policies became clear when the first family allowances were introduced: in 1935, a one-off grant was paid – like the marriage loan, in vouchers, not cash – to fathers of needy 'valuable' families with at least six children aged under sixteen. Recurrent cash allowances were introduced for low-income 'valuable' families in 1936, initially for only the fifth and subsequent children. Finally, from 1938 allowances were paid for the third and subsequent children, to try to breach the standard two-child family pattern. These schemes were financed from marriage loan repayments and savings on unemployment benefit after 1933. Increased taxes on the childless financed other benefits and tax rebates for families. Family allowances went to the father; according to Bock, 'the purpose of the subsidies was not to raise the status of mothers in relation to fathers but ... to raise the status of fathers in relation to bachelors' (1994: 165).

Yet it was precisely the *status* of mothers that the regime aimed to raise, with various symbolic gestures honouring the 'German mother'. Mothers of large families admittedly received some material benefits: in 1934, the Darmstadt local authority, for example, issued 1,500 mothers of at least three children each with vouchers for free theatre tickets. More typical, however, was the Nazis' appropriation of Mother's Day in May as a festival celebrating the 'German family'. Another symbolic award followed in 1934, when mothers of at least three children under ten received Honour Cards bearing the inscription, 'the most beautiful name in all the world is Mother', and requesting all shops and offices to give them preferential treatment – allowing them to jump a queue (Stephenson, 1975: 48) [Doc. 26b]. Clerks in government offices were reminded to favour mothers with small children.

The ultimate honour came with Hess's announcement in autumn 1938 that three million 'valuable' prolific mothers would be awarded the Honour Cross of the German Mother at ceremonies attended by NSDAP dignitaries. There were three grades of cross: bronze, for mothers of four or five children; silver, for six or seven; and gold, for eight or more children. The parallel with Germany's highest military honour, the Iron Cross, was clear. Members of the Hitler Youth were ordered to salute women wearing the Mother's Cross, and Himmler enthused: '... one day it'll be the greatest honour in Greater Germany. Sentries will have to present arms to a woman with the Mother's Cross in gold ...' (Stephenson, 1975: 50). But in their zeal to honour prolific mothers, authorities sometimes neglected to investigate their 'value', regardless of the guidelines for awarding the Honour Cross [Doc. 6]. Complaints were made that 'asocial' women were receiving it, and that some 'valuable' mothers were therefore refusing to accept it.

Even with legislation and the Nazis' intricate medico-racist bureaucracy, the problem of identifying both the allegedly deserving and undeserving surfaced also in the League of Large Families (*Reichsbund der Kinderreichen* – RdK). The RdK, inherited by the Nazis, was a propaganda organization to promote the ideal of a nation of families 'rich in children' ('*kinderreich*') [Plate 1]. Its leadership council included NSDAP notables, and officials of party and state with four or more children were urged to join, to set an example to professional, managerial and white-collar workers, who were clearly reluctant to have large families. In December 1937, the first Honour Books of the German Family were presented to RdK members in Berlin, by four hundred members of the *Bund Deutscher Mädel* (BDM – League of German Girls), to impress on them the importance of large families. Nevertheless, there were complaints that many 'Aryan' large families were feckless and scarcely 'valuable'. The press was instructed to emphasize that 'Aryan' large families whose conduct was anti-social were not '*kinderreich*' but were merely '*Grossfamilien*' (big families). Some regions introduced tighter scrutiny to distinguish between the two.

The results of all the propaganda and incentives were poor. Certainly, the birth rate rose after 1933, but it remained stubbornly below early 1920s' levels, far short of pre-1914 rates (Table 2.1). Marriage loans perhaps boosted the birth rate in immediate terms, but, as Angus McLaren says, 'birth rates rose after 1933, but not because of Nazi pro-natalist policies: fertility increased in every country (except France) once the worst years of the Depression had passed' (1990: 238). By the late 1930s it was clear that loan-aided couples were no more likely than others to have large families. This was hardly surprising, with 84 percent of loan applicants coming from poorer families (Mühlfeld/Schönweiss, 1989: 207). In fact, the rise in the birth rate was principally consequential on the rise in the marriage rate (Table 2.1):

> in 1920, there was an average of 2.3 children per family; in 1940, this 'quota' had sunk to 1.8 children. Thus even the National Socialists could not halt the trend towards 'two-child marriages', which according to the opinion of population policy experts would undeniably lead to 'the death of the nation'. (Wippermann, 1998: 182)

The government's reluctance to spend freely to promote the policy which was, it claimed, vitally important to it, paid commensurate dividends. The RdK symbolized this policy, charged with encouraging 'valuable' large families with virtually no resources besides its purely decorative Honour Book. As Pine says, 'the *kinderreich* stood behind the "old fighters" [of the NSDAP] and behind the war-wounded in terms of benefits, so that their preferential treatment often failed to appear in reality' (1997: 95).

Low incomes were undoubtedly critical in discouraging poorer families from having larger families, while most middle-class families were inclined to family limitation. The birth rate is evidence that, however hard the Nazis tried to encourage large families, women were not 'forced to bear children'.

Motherhood in 'hereditarily unhealthy' and 'asocial' families

Gisela Bock is fully justified in saying: 'Nazi pronatalism for desirable births and its antinatalism for undesirable ones were tightly connected' (1984: 276). The Nazis aimed to eliminate the possibility of mother-hood in families which they considered 'worthless'. The mass murder of Jewish women and children in extermination centres was the ultimate expression of this. Earlier, creeping discrimination and persecution had, for example, excluded Jewish children from school celebrations on Mother's Day, and had, in March 1936, denied family allowances to large Jewish families. In 1939, it was brutally emphasized that the strict prohibition of abortion for 'Aryans' did not apply to Jews, whose repro-duction was regarded as undesirable.

Jews were the supreme 'racial enemy' targeted for elimination from the German 'racial body', but there were other 'racially worthless' groups, in particular most, but not all, Roma and Sinti 'Gypsies' and a very few Black Germans, who were persecuted. Further, in the 'Aryan' majority, many who were classed as genetically 'worthless' or else 'asocial' were married with young families. In fact, Nazis and others believed that the 'valuable' tended to have small families while the 'worthless' and feckless were prolific. These had to be prevented from further procrea-tion, while childless 'hereditarily unhealthy' or 'asocial' persons were to be prevented from reproducing at all. The propagation of those who were a 'burden' on the community – through their failure to contribute to its wealth and well-being, through criminality, or through their need for institutional care – was estimated to cost a fortune [Doc. 7]. Therefore while ideological prejudice conditioned attitudes to both the 'valu-able' and their antithesis, 'life unworthy of life' ('lebensunwertes Leben'), there was also a balance-sheet mentality which costed individuals' and families' economic value. Those who failed on either 'racial hygiene' or cost-effectiveness criteria were to be prevented from creating new life similar to their own, and then perhaps to have their own 'unworthy' life prematurely terminated by 'euthanasia'.

Eugenics, as a modern scientific discipline, seemed to many appropriate in an age of technological advance. As Atina Grossmann says, 'many committed sex reformers and birth controllers came to see sterilization as a positive social good and a cost-efficient method of reducing expensive "social ballast"' (1995: 71). The first major legislation on racist population engineering, on 14 July 1933, came on the same day as the 'Law Against the Establishment of Parties' declared that 'The National Socialist German Workers' Party constitutes the only political party in Germany' (Noakes/Pridham, 1983: 167). The one-party state ensured that Hitler's government could legislate by proclamation, without formal opposition. The 'Law for the Prevention of Hereditarily Diseased Offspring' (14 July 1933) introduced 'eugenic sterilization' where 'there is a strong probability that his/her offspring will suffer from serious hereditary defects of a physical or mental nature'. This had broad application:

> Anyone is hereditarily ill within the meaning of this law who suffers from one of the following illnesses: (a) Congenital feeblemindedness. (b) Schizophrenia. (c) Manic depression. (d) Hereditary epilepsy. (e) Huntington's chorea. (f) Hereditary blindness. (g) Hereditary deafness. (h) Serious physical deformities. . . . In addition, anyone who suffers from chronic alcoholism can be sterilized.
> (Noakes/Pridham, 1986: 457)

Several of these categories, in particular (a), were open to interpretation. Medical practitioners were obliged, from December 1933, to report patients with these ailments, as the prelude to an application for sterilization. Those defined as candidates could be compelled to submit to sterilization if they tried to resist [Doc. 8].

It was, however, logistically impossible to monitor everyone intending to marry, even with doctors required to report on their patients. The Certificate of Suitability for Marriage, designed to apply to the entire population, was in practice required only of applicants for marriage loans and those suspected by health or social service authorities of being 'flawed'. In one Berlin district between 1934 and 1940, nine percent of intending couples had to apply for the Certificate, and half of them were denied it, while almost four percent of those applying for a marriage loan (113,543 individuals) between 1934 and 1941 were also rejected – and would probably be prohibited from marrying. Sixty percent of these (between 1935 and 1941) were women (Heineman, 1999: 24–25). These procedures discriminated against women, because in some cases the woman but not the man was tested to assess fertility. Further, while sexual promiscuity was 'normal' in men, it was regarded as delinquent in women and was often a reason for grading women as 'asocial'. The 'double standard' in sexual morality persisted with catastrophic results for some women: firstly, they were irreversibly rendered 'unfruitful' (*unfruchtbar*); secondly, 'asocial' women who were sent to a concentration camp were often forced into prostitution there.

There was strong pressure on women failing the Marriage Health Law's test to undergo sterilization. If they were already pregnant, abortion would, from 1935, precede sterilization. It was difficult to resist when the criteria for it included a doctor's examination and his/her recommendation in favour of sterilization. Cases were adjudicated in the many Hereditary Health Courts, whose proceedings, like doctors' evidence to them, were confidential: patients did not receive a record of the case which decided for or, relatively infrequently, against their sterilization. During the Third Reich, some 400,000 sterilizations were performed under the 1933 law, about half each on men and women; in addition, an unknown number of sterilizations of 'racial enemies' occurred in concentration camps and other institutions where normal legal processes were ignored (Bock, 1986: 8). Bock argues that women were particular victims of this policy. Certainly, more women than men died as a result of the operation – 70 of the 89 deaths in 31,002 operations in 1934 were of women (Mühlfeld/ Schönweiss, 1989: 173) – and women were more likely than men to be adjudged 'feeble-minded', because of their sexual behaviour or their lifestyle. Heineman adds that 70 to 80 percent of the women were single, and that sterilization could damage their marriage prospects because they were infertile (1999: 30). The grounds for sterilization often resulted in their being institutionalized, in a psychiatric home or a workhouse. From December 1937, they might be sent to a concentration camp to join the army of forced labour.

It was, however, not only single persons who were regarded as a biological threat. Married couples and whole families were assessed as 'worthless' or 'asocial' and subjected to official scrutiny. Local health departments created massive card indexes of both individuals and families in these categories and constructed genealogical tables which 'proved' that vast clans of 'asocials' existed and interbred with each other, perpetuating their flaws in large families. On this basis, local authorities initiated schemes for dealing with the 'asocial', whether through slum clearance to destroy their communities, through restrictive and insanitary camps for 'Gypsies', or through purpose-built colonies for regulating 'asocial' families. The Hashude colony in Bremen tried to distinguish 'asocial' families which were capable of improvement from those which were not. One criterion for deciding if a family was 'asocial' and therefore requiring 're-education' was if children were neglected and the household was not managed in an orderly way. This was regarded as women's reponsibility, and 'success in the education of the housewife and mother was considered a crucial step forward, because the running of the household, the example set to the children and the health of the family depended almost exclusively on the behaviour of the woman' (Pine, 1995: 191) [Doc. 4]. Families which could be turned into orderly, productive units were returned to the community as potentially useful members. Those which were incorrigible – 'workshy', slovenly and dependent on state aid – might be sent to a concentration camp.

One reason for the high marriage rate in 1939 (Table 2.1) was the revocation, on 31 August 1939, of the clause in the Marriage Health Law requiring couples to undergo a medical examination and acquire the Certificate of Suitability for Marriage. By this time, large numbers had already been sterilized. With war imminent, the government aimed to encourage young men liable for conscription to marry in haste and beget a child before leaving for the front, perhaps never to return. The SD (*Sicherheitsdienst* – security service) reported in late 1939 that 'hereditarily unsound' people had been exploiting this relaxation of the law (Stephenson, 1975: 44). In all probability, between 1935 and 1939 some couples had chosen not to marry to avoid risking an examination whose result might be enforced sterilization. In autumn 1939, they took the opportunity inadvertently offered to them.

Birth control: contraception and abortion

Control of fertility is a precondition of women's enjoying equal opportunities with men. Even if there are other constraints – lack of money or education, for example – effective birth control liberates them from the tyranny of unpredictable pregnancy. In invading the private sphere, Nazis tried to deny women self-determination and choice by restricting access to birth control for 'valuable' women and by imposing birth control on the 'worthless'. While men were undoubtedly affected by these policies, Bock is right in saying that women were particular targets of both pronatalist and antinatalist Nazi policy because of their biological role as childbearers.

It was no coincidence that Germany's birth rate declined during the 1920s, at a time of limited new rights and opportunities for women: there was obviously increasing resort to birth control, with more effective contraception and a higher rate of abortion. Yet old traditions persisted: in the 1920s, 'the most popular method of preventing conception was *coitus interruptus*' (Usborne, 1992: 29), partly because mechanical devices like the condom or cap were expensive, required forethought or, in the case of chemical pessaries and intrauterine devices, could cause infection. In addition, and influentially, both the Evangelical and Catholic churches were utterly opposed to abortion and hostile to contraception. The former condemned 'any limiting of births on grounds of selfishness, convenience or pleasure', while Pope Pius XI called contraception 'a shameful and intrinsically immoral . . . criminal abuse' (Stephenson, 1975: 60). However, the establishment in the 1920s of birth control advice centres, many sponsored by the SPD or KPD, spread knowledge about modern contraception, providing cheap contraceptives and sometimes arranging abortions. There were also informal traditional facilities, like a 'wise woman' in a small community, who assisted with abortion.

Nevertheless, abortion was not freely legally available, although the law governing it was reformed in 1926–27 to mitigate the severe penalties prescribed by the Criminal Code and to permit abortion on medical grounds, especially where the woman's health or life was at risk. This made 'Germany's abortion law the most lenient in Western Europe' (Usborne, 1992: 174). Further, contraception was neither fool-proof nor universally practised, which left many women seeking an abortion – so many that James Woycke writes of an 'abortion epidemic' in early twentieth-century Germany (1988: 68–89). Doctors estimated an annual rate of half a million abortions in the 1920s, rising to perhaps one million during the depression as financial crisis hit many families. The majority of women undergoing abortion were married; they belonged to every class and station.

For the Nazis, abortion among the 'valuable' was a crime, and in 1933 the paragraphs of the Criminal Code which had been repealed in 1926 were reinstated in more Draconian form, punishing with a severe prison term both the woman undergoing an abortion and anyone assisting her. Nevertheless, a few abortions were permitted in the Third Reich where the life of a 'valuable' mother was at risk from a continuing pregnancy. But most birth control advice centres were closed down in 1933 along with the political parties which sponsored them: the 'Law for the Protection of the People and the State' (28 February 1933) was invoked to close down 'Marxist' birth control centres (Noakes/Pridham: 1983: 142). Some survived for a time, precariously and in great secrecy.

Yet, although the availability of contraceptives was curtailed, there was no formal ban on their production and distribution before the Second World War. It is therefore misleading to say, without qualification, that 'birth control', meaning contraception, was 'outlawed' or 'prohibit[ed]' (Koonz, 1987: 7, 186, 285) or that 'contraception . . . [was] illegal' (Nolan, 1997: 332), at some unspecified time. Nazi population experts knew that contracting a sexually transmitted disease could result in sterility, and that the condom had obvious protective value. Kirkpatrick reported that from 1933 'pressure was exerted' to have machines dispensing condoms removed, but that 'in Berlin, at least, public health takes precedence'; in 1937, these machines existed throughout the city (1939: 133). When, in wartime, the Himmler Ordinance of January 1941 prohibited the production and distribution of contraceptives, the military authorities had the condom exempted because of its value in preventing disease. Nevertheless, the loss of young men in wartime – with their reproductive potential often hardly exploited – along with a renewed decline in the birth rate (Table 2.1) – led to the introduction in 1943 of the death penalty for abortionists, even if it was rarely invoked.

Even before the war, the campaign against abortion intensified, particularly with Himmler's creation in 1936 of a Central Office to Combat Homosexuality and Abortion which kept detailed files on women who had had abortions and the doctors, midwives and others who had performed them. In 1937, prosecutions of abortionists were nine times higher than in 1936, due to strenuous *Gestapo* activity (Pine, 1997: 20). Yet it was no easier to eradicate abortion than to prevent contraception. The Nazis 'were as helpless as previous regimes in trying to prevent criminal operations' (McLaren, 1990: 238). The *Gestapo* might target and entrap suspected abortionists, but its officers could not police the entire population. Beyond that, trying to eradicate a long tradition of *coitus interruptus* was not remotely realistic. Himmler, especially, tried to discourage and restrict birth control, especially through the SS's *Lebensborn* (Fount of Life) organization, with its network of residential homes for 'valuable' expectant and nursing mothers, including SS officers' wives, which, in wartime, accommodated 'racially valuable' eastern European children cruelly abducted from their families. Contrary to popular myth, *Lebensborn* homes were neither 'stud farms' nor bordellos for SS men. They were integral to Himmler's campaign against abortion because they provided a home and care for single pregnant women and mothers who had no other refuge. Nevertheless, learning in 1940 that high rates of abortion persisted – over half a million a year, comparable with pre-1933 rates – he resolved to intensify *Lebensborn*'s role in combating it, if he could attract the necessary funds [Doc. 9].

During the 1930s, rural families still had, on average, more children than urban families. Constraints of both space and employment in the towns encouraged family limitation, while knowledge about and access to modern contraceptives were more available there. Further, in the countryside, the influence of the Christian churches was stronger. Nevertheless, traditional forms of contraception (including sexual abstinence) were practised in rural areas, and Nazis worried that even rural families were becoming smaller. They were also disturbed by the higher incidence of death among infants and young children in the countryside than in the towns, which they believed, probably correctly, was partly caused by the overburdening of rural women [Doc. 11]. It was probably also partly due to ignorance about modern methods of childcare and the persistence of harmful superstitions and a lack of personal hygiene. The zeal with which Nazi welfare authorities sent social workers both to assist rural pregnant women and to deter abortion helped to achieve a lowering of infant mortality rates [Doc. 5] (Table 1.1). It perhaps also inhibited women from resorting to traditional remedies, like infanticide; but 'child murderers . . . girls from the countryside who had killed their new-born babies', could be found in Hamburg's Fuhlsbüttel jail in the 1930s (Kaminsky, 1999: 237).

The 'abortion epidemic' perhaps indicated that infanticide had overwhelmingly been superseded by preventive means during a pregnancy. On the other hand, the greater difficulty in – but not impossibility of – obtaining contraceptives probably also guaranteed greater resort to abortion, regardless of Himmler's and the *Gestapo*'s efforts [Doc. 9]. By 1933, many German women were accustomed to controlling their fertility and they would not relinquish this, even with doctors obliged, from 1935, 'to report all miscarriages, premature births, and terminations for medical reasons' (Grossmann, 1995: 150). Certainly, every effort was made to ensure that those involved in an abortion were punished – at least with a jail sentence – and stigmatized, for example by being denied the Mother's Cross, if they were otherwise eligible [Doc. 6]. This haunted women who, to their distress, had genuine miscarriages which might put them under suspicion of having had an abortion. In late 1939, the SD reported an abnormally high incidence of miscarriages, probably due to both an increase in rural women's burdens, with men conscripted, and anxiety about men at the front. But, suggested the SD, some 'miscarriages' might have been deliberately induced, although the evidence was merely circumstantial [Doc. 9]. In Nazi Germany, many women continued to employ birth control techniques, whatever the difficulties or the sanctions; the evidence lies in the birth rate (Table 2.1).

'Sexual deviants': single mothers, lesbians, prostitutes

Women who did not conform to Nazi prescriptions for family life and reproduction, but who were neither 'asocial' married mothers nor persecuted as racially 'worthless', could, even as 'Aryans', be 'without value' because they were regarded as 'sexual deviants' – they deviated from the official norm. Discrimination against single mothers and prostitutes was nothing new: legally, the unmarried mother had no rights over her child; socially, she was stigmatized. Prostitutes were social outcasts, causing anxiety because their trade publicly affirmed aspects of sexuality condemned by the churches and not openly acknowledged in society. Their status was ambiguous because paragraph 361.6 of the Criminal Code 'outlawed prostitution but condoned it as long as it was contained by police surveillance' (Usborne, 1992: 83). Female homosexuality was even more of a taboo; polite society ignored it, although in the 1920s it had a higher profile in larger cities, with clubs and other facilities for lesbians newly available.

Heineman argues persuasively that 'women were described as asocial mainly on the basis of their sexual behavior or demeanor, while men earned the term mainly on the basis of criminality, chronic unemployment, or failure to support their families' (1999: 28). The 'double standard' in sexual morality thrived, then, in a party affecting to despise 'bourgeois morality and custom'. Prostitutes were officially regarded as morally degenerate 'asocials' to be denied the benefits offered to conformist 'Aryan' women [Docs 3 and 6], yet Nazi men, like others, enjoyed their services. Lesbianism was mostly ignored except when it served a political purpose. In particular, the Nazi regime stigmatized as lesbians the leaders of the pre-1933 women's movement as part of their vilification of liberal 'women's rightists'. Yet Goebbels, for one, enjoyed 'lesbian displays' at the notorious 'Salon Kitty' in Berlin.

Above all, there was the thorny issue of the status of single mothers. In the 1930s, the illegitimacy rate declined from 1920s' levels because marriage loans enabled some pregnant women to marry before the birth, while some women branded as 'promiscuous' were sterilized (Table 2.1). From 1933 there were differing views, ranging from 'absolute condemnation of the unwed mother, through acceptance under certain conditions, to open encouragement to have a child outside wedlock' (Klinksiek, 1982: 94). Where a single woman continued with a pregnancy, she posed dilemmas for both herself and the regime. Morally, she was unchaste, a loose woman to be classed as 'asocial' and treated accordingly. However, any 'valuable' child was welcome, even if its mother was single. If both parents were 'valuable', the child was nurtured and valued. If the mother refused to divulge the father's identity – as she might in wartime, if he was a foreign worker – there was doubt about how to treat both her and her child.

Hitler's government began to ease conditions for single mothers from 1933, when tax changes both gave them relief on earnings to help to maintain a child and exempted them from marriage loan taxation. It was cautious, however, because toleration of illegitimacy had been promoted by the KPD and was denounced by conservatives and the churches. Nevertheless, in the mid-1930s a debate raged about how to treat a woman in the public service who had an illegitimate child: should she be dismissed, or should she even be punished at all? In May 1937, Gürtner, Minister of Justice, ordered that single women could choose to be addressed as 'Frau' (Mrs) rather than 'Fräulein' (Miss). Then in early 1939 it was decreed that a woman having an illegitimate child should not be punished by dismissal. But while some 'valuable' single mothers and their children were treated less judgementally, the stigma associated with illegitimacy persisted.

The partial easing of official prejudice against single mothers and their children prompted rumours about official encouragement to young women to 'give the *Führer* a child' by a 'valuable' consort, whether within a stable relationship or not. Himmler and his SS (*Schutzstaffeln* – Protection Squads) are particularly associated with this. Especially during the war, the SS leadership campaigned for equal treatment for married and single 'valuable' mothers, and its *Lebensborn* homes welcomed both. Himmler had already declared, in 1938, that he, through *Lebensborn*, would assume guardianship of all 'valuable' illegitimate children whose mothers were alone and vulnerable. Then Hess announced in December 1939 that the NSDAP would assume guardianship of illegitimate children whose fathers perished in the war, because

considerations which are justifiable in normal times must for the present be overlooked. . . . What use is it if a nation is victorious, but through the sacrifices made for that victory it dies out? . . . The life of the nation comes before all principles thought up by men, all conventions which carry the mark of recognized custom but not of morality, and before prejudice. The highest service a woman can render to the community is the gift of racially healthy children for the survival of the nation. (Stephenson, 1975: 66)

The SS went further. Its newspaper, *Das Schwarze Korps* (*The Black Order*), quoted Himmler's view that men could go into battle with equanimity only if they had fathered children, while women who refused to serve their country by bearing soldiers' children, even outside marriage, were comparable with army deserters. By contrast, those bearing illegitimate children could be confident of state support. This created a furore, with the Catholic Church, in particular, condemning Nazi incitement to contravene Christian teaching. Some NSF leaders, too, were openly critical. But the NSDAP offered a cash grant to single women in full-time work who had a child, on the same basis as to a man who fathered a child within marriage, and the government paid grants to 'valuable' impecunious unmarried mothers. From November 1941, the unmarried bereaved could apply for a 'postmortem marriage' if there had been a firm engagement at the time of the man's death in action (Kundrus, 1995: 362). This would legitimize any child of the couple, and it enabled the woman to draw a widow's pension.

This was far removed from branding single mothers as 'asocial' because of their sexual conduct, and classing them as little better than prostitutes. Heineman argues, however, that Himmler and the SS were a radical minority set on overturning conventional morality, whereas Hess, the NSDAP and the government continued to regard marriage and the family as forces for stability that should be protected, even if, particularly in wartime, the 'valuable' single mother and her child should be cherished. Certainly, Himmler believed that male members of the racial elite, especially SS men, had a destiny which transcended laws and the churches' teachings. Particularly 'valuable' women could, he said, have such men provided as 'conception assistants', a scheme initiated in wartime. Contrary to popular mythology, few women responded, and, as another tactic, Himmler and Bormann planned to encourage bigamy after the war 'to safeguard and improve the racial qualities of the Greater German Reich' at a time when many young men had been killed (Stephenson, 1975: 70). Hitler, too, came to favour this idea.

In Germany, as elsewhere, lesbians were regarded as deviant and abnormal because they did not conform to heterosexual social norms. Many felt greater need to conceal their sexuality after 1933 than before, with the result that some lesbians married gay men, as camouflage for both, while others married heterosexual men. Yet while gay men were brutally persecuted, homosexual women escaped comparable treatment. Although homosexual relations between men were an offence, under paragraph 175 of the Criminal Code, lesbianism was not mentioned, and attempts by law officers in the 1930s to extend paragraph 175 to include women were unsuccessful [Doc. 10]. This was because 'lesbians were not taken seriously' (Kundrus, 1996: 496). Because men, including doctors, believed that women were sexually passive, they did not regard women who breached heterosexual norms as saboteurs of population growth in the way that they – and Himmler in particular – regarded gay men. The rationale was that lesbian women could still conceive and bear children, and many did. Lesbians were, however, regarded as dangerous if they were in a position of authority, like teaching or leadership in a youth organization, where they might influence their subordinates and divert them from heterosexuality.

Lesbian relationships developed, in deepest secrecy, in women's prisons. But lesbians in concentration camps were not forced to wear the 'pink triangle' badge that cruelly distinguished gay men, because, when a lesbian was incarcerated, it was not primarily because of her sexuality but because she was either non-'Aryan' or 'politically unreliable'. A lesbian might be imprisoned for these reasons, or because she was a prostitute and therefore 'asocial', but Claudia Schoppmann believes that 'this is not convincing proof that such women had actually been arrested and gaoled because of their homosexuality' (1995: 15). Nevertheless, if a lesbian was incarcerated, she might be sadistically punished by being forced to 'work' as a prostitute in a bordello for men, including male homosexuals for whom this was part of their 're-education'.

In most societies, prostitutes are despised yet seemingly indispensable. Between the wars, there were particular reasons for demonizing female prostitutes. What Shorter calls 'a whole revolution in extramarital sexual behavior' in later nineteenth-century 'Europe and America [caused] a huge increase in all venereally transmitted infections', in all classes (1982: 265). Prostitutes became infected because of their clients' numbers and social diversity, and they then transmitted the infection. Until sulphonamide drugs were widely available to combat gonorrhea, from 1936, and penicillin was used to cure syphilis from 1943, there was a massive increase in the spread of sexually transmitted diseases, and, with them, infertility among women of all classes who were infected by husbands who had visited prostitutes before or during marriage. For Bock, one motive for the marriage loan scheme was to enable men to marry earlier and thus reduce their dependence on prostitutes' services. Prostitutes, then, were not merely 'asocial' because they deviated from the norm; they were also dangerous, given the implications of disease-bred infertility for the birth rate. Lenz, a Nazi population expert, estimated that more than 100,000 births were lost annually as a result of infection, although others suggested 40,000 (Kirkpatrick, 1939: 132; Stephenson, 1975: 68). To try to combat high rates of infection, control of prostitution had in 1927 been transferred from the police to local health departments, with the emphasis on treating both infected women and their clients.

From 1933, however, there was renewed emphasis on police targeting of street prostitutes because they set an unwelcome example to the young and because they allegedly caused offence to law-abiding citizens. The 'Law for the Protection of the People and the State' enabled police forces to arrest many known prostitutes. In May 1933, soliciting and behaviour resembling it became an offence. Other restrictions followed and the ban on houses of prostitution, or bordellos, issued in 1927, was reiterated. Nevertheless, Kirkpatrick reported that even in 1937 there was no uniformity, with 'a policy of complete repression' attempted in some smaller communities while 'to all intents and purposes *Bordelle* still existed' in larger cities (1939: 130–31). Local health or social service departments were left to pursue individual women, classing them as 'asocial'. Some, like Hamburg's, acted assiduously, assuming legal guardianship of women 'at risk': the relevant official described most of her charges as 'prostitutes' (Heineman, 1999: 27). They were overwhelmingly single, with no man willing or able to protect them. Prostitutes were routinely categorized with vagabonds, the mentally ill and the feckless, and were equally routinely subjected to sterilization. Many were incarcerated in jails or concentration camps.

Yet there was no serious attempt to eradicate prostitution in Nazi Germany. Both the women and their pimps were officially despised, but their trade continued, under stricter control and police surveillance, especially from September 1939. During the war, separate bordellos were opened for members of the *Wehrmacht* (armed forces) and for foreign male workers in Germany who were to be serviced by foreign women. This was consistent both with the regime's fear of an epidemic of sexually transmitted diseases in wartime and with its attempts to prevent sexual contact between 'valuable' Germans and others. With several million non-'Aryans' forced to work in Germany during the war, there was constant official anxiety about the opportunities for 'prohibited contact' between them and German women left at home while their male relatives were in the *Wehrmacht*.

Wartime marriages and wartime liaisons

During the Second World War, millions of men were absent from home for ever lengthier periods; many were captured and became prisoners-of-war (POWs), while over three million died. For the survivors, marriages involving servicemen came increasingly under strain. At first, enlisted husbands were allowed regular home leave in the hope of stimulating conceptions. But it was often hard for men who had faced mortal danger to appreciate that civilians, too, had difficulties. Women knew that men at the front were both in danger and under military discipline. Yet they expected some understanding of their own plight, particularly once bombing had put civilians, too, in the front line. Further, they expected a soldier home on leave to be carefree, when he often remained obsessed by his own experience and treated life at home as if it were removed from reality [Doc. 25]. One devoted young wife was puzzled when her husband eventually had home leave in 1942: 'then it suddenly struck Inge that something had changed between them. Were they still the same people? Which of them had changed?' He died of gangrene after being wounded in the last weeks of the war. In five years of marriage, they had spent a few fleeting months together (Szepansky, 1986: 53).

With many German men aged 18 to 45 away from home, German women had not only to carry the burdens of war but also to try to entertain and comfort themselves, perhaps by forming new relationships with available men. There might, for example, be an army unit stationed nearby, whether in the woman's home environment or if she had been evacuated elsewhere. Szepansky describes how 'I visited a dance-café . . . in the largely destroyed centre of Berlin. It was hopelessly full, with young girls, mature women, men in uniform, front-line soldiers of every age on leave, all in search of some entertainment. Eventually I found a seat beside an airforce officer . . .' (1986: 27–28). Many women found men in uniform a source of interest and diversion – and sometimes also a source of sexual infection. There was particular anxiety about women and girls who frequented railway stations and barracks in the hope of meeting soldiers. Paradoxically, the government itself had facilitated the forming of non-marital and extra-marital sexual relationships. Removing men from home introduced them to women elsewhere, in Germany and in occupied countries. Bringing into Germany millions of men as POWs or forced labourers provided women with a new focus of social and sexual interest. There were also female foreign workers, who sometimes appeared sexually attractive to adult and teenage German males. 'Prohibited contact', as any social or sexual intercourse between Germans and foreigners was called, was obvious from the arrival of Polish workers in 1939 and generated the utmost concern among NSDAP leaders.

While sexual attraction was sufficient motive for a relationship, there were often other reasons. In rural areas, particularly, a foreign worker – often a Pole – lived and worked in close proximity to his German employer's family. Sometimes, regardless of relentless propaganda about eastern European 'subhumans' ('*Untermenschen*'), genuine affection developed. A farmer's wife whose husband was away might voluntarily embark on a sexual liaison with a foreign worker allocated in his place, or else she might accept it as the price of having a compliant worker without whose labour the farm could not function [Doc. 12b]. In the towns, too, a woman alone might become friendly with a foreign worker, especially as he became more confident once the war turned against Germany. To the Nazi authorities such relationships constituted 'racial pollution'. The well-publicized penalties for offenders 'were also an instrument of repression against the German population, especially against women . . . [showing] how patriarchal conceptions of power were realized' (Münkel, 1996: 412). Certainly, they demonstrated a gender-based double standard: although German men risked a concentration camp sentence for having sex with a foreign woman, they often suffered little more than official disapproval, while a 'racially inferior' foreign man would probably be hanged and his 'Aryan' lover perhaps sent to prison or a concentration camp after being ritually abused by Nazi vigilantes, usually by having her head shaved in public, until Hitler ordered in 1941 that this be stopped [Doc. 12a]. Some women who had 'forbidden contact' with foreign workers were branded as 'asocial', and forced into prostitution in a concentration camp. The treatment of an 'Aryan' woman who had a foreign lover indicates the ferocity with which even the 'valuable' were punished when they violated Nazi racial prescriptions. There could be few sins greater than 'polluting German blood', as the invasion of a 'valuable' woman's body by a 'racial enemy' was characterized.

Partly to combat this, and because both the marriage and birth rates sank during the Second World War, as in 1914–18 (Table 2.1), there were desperate attempts to bring 'valuable' young people together through tactics like engineering postal romances between front-line soldiers and young women at home, using 'letter centres' organized by the *Reichsbund Deutsche Familie* (National Association of the German Family, formerly the RdK) as match-making agencies, and sanctioning weddings by proxy or by telephone. The problem was that, with men away and women at home, those reaching marriageable age after 1939 had limited opportunities for meeting a partner. Where 'war marriages' were contracted, they might not last, even if the husband survived: after the war, the spouses were often like strangers because of long separations, and many divorced. Even if they married, many women did not want to bring children into a war-ravaged world because 'their fathers would fall in battle and their mothers under the rubble of the cities, and even if the children themselves did not meet an agonizing death in the bombing, they might well be left orphans . . .' (Beck, 1986: 86).

The pressures of war meant that reduced health and social service departments often could not process cases which in peacetime would have classed wayward women as 'asocial' or 'deviant'. Single women were a major problem, but so was a rising level of adultery among married women. Sanctions were invoked, like the withdrawal of family allowances from adulterous wives, and in 1942 a new crime of 'insult of husbands at the front' permitted the prosecution of the male lover but not the wife, to try to maintain the marriage. Where the husband had been killed, from March 1943 his adulterous widow might have her pension cancelled as a result of a 'postmortem divorce' (Kundrus, 1995: 391–93). None of these sanctions prevented the forming of irregular relationships up to and beyond the end of the war. As German women found new partners on the home front, so German men formed social and sexual relationships where they were billeted, both in Germany and in occupied countries. For the vanquished – including German women in 1945 – the victors, even as enemies, sometimes had a magnetic aura of success and confidence, as well as access to otherwise unavailable commodities, especially food. The party which had lauded the 'Aryan' family as the 'germ cell' of the nation and devised reverential rhetoric about 'German marriage' was itself, through the rapacious pursuit of foreign hegemony, responsible for the breakup of families and the breakdown of the conventional moral order.

3

Women at work

Patterns of employment from depression to war

As Bock rightly says: 'The National Socialist regime did not exclude women from employment. Even though this has often been demonstrated since the 1930s, the myth persists that during Nazism women were fired *en masse*, by force, and for the sake of motherhood' (1994: 158). For example, contemporary Marxist commentators spoke of women being 'squeezed out of the factories and offices, from the civil service and the professions. In their stead men were employed . . .' (Lode, 1938: 42). The myth indeed persists: 'from 1933 to 1939 middle-class women were pushed out of jobs in the public and private sectors' (Nolan, 1997: 331). This camouflages the extent to which middle-class women remained in employment. Germany's economy, in both its modern industrial and its traditional rural sectors, could not function effectively without substantial numbers of women. But the catastrophic effects of the great depression, following America's stock market crash in October 1929, hit Germany severely because, after receiving massive American loans and investment in the 1920s, Germany was peculiarly dependent on America. The depression's major symptom, mass *un*employment, promoted the illusion that women's presence in the workplace threatened men's livelihood. It was no coincidence that 1932 saw both the highest rates of unemployment in Germany and the NSDAP's major electoral triumphs. The NSDAP waged propagandistically skilful campaigns before the national elections and the two Presidential and various *Land* and local elections in 1932, promising, among other things, 'jobs first for the fathers of families' and a reduction in the employment of women, especially married women, outside the home.

In January 1933, there were 6,013,612 Germans registered as unemployed, and probably at least a million more jobless, in a population in work or seeking work of some thirty-two million (*Statistisches Jahrbuch*, 1935: 318). Were women worse affected by the depression than men? Mason contends that they were, but others suggest that unemployment among men was proportionately higher. Winkler adds that many more women than men worked part-time or, in the depression, on short-time (Table 3.1). Both sexes were unemployed in large numbers, but women who remained employed while men were jobless were conspicuous and were, to conservatives and Nazis in particular, an affront. Above all, the working married woman – the 'double earner' (*Doppelverdiener*) – faced hostility, not only from men but also from single women with themselves and perhaps dependants to support. On 30 May 1932, Brüning's government legislated to permit the dismissal of married women public servants if 'their financial maintenance seemed . . . to be guaranteed in the long term' (Stephenson, 1975: 153). The overwhelming majority of *Reichstag* deputies of both sexes supported this. Thus even before Hitler became Chancellor there was massive resentment against employed women – especially if they were married – in time of high unemployment, and a Weimar government enacted legislation discriminating against married women public service employees.

Table 3.1   Employment in 1932

	Men	Women
Unemployment	45.6%	32.7%
Short-time working	20.8%	32.8%
Full employment	33.6%	34.5%

(Winkler, 1977: 193)

Hitler's government therefore reflected substantial public opinion in calling for women to return to home and family life. Focusing on areas where resentment about women's recent invasion of traditional 'male' bastions was acute, it extended the law of 30 May 1932 with legislation on 30 June 1933 which made mandatory the dismissal of married women in the public service with a husband in state employment. Violating Article 128 of the Weimar Constitution, the law sanctioned lower pay rates for women than for men, and it made women ineligible for permanent state employment until they were aged 35. Thus discrimination against married women was broadened in June 1933 to target women public service employees generally. This suggested that Nazi aims in population development and employment policy would be compatible and mutually reinforcing. Marriage loans were, after all, introduced in the 'Law to Reduce Unemployment' (1 June 1933); they were conditional on prospective wives relinquishing work on marriage, to ease the straitened labour market.

While the depression persisted, until the mid-1930s, mass unemployment seemed justification – beyond reproductive considerations – for the proclaimed Nazi policy of removing women, particularly married women, from jobs outside the home in order to give men (actual and potential 'fathers of families') priority in employment [Doc. 13], while recalling women to their 'natural sphere' of home, family and 'womanly work'. Yet Mason is right to ridicule this: 'the stance of the Nazi Party on the question of *married* women's work resembled that of King Canute as he faced the incoming tide. . . . The campaign against *married* women who worked was . . . a largely ineffectual and deeply irrelevant exercise in paternalistic and male chauvinist demagoguery', whose most significant impact was on the few married women in the professions and the bureaucracy (1976, I: 93–94, his emphasis). Otherwise, pressure was exerted on some employed married women at local level, but there was no legislation against working married women in private industry or trades. Indeed, there was no legislation against women's employment as such, suggesting that ideological considerations played a subordinate role to other anti-liberal prejudices. For Nazis and conservatives opposed not women's employment in general, but the employment of women in jobs with higher status and pay – the more attractive work that men had traditionally monopolized, and from which many of them wished to exclude women. Until 1939, the Third Reich witnessed a partial attempt to redress the balance that many male professionals and students felt had tilted in favour of women and against themselves. But, especially after the worst of the depression, men did not aspire to oust women from low-paid jobs on production lines, in domestic service or in low-grade clerical work.

From the mid-1930s, rapid economic revival brought increasing short-ages of labour, first in some sectors and then throughout the economy, indicating that German male workers would not suffice for the regime's ambitions. Women were therefore increasingly encouraged into employ-ment, even in what had previously been termed 'men's jobs'. Particularly with the exclusion of non-'Aryans' and political opponents of both sexes from influential or promoted positions, through purges in 1933–34, new opportunities emerged. This confirmed that women were regarded as a 'reserve army' for deployment wherever shortages in male personnel appeared, and only for as long as those shortages obtained. By 1939, there were 50 percent more women employed in industry than there had been in the depressed year of 1933 (Table 3.2), with increases in other sectors, too, especially clerical work and service industries.

Table 3.2   The number of women working in industry, 1933–38

Year	Number of women in industry		Annual increase (%)		Women per 100 workers in industry		
	Actual	Index	Men	Women	Total	Producer	Consumer
1933	1,205,000	100.0	–	–	29.3	11.4	50.1
1934	1,408,000	116.8	30.9	16.8	27.0	10.3	49.7
1935	1,463,000	121.4	12.3	3.9	25.5	9.8	49.2
1936	1,549,000	128.5	10.5	5.9	24.7	9.2	49.4
1937	1,749,000	145.1	9.4	12.9	25.3	9.6	50.1
1938	1,846,000	153.2	6.1	5.5	25.2	9.9	50.8

(Bajohr, 1979: 223)

Whereas both the 1925 and 1933 censuses had shown 11.5 million women either working or seeking work, in May 1939 there were 12.7 million employed women (Table 3.3). Yet in 1939 almost half of all German women classed as 'fit for work' were not employed, of whom the overwhelming majority were married: whereas almost 90 percent of single women were in work, as employees, proprietors or 'assisting family members' in small businesses, including farms (Overy, 1988: 426), almost two-thirds of married women of working age were not employed (Table 3.3), including more than one-third of childless married women (Bajohr, 1979: 25). By the later 1930s, there were strenuous efforts to attract more married women into work, with half-day shifts and the promise of more crèches – a promise never adequately fulfilled. Nevertheless, 37 percent of all employed persons in 1939 were women, and in the service sector the figure was even higher (Wippermann, 1998: 184). Further, in Greater Germany in 1939 [Map 2], there were two million more employed married women, out of a total of 6.2 million, than there had been in 1933's Germany [Map 1] (Frevert, 1989: 218).

Table 3.3   The number of employed married women, 1925, 1933 and 1939 (in millions) (Germany by its borders at 31 December 1937, without the Saarland)

Census year	Employed women (total)	Employed married women	Married women as % of employed women	Of 100 working women, those married
1925	11.5	3.6	32	29
1933	11.5	4.2	36	29
1939	12.7	5.2	41	33

(Bajohr, 1979: 25)

The 1914–18 war had shown that civilian workers were vital in wartime, especially in supplying the armed forces with weapons and other provisions. But it had also shown that women's employment had hardly increased overall, merely that working women had moved into war-related industry from other sectors. With the reintroduction of rearmament and conscription in 1935, strategists devised plans for employment in essential industries in any future war, consistent with their conception of a 'total war' in which the entire nation's resources would be concentrated on the war effort [Doc. 13]. Once the mass unemployment of the depression had receded, in the mid-1930s, the prospect of a shortage of labour in many sectors loomed. By the end of 1938, with virtually full employment, employers were offering incentives to retain workers. The plight of small farmers was desperate, with farmhands and also farmers' sons and daughters migrating to the towns, leaving older family members to struggle on. By 1939, the available *and willing* reserves of female labour had patently been exhausted, while increasing recruitment in one sector meant a loss to another. Conscription into the armed forces and Nazi service organizations only exacerbated these problems. Therefore Germany's labour resources were already at full stretch even before millions of men were conscripted into the *Wehrmacht*.

The employment question in wartime

The wartime withdrawal of men from civilian life and work continued for five and a half years, leaving to women many jobs traditionally performed by men, in increasingly difficult circumstances. Yet women's recorded numbers in employment remained around the 14 million mark – the 1939 level in Greater Germany – and even in 1944 reached only 14.9 million (Wippermann, 1998: 184). This is attributed particularly to the importation of several million foreign workers, mostly brought to Germany by force to work under German supervision and to compensate for the loss of German male labour. By late 1939, an influx of Polish POWs and coerced civilians allowed the government to defer a decision on the sensitive issue of labour conscription for German women. Both POWs and civilians from western Europe arrived in and after 1940, and from 1941 large numbers of forced workers from the Soviet Union were brought to Germany.

The exploitation of foreigners mitigated but did not solve the regime's key labour problem: how to mobilize more 'valuable' German women for the war effort without using coercion [Doc. 13]. While the *Wehrmacht's* campaigns were overwhelmingly successful, until late 1941, this question was important but not critical, and the regime relied on propaganda and appeals for volunteers [Plate 4]. The idea of labour conscription for women was repeatedly discussed, but it was not enacted until January 1943. Even then, it affected only women aged 17 to 45 at first, it permitted many exceptions, and it was imperfectly enforced. Conventional wisdom is that this derived from Hitler's reluctance to risk women's reproductive health by forcing them into factory work, but other factors were clearly at least as important. Firstly, Hitler believed that unwilling and inexperienced female workers would be of little value, especially in compensating for skills' shortages. And secondly, Hitler and some of his circle were reluctant to risk antagonizing women and their families: middle-class women and their husbands, particularly, resisted appeals for more female labour in industry and found loopholes in the 1943 legislation [Doc. 14].

The lengthy debate over labour conscription for women derived from the perception, both in government and among the public, that there was a large female reserve of labour waiting to be tapped. A particular irritant was the inequitable treatment of different groups of women. To try to prevent discontent at home, women whose husbands were conscripted received an allowance of up to 85 percent of their previous remuneration, to compensate for the loss of a man's income (Noakes, 1998: 314–15). But this applied only to women who were married and not in work, and whose husbands were not already in the *Wehrmacht*, when the war began. It was not designed to enable employed married women to leave work and live on their allowance; nor was it intended that a hasty marriage should exempt young women from the need to work. Women already in work received an allowance reduced according to how much they earned. Further, farmers' wives, as 'assisting family members', did not normally receive the allowance. Thus the largest group of women able to avoid being drafted into war work were women – with or without young children – who had not previously needed or wanted to work. They might even have a maid for household chores. During 1940 and 1941, loud complaints were heard about how some wives of conscripted soldiers led an increasingly harassed life, juggling job, household and family, while others relaxed in cafés or on the tennis courts.

It is difficult to assess how justified these complaints were. Most were anecdotal, based on individual local examples. Yet many similar complaints reached authorities across the country, in employment offices or in one of the many intelligence-gathering organizations, especially Himmler's SD [Doc. 14]. Albert Speer, Minister for Armaments, 1942–45, certainly believed that considerable untapped resources of female labour remained. Goebbels agreed, as his reference to women in his 'total war' speech in Berlin on 18 February 1943 showed. The eighth of his ten questions to his invited audience was: 'Do you, and especially you, the women, want the Government to ensure that German women, too, devote all their energy to waging the war, by filling jobs wherever possible to free men for action and thus helping their men at the front?' (Michalka, 1985: 297). Nevertheless, compulsory registration by women at employment offices probably yielded more paperwork than additional workers. Most of those registering claimed exemption from work, on grounds of either health problems or family responsibilities. According to Winkler, by the end of June 1943, 3.1 million women had attended an employment office, of whom 1,235,000 were declared suitable for work. Of these, more than half (672,000) had household responsibilities which enabled them to work only part-time (1977: 137). Of those who took up full-time work, 'by the end of the year, half had produced medical excuses' (Heineman, 1999: 63) [Doc. 14].

Germany's problem was that its resources – both human and material – were stretched even in the war's early, victorious stages. Once Germany embarked on a long war on several fronts, with, as in 1914–18, limited assistance from allies and against increasingly formidable adversaries, even the exploitation of occupied countries' resources – both human and material – was not enough for its needs. And with increasing territorial losses in 1944–45, access to these areas' resources was increasingly lost. Eleanor Hancock argues that the government overestimated the number of women available for work. Goebbels 'pared German life on the home front down to the essentials and . . . freed staff. Yet he was not able to free the numbers which both he and Speer believed possible in July 1944. The reservoir of staff they believed existed proved elusive' (1991: 158). Wippermann attributes this partly to the government's reluctance to fund 'canteens, crèches and other social services' to bring more women into work (1998: 184). Heineman argues that few additional married women joined the labour force, and that 'women born roughly from 1918 to 1928 who remained single during the war contributed to it more directly than any other group of German women' (1999: 64). But Richard Overy believes that there simply were not more women to be mobilized, particularly once the crises of bombing and evacuation dispersed many from their homes. The employment figures did not tell the full story: only 'older women and women with small children' were left to be coerced into full-time work. Apart from the 3.5 million working part-time, there were also women volunteers with the Red Cross or the NSV, while young women in the Labour Service and other service schemes were not included in the employment figures. In concurring that foreign workers were ruthlessly exploited for the German war effort, Overy believes that that 'does not detract from the fact that the National Socialist state imposed heavy burdens on German women workers from the start of the war' (1988: 430–32). By 1942, women comprised 52 percent of the native workforce (Noakes, 1998: 302). This proportion would only increase.

There undoubtedly were women who avoided being drafted, cajoled or shamed into work in wartime. Some had young children, others were evacuated to areas remote from war industry, and, in the increasingly chaotic circumstances of 1944–45, still others were able to abscond. For example, an 'asocial' young woman from Hamburg, having served a short concentration camp sentence for malingering, 'utilized the social upheaval after bombing raids' to change her identity, travel far from home and survive as a black marketeer (Kaminsky, 1999: 335). Nevertheless, hundreds of thousands of single women, particularly, were conscripted into service schemes to assist both military and civilian authorities, while both foreign women workers and women prisoners in labour and concentration camps served as slave labour. Beyond that, millions of German women worked full-time or part-time, in every sector of the economy [Plates 5 and 6]. In Hamburg in 1944, a survey of 'unemployed' women eligible to be conscripted concluded that perhaps four percent of them could realistically be drafted into work (Büttner, 1993: 40). As Schupetta astutely comments, 'it is amazing that the number of employed women remained constant or even rose slightly, right up to the end of the war. It is hard to comprehend how much effort it must have cost women to overcome all [the difficulties involved]' (1981: 297).

The modern economy: industry

Women industrial workers formed about half of the workforce in consumer goods industries throughout the 1930s, but only around 10 percent in producer goods industries (Table 3.2): they were far more numerous in textiles' production than in armaments factories. The consumer goods industries, including textiles, foodstuffs and paper-making, where women comprised half of the workforce, suffered recession from 1929 but were less severely hit than producer goods industries. Workers in these heavy industrial sectors, almost 90 percent of whom were men, were particularly affected by unemployment. However, government policies to promote economic recovery gave them an advantage. The building industry and metal trades, where few women were employed, had been devastated in the depression. Basing recovery on preparation for rearmament meant both manufacturing steel and building motorways (*Autobahnen*) for transportation. Therefore, the *proportion* of women employed in industry declined in the early years of Nazi rule. But that camouflages the increase in the absolute numbers of women employed in industry from 1.21 million in 1933 to 1.85 million in 1938, a rise of over 50 percent (Table 3.2) [Doc. 13]. Not all women industrial workers were in factories; some were 'home workers' who assembled items, like 'Inge D.', who helped her mother from the mid-1930s, making packaging for armaments industry batteries. It was monotonous work, and there was heavy pressure to meet rising daily quotas (Szepansky, 1986: 51).

In factories, many women staffed the new assembly lines [cover picture], and employers were reluctant to lose their cheap and generally compliant labour. During the 1930s, mechanization enabled women to invade 'men's industries', like iron and steel-processing and precision engineering, and, while their proportion in consumer goods industries remained steady (Table 3.2), their *absolute* numbers in these traditional fields declined, with attempts to throttle back consumption in order to give priority to war industries. Most women industrial workers worked from necessity rather than choice, and they were restricted almost exclusively to unskilled or semi-skilled jobs. The craft and supervisory positions were still a virtual male monopoly. Even if women factory workers' wages were around twice those of female agricultural workers (Tröger, 1981: 256), in 1939, an unskilled man normally earned 50 percent more than an unskilled woman (Focke/Reimer, 1979: 161). As Mason says, 'the role of the housewife really did seem preferable to most women who were not forced by their economic circumstances to seek regular employment in the modern capitalist sectors of the economy – such employment brought few rewards and many additional strains' (1976, II: 7). Where men's and women's wages were equalized, the intention was to deter employers from hiring women, whether to protect men's jobs in time of unemployment or to prevent the employment of women in industries potentially harmful to their reproductive health. But whatever efforts were made by the German Labour Front (DAF) to improve factory amenities, through its 'Beauty of Labour' programme, or – through its women's section – to deploy factory social workers to monitor 'Aryan' women's health and assess their problems, for married women workers the 'double burden' of employment and housekeeping remained crushing.

To mitigate the reproductive effects of this, the DAF trained female social workers to ensure that 'Aryan' pregnant factory women workers' health was safeguarded, and under the 'Law for the Protection of Mothers in Gainful Employment' (17 May 1942), 'Aryan' women were given leave, an allowance and medical care around the time of the birth (Noakes, 1998: 336–38). Emphasis was laid on improving 'Aryan' women workers' attention to hygiene, and industrial social workers ran courses in housekeeping, childcare, cooking and sewing to enhance their household skills. Because working-class women rarely attended the NSF's homecraft courses, reaching them through their workplace was regarded as vital. Nevertheless, some large firms excluded DAF-accredited social workers, continuing to use their own staff instead, although small and medium-sized firms were less able to prevent DAF social workers from operating on their premises, purveying Nazi ideological nostrums as well as practical advice.

In wartime, the government attempted to attract more women into war-related industry, while both working conditions and public transport deteriorated [Plate 4]. Many failed to respond to appeals to volunteer precisely because they feared conscription into a factory. And, as employers reported, women who worked part-time, or were unaccustomed to factory work, or were simply reluctant to work in a factory, were sometimes more trouble than they were worth. Further, they caused unrest among existing employees who, with the suspension of some labour protection measures, worked increasingly long hours, including shift-work, and were not – like the conscripted – able to retire on becoming pregnant. Industrial employers preferred an allocation of foreign workers, especially eastern 'subhumans' to whom welfare considerations did not apply and whose costs were much lower. Yet, as Overy shows, the number of German women working in producer goods industries doubled between

May 1939 and May 1943, while those in consumer goods industries increasingly worked on orders for the *Wehrmacht* (1988: 426–27). This was part of an increasing reallocation of labour from civil industries to war-related industries in wartime. DAF attempts to shield 'Aryan' women from the increasing demands of war industry were partly successful; and, as Winkler points out, where, in 1944, women were made to work longer hours, 'this was accompanied by diminishing productivity' (1977: 162). Genuine exhaustion was as important a reason for this as foot-dragging.

The modern economy: white-collar and clerical work

According to Tröger (1984: 244), as women were to staff monotonous, minimally-skilled production line work in industry, so they were to perform mechanized clerical work, above all at the typewriter. In 1936, 95 percent of shorthand-typists, but only 13 percent of bookkeepers or cashiers, were women (Winkler, 1977: 55). Women remained at the lower levels of clerical work, with limited skills and prospects; the rationale was that high-level training and expertise would be wasted when they married – a common argument used for reserving more attractive opportunities for men. Nevertheless, young women from the middle classes or skilled working class aspired to an office job rather than work in a factory, in domestic service, on a farm or in a trade. Many, then, rejected both traditional women's occupations and industry, instead embracing an expanding modern opportunity.

An 'office job' or 'clerical work' covered a variety of urban occupations. Some were in the private sector, in banks, insurance companies, and in office work for industrial concerns like Krupp or Siemens. Especially with the economic upturn, office work in the public sector, too, burgeoned, at central, *Land* and local government levels, including the *Reichsbahn* (state railway), the telephone and postal services and a wide range of social and child welfare offices. The NSDAP and its affiliated organizations and service projects required clerical workers who could deal with correspondence and filing, as did children's homes, hospitals, prisons and concentration camps; many of these employees were women. Between 1933 and 1939, the number of women office workers increased from 1.6 million to 1.9 million. Among all female vocational trainees in 1940, 72 percent were taking courses in various kinds of clerical work (Tröger, 1981: 258–59).

Employment of another group of white-collar workers, shop assistants, expanded with the development of consumerism in the inter-war years. In 1936, almost 80 percent of these were women who, like office workers, took pride in their status as non-factory workers (Winkler, 1977: 55). This included young women from a manual working-class background, as well as middle-class women. Like office workers, they viewed their job as a stop-gap between school and marriage, and few expected to have to work after marriage. Possibilities for career advancement were slim, but, on the whole, pay was reasonably attractive and conditions of work were far preferable to those in a factory. As Mason points out, 'employment of this kind was clearly sought after. . . . This was the only sector in which the employment of women increased rapidly and steadily throughout the inter-war years . . .' (1976, II: 8). There were not, in this kind of work, the shortages of female labour that would become apparent elsewhere from the later 1930s.

The war generated a huge demand for women in white-collar work. Men in 'non-essential' office jobs could be more easily spared for military service than skilled factory workers, and the wartime bureaucracy – with new taxes, rationing and various other controls – necessitated the employment of legions of office workers. For example, in offices dealing with the complex calculation of myriad individual wives' allowances, 'when skilled personnel were drafted, inexperienced office workers took their place; meanwhile, the caseload exploded' (Heineman, 1999: 62). Areas like the postal service and public transport, too, needed replacement staff for conscripted postmen, tram conductors and railway ticket salesmen [Plate 6]. Some women were drafted into these areas, either by local authorities or through the Labour Service and its wartime extension, Auxiliary War Service. This allowed some rural young women to escape from farm work into more congenial employment – as they saw it – provoking anger in the farming sector. Other women volunteered for clerical work to avoid being drafted into factory work. For some, it was a liberating experience: working at a busy ticket counter in a rail station, 'Elvira L.' felt that at last 'I am Somebody. . . . Words cannot express the effect which employment had on my attitude to life' (Szepansky, 1986:

162). Others served as clerical workers with the *Wehrmacht*, to release men for the fighting front.

The modern economy: the professions

In addition to school-teaching, where women were well-represented at all levels, in 1930 over five percent of medical doctors were female, although women's numbers remained below one percent among university lecturers and in the legal profession. Some professional women were married, but the vast majority – 121,000 out of 128,000 in 1933 – were unmarried (Stephenson, 1975: 149, 152–53). Dominated by men with conservative prejudices, the professions – especially law and medicine – were often unwelcoming to women. The depression increased male demands for the exclusion of women – and Jews and socialists – from their ranks. As Jarausch says, 'the overcrowding hysteria of the early 1930s made gender into a divisive issue, exaggerating the numerical impact of female inroads into male domains' (1990: 105). In particular, the 7,000 married women *Doppelverdiener* in desirable public service positions became a scapegoat for the shortage of opportunities for younger men (Stephenson, 1975: 151). After January 1933, the few women in high-level posts were dismissed and were overwhelmingly replaced by men, even in girls' senior schools.

But Nazi racial and political prejudices took precedence over male chauvinism. The 'Law for the Restoration of the Professional Civil Service' (7 April 1933) permitted the dismissal of non-'Aryans' and the 'politically unreliable' (Noakes/Pridham, 1986: 223–25). Women in these categories – Jews, socialists, pacifists and feminists – were strongly represented among high-achievers. For example, some 13 percent of women doctors were Jewish (Kaplan, 1998: 26). Therefore many women professionals were vulnerable less as women – even married women – than as perceived racial or political 'enemies'. German professional and academic life was impoverished – and British and American life enhanced – by the emigration of some of these. For example, the distinguished pharmacologists, Marthe Vogt – a Gentile who loathed Nazism – and Edith Bülbring, a '*Mischling*', enriched their profession in Britain. But, at first, some *émigré* professionals took the only jobs they could find: in America, 'a woman doctor from Berlin ended up peeling potatoes in someone else's kitchen', while a woman holding 'a doctorate in political economy ... kept the family afloat by working as a secretary' (Quack, 1991: 107, 103).

Despite propaganda against women professionals, reliable Nazis were retained in post or promoted. Gender segregation, already strong in professional organizations, was enforced, and some Nazi women made careers in the women's section of the civil servants', doctors' or lawyers' associations, or in organizing women teachers – much the largest women's professional group – in the NSLB (*NS-Lehrerbund* – Nazi teachers' league). While all professionals were potentially influential over patients, clients or students, teachers were in a particularly sensitive position, guiding both pupils' learning and attitudes. With women still, in 1939, accounting for 68 percent of girls' senior school-teachers – two percent less than in 1931 – monitoring their political attitudes was a priority (Stephenson, 1975: 166–67). Yet when teachers joined Nazi organizations, it was often to protect their position; saying that '27,000 members of the NSLB were active in the *NS-Frauenschaft* in 1936' (Said, 1981: 123) overestimates how 'active' some were [Doc. 15a and c]. In Hamburg, even in 1939, 'a large number ... of women in the public service still were not involved in the NSDAP or one of the party organisations' (Lohalm, 2001: 53).

Some officials in women's professional organizations were married, demonstrating that marriage was no obstacle to advancement for loyal Nazis, although married women doctors were under attack. Kater shows that in January 1934 married women doctors were 'formally' denied state employment. Yet the boasted intentions of the Nazi doctors' leader 'to rid the nation gradually of all female doctors' were illusory, while 'few married women doctors actually suffered in the end' (1989: 93). The fate of women professionals varied: women lawyers and higher civil servants were unlucky in being brought to Hitler's attention. In 1936 he decreed women's exclusion from the judiciary and the bar – where very few had worked – although he accepted women lawyers in administrative posts or private practice. In 1937 he decreed that only men should be appointed to the highest public service positions, with exceptions possible in 'womanly' areas like education, health and welfare.

Therefore it is incorrect to write about 'the exclusion of women from academic and professional work' (Proctor, 1988: 123). Women remained conspicuous in the professions, although overwhelmingly at their lower levels. There were exceptions, like two women appointed to university chairs in engineering and dentistry in 1938 and 1939, respectively, and the later 1930s provided new avenues for women graduates, albeit mostly within the gender-specific limits of Nazi women's organizations. A few women were among the doctors, lawyers and bureaucrats who prostituted their professional training in the sterilization and 'euthanasia' programmes. The same was true of nursing and social work, where most employees were women. Many nurses were Roman Catholic nuns, but from 1936 there were also the Nazi 'Brown Nurses'. With new occupations relating to the 'racial and hereditary health' qualifications for both citizenship and marriage, the massive card indexes used to identify and monitor both the 'valuable' and the 'worthless' depended on expert information from social workers and professional researchers [Doc. 7].

During the war, restricting women to 'womanly' areas was increasingly impractical, and many women graduates enjoyed unprecedented opportunities. For example, women teachers benefited from a relaxation of earlier restrictive legislation: many who had been retired returned, with some recruited for promoted positions, including school headships and senior administrative posts. Women doctors were also in demand, replacing conscripted male doctors in hospitals and practices in Germany and working in the NSV, the girls' service organizations and the occupied east. Undoubtedly, however, most of these opportunities would have been withdrawn had Germany won the war.

The traditional economy: domestic service

Between the wars, many girls still entered domestic service as maids in a middle- or upper-class household. In 1933, 1.2 million domestic servants were the third most numerous category of women workers (Wittmann, 1981: 42). For Nazis, domestic service for women, and especially for young women, seemed particularly appropriate. It was in the home – albeit not a maid's own home – while the duties involved habituated maids to orderly housekeeping and childcare, thus preparing them for marriage.

In 1939, there were 1.5 million domestic servants, 99 percent of whom were female. Almost one-third were in the 14 to 18 age group, while a further near-third were aged between 18 and 25: this occupation was chiefly for young women between elementary school and marriage. More than two-thirds of them resided in their employer's home (*Statistisches Jahrbuch*, 1941/42: 39, 53). For resident domestics, particularly, life was both restrictive and oppressive: they were almost always on call; they were poorly paid; they had to obey house rules, possibly including a curfew; and the work could be very heavy indeed. For the regime, the restrictions had the attraction of disciplining young women, making them unlikely to develop 'asocial' habits. Partly for this reason, the work designated for girls and young women in Nazi service schemes included domestic service. Further, encouraging the employment of maids was partly to reduce demands on industry for household labour-saving devices at a time when rearmament was the priority.

To encourage employment of domestic servants hit by the depression, the government introduced tax relief for employers in 1933. But there was a perceived problem when the infamous 'Nuremberg Laws' prohibited maids aged under 45 from working in Jewish households [Doc. 23]. This meant temporary unemployment for some, but, as demand for workers in industry and business revived, domestic servants were recruited into these sectors which often had better conditions and always had better pay. Winkler describes how 'in cities, the aim was to replace domestic servants who had gone into industry with maids from regions with a lower level of wages, like Silesia' (1977: 56). But many of those classed as 'maids' were essential workers on farms, and losing their labour to the towns was disastrous for farmers. The increasingly dire shortage of young women for work in agriculture and domestic service was a major reason for the expansion of the women's Labour Service from the mid-1930s and the introduction of the *Pflichtjahr* (Compulsory Year of Service) in February 1938.

During the war, much was made of the continued employment of domestic servants – including some 100,000 Ukrainian women (Hancock, 1991: 41) – when industry was short of labour. But however unattractive domestic service was, many women preferred it to conscription into a wartime factory. Further, for a woman left to run a small business, when her husband and male assistants had been conscripted, and when she also had household chores and perhaps children to look after, the only solution was to employ a domestic servant who could assume her duties in the home while she devoted herself to the business. Thus, the *Hausgehilfin* (maid) could become a substitute for a family member or male employee. The persistence of domestic servants was not necessarily an indication that the leisured, far from contributing to the war effort, were depriving it of labour, although this undoubtedly did happen. Some small family businesses were able to continue for much of the war only because of the assistance of a domestic servant. Where there was none available, the business might eventually close because of a shortage of personnel. This was more likely once domestic servants became liable for labour conscription in September 1944.

The traditional economy: small-scale farming

A farmer's wife and daughters were traditionally essential to the management of his land and stock, often to the detriment of their health [Doc. 11]. As Münkel says, 'National Socialist agrarian policy could not possibly achieve its self-imposed goals without the utilization of female labour on the land' (1996: 429), especially on small and medium-sized farms where, in 1933, the 4.4 million women in agriculture mostly worked (Corni/ Gies, 1997: 283), and where labour-saving machinery was only slowly being adopted. Daughters usually worked as unwaged 'assisting family members' until they married, probably into a farming family in the same district. If there was not enough work at home, they might work either in a nearby town or on a local farm, or else enter domestic service. In poorer rural households where the husband commuted to work in a nearby industry or craft, the women worked on the family's plot of land. For the more prosperous, marriage 'represented . . . a contract between the two households. Material factors were to the fore, with the participants assuming that love and affection would automatically arise at some future date' (Wilke/Wagner, 1981: 137). The most valued assets in a daughter-in-law were physical strength and willingness to work long hours.

Between 1933 and 1939, women's numbers in agriculture increased by some 230,000 while men's fell by 640,000, so that in 1939 women accounted for 54.5 percent of the workforce (Overy, 1988: 428). But also between 1933 and 1939, 61,000 female agricultural workers migrated to the towns (Tröger, 1981: 258). This reflected the growing demand for industrial labour; hired hands abandoned rural employment, leaving women on farms to shoulder an increasing proportion of the work. Farm workers' long hours, low pay and physical exhaustion tempted many into factory work, where women's wages were roughly twice those in agriculture (Tröger, 1981: 256); certainly, some rural sons and daughters saw in the demand for industrial labour an escape route from farming. Assistance from the service schemes afforded temporary relief; nevertheless, many small farms had desperate labour problems even before the war.

The conscription in wartime of farm hands and often proprietors might leave a farmer's wife struggling to run the farm [Doc. 16]. The *Reichsnährstand*'s (National Food Authority's) magazine, *Die Deutsche Landfrau* (*German Rural Woman*), its radio programmes and its local officials supposedly offered her practical advice, but made little practical difference. Officials visited farms mostly to check that regulations were being observed, rather than to monitor problems, and farmers' wives were often unable to attend meetings held to dispense advice. There was resentment that a farmer's wife was not eligible for the allowance paid to soldiers' wives, unless the farm's income had diminished significantly, or unless she could find a farm hand to hire, which was increasingly unlikely. Providing her with young women from the *Pflichtjahr* or Labour Service schemes was not always welcomed, partly because of the recruits' limited period of service and inexperience of farm work.

The remaining solution was to employ foreign workers, who often had farming experience and were reasonably reliable workers. It was not simply misogynist prejudice to recognize that a farmer's wife 'is not able to take over all the work which the mobilized farmer was accustomed to do' (Stephenson, 1987: 357). Labour-intensive work, when farm machinery and draught animals were increasingly unavailable in wartime, demanded considerable physical strength, strength beyond that of a worn-out farmer's wife [Doc. 16]. Attempts from 1943 to deploy conscripted German women on farms foundered on the unsuitability and unwillingness of the recruits, and women evacuees from urban areas, billeted on farms, often refused to help. By summer 1943, with the enlistment of most male farm hands, foreign workers were the only reliable assistance available. Thus, on a farm nominally run by a woman whose husband had been conscripted and who was increasingly unable to cope, foreign workers might be effectively in charge. They would soon realize that the farm depended on them, and bargain with their hosts accordingly, perhaps for improved accommodation and more food, or perhaps for sexual favours. Social and sexual relationships developed between Germans and foreigners living and working together on the land, demonstrating the ineffectiveness there of Nazi propaganda about 'racial value'. Foreign workers were judged overwhelmingly on their utility as workers.

In Körle, a village in northern Hesse – probably like rural Germany generally – 'the absence of men during the war greatly enhanced the women's role and influence. Women now acted as household heads and did work which had been reserved for men. . . .' But was this an advantage when previously 'men undertook the *heavy* work and women the *lighter* work', and 'more and more women were forced into [heavy work] during the war' (Wilke/Wagner, 1981: 131–33, 143, their emphasis)? Young women were already reluctant to marry into farming families because of farmers' wives' excessive burdens. In wartime, the position deteriorated, as remaining men were conscripted and 'the farms were largely denuded of male labour' (Schnabel, 1986: 574) [Doc. 16]. By 1944, all machinery and most draught animals had been requisitioned. The SD believed that conscripting a farmer meant that his wife would 'on the one hand have to cope with the extra work, and on the other hand see her income diminish because she cannot take over all the enlisted farmer's work' (Stephenson, 1987: 359). She might then resort to subsistence farming, or, exceptionally, she might pack up and leave. Either way, the supply of food to the towns progressively deteriorated.

4

Education, socialization, organization

Education and opportunity

If control over fertility is a precondition of women's freedom of life choices, equal educational opportunity is also fundamental, especially for women aiming for a career requiring a formal qualification. But in the 1930s, for most German girls, education remained a grounding in literacy and numeracy, with little intellectual input. Hitler pronounced that in girls' education, as in boys', 'the chief emphasis must be on physical training, and only after that on the promotion of spiritual and, finally, intellectual values. Future motherhood must be the unalterable objective of girls' education' (1936: 459–60). Nazi leaders endorsed conservatives' view that women's 'nature' was unsuited to academic study. Not only was rational and theoretical academic work alien to women, with their inherently emotional and instinctual outlook [Doc. 1b], but, by opening absorbing career opportunities, it would divert them from motherhood. Accordingly, in state schools there was explicit preparation for homemaking. Further, 'racial biology' became compulsory for girls, as for boys, to instruct them in the 'scientific' basis of Nazi racial prejudices, which also perverted subjects like history, geography and mathematics. Additionally, girls were encouraged or obliged to undertake six months' or a year's service, usually on leaving school, before embarking on employment or further education.

At the *Volksschule* (elementary school), ideology was incorporated into school subjects: learning, from childhood, about Germany's history, geography, language and culture, was the ideal medium for instilling ideas of German superiority, the NSDAP's 'mission', the 'injustice' of the Versailles territorial settlement, and the plight of Germans living under foreign rule. In the *Mittelschulen* (middle schools) for 10 to 16 year-olds, elementary school subjects largely continued, but with more theoretical input. Shorthand and typing were compulsory for girls not taking a second foreign language besides compulsory English. In both elementary and middle schools, girls were prepared for traditional 'womanly' roles. Yet the permeation of learning by Nazi ideology was patchy: delays in replacing pre-1933 textbooks left teachers with some discretion about how far they taught Nazified versions of school subjects.

For 'a good ten percent of the girls in any age-cohort', there were academic senior schools (Speitkamp, 1998: 202). Jewish girls were particularly well represented there and in universities: in 1932, seven percent of women students were Jewish (Kaplan, 1998: 11). In April 1933, a quota was set for Jewish students at senior schools and universities of 1.5 percent of new enrolments and five percent of students on course, to meet widespread criticism that Jews were 'overrepresented' in both universities and some professions (Speitkamp, 1998: 215). This blighted many talented individuals and encouraged young Jews to emigrate, although Marion Kaplan believes that their diminishing numbers owed more to discrimination and bullying in the classroom. Ruth Bednarski, for example, 'is no longer an exceptionally gifted and also highly intelligent pupil; Ruth is a Jew' (Jureit, 1999: 335). Non-'Aryan' pupils were victimized, by being excluded from activities like swimming and pilloried as 'racial enemies' [Doc. 17a and b]. In May 1932, there were 6,317 Jewish girls in Prussian state senior schools; by May 1936, only 26 percent of them remained (Kaplan, 1998: 98). In November 1938, remaining Jewish pupils were excluded from state schools and confined to separate schools for Jews only, until these were closed in June 1942. Similarly, in March 1941, the exclusion of Sinti and Roma children from schools was ordered if they 'posed a moral or other threat to their German classmates' (Wippermann, 1998: 158).

Few girls from an urban working-class or humble rural background attended academic senior schools, far less universities. Nevertheless, during the 1930s, girls comprised over one-third of senior school pupils, and women attended universities and colleges in conspicuous numbers. Saying that 'German women under the yoke of Hitlerism . . . may not study at universities' (Lode, 1938: 46) was erroneous: 'Aryan' girls and women were not denied an academic education in Nazi Germany, but they were guided and sometimes forced into 'womanly' areas and out of disciplines regarded as men's domain, including the classics and some science subjects. This patriarchal policy appealed to many non-Nazis, not least those whose daughters attended confessional schools. Although these church-sponsored schools were under increasing attack, as late as 1940 some still survived. Economic priorities, however, particularly in wartime, demanded more graduates, especially in medicine and the sciences, demonstrating the practical deficiencies of Nazi policy: as with employment policies, so with academic education, women were a resource to be tapped when necessary and dispensed with when there were sufficient men.

By 1933, almost 20 percent of a student body swollen dramatically through the jobs' famine was female. High graduate unemployment convinced many non-Nazis that student numbers should be forcibly reduced. The Nazis' priority was to protect 'valuable' men's study opportunities; therefore groups whose presence in universities was unpopular with male students and professionals were targeted with quotas. While Jews' numbers were restricted, male Nazi students hoped for women's exclusion from universities: 'the essential antifeminism of the Nazi student leadership was . . . deeply ingrained' (Giles, 1985: 278). In December 1933, an annual intake of 15,000 for universities and colleges was decreed, with women restricted to 10 percent of it: yet women's representation throughout the 1930s was consistently above 10 percent. For example, in 1934 they comprised 12.5 percent of all new college admissions and 15.3 percent of university admissions (Deutsche Hochschulstatistik, 1934/35: *4–*5). Saying that 'the number of women students dropped steadily' (Nolan, 1997: 331) ignores the steady decline until the later 1930s in male students' numbers (Pauwels, 1984: 146–47). And with the conscription of young men in September 1939, women students' numbers once again reached 20 percent; by late 1940, they stood at 30 percent, and in 1943/44 at 49.5 percent (Lück, 1979: 119; Stephenson, 1975a: 54).

Unlike academic boys' schools, where the classics dominated the curriculum, girls' senior schools emphasized modern languages and steered pupils towards 'womanly' careers in teaching, homecraft or childcare [Plate 2]. Although co-education was discouraged before 1933, the few girls keen to study the classics could attend boys' schools. Nazi hostile propaganda focused on both these and pupils at girls' senior schools who were, allegedly, being diverted from their 'natural' disposition to marry and have children. Accordingly, Hedwig Förster, a Prussian Education Ministry official, announced in 1933 that the curricula of girls' senior schools would be reformed, to de-emphasize intellectual and abstract subjects and stress subjects relevant to a career in practical occupations, like social work. She conceded that women would figure in other 'caring professions', like teaching and medicine, for which academic schooling and university courses were necessary.

But the Nazis did not have 'a developed education programme' in 1933; instead, they made piecemeal changes to the variegated pattern of girls' senior schools during 1933–37 (Lück: 1979: 59). For example, from 1935 needlework was added to the curriculum, but, also in 1935, home-craft was removed from it because of academic demands. Girls would instead learn at home, to enable them to pass a simple test. Eventually, comprehensive reforms created a unified curriculum which reflected the NSDAP's inherent anti-intellectualism and its determination to prepare women for homemaking. In 1937–38, senior schooling was shortened by a year, to eight years, and a new national system was created for both sexes. Four years at elementary school were followed by five general senior school years, before the final three years of specialization. In the general years, the difference between boys' and girls' curricula was that boys studied Latin while girls had needlework and music. In the final three years, however, there was a major difference: girls had no opportunity to specialize in science subjects or mathematics. Instead, they could choose between foreign languages and homecraft, which included nursing, social work, household management and childcare. The ideologically-correct homecraft stream did not qualify girls for university entrance; nevertheless, propaganda depicted it as a major innovation with rigorous theoretical and practical aspects.

Yet by this time preparation for war demanded that women acquire what were normally 'men's skills'. In January 1939, homecraft stream graduates became eligible for university if they passed examinations in various academic subjects, and in August 1939 they were declared eligible for university on equal terms with languages' graduates, as from Easter 1941. This was a botched and belated response to the need for women graduates which had been evident since 1936. Ursula von Gersdorff has written of 'the neglect of women's education, a sin of omission' (1969: 71). Yet it was not 'omission' but deliberate government policy which introduced fluctuating arrangements and denied girls equal educational opportunities. One example was their exclusion from the elite Adolf-Hitler-Schools, while out of ninety-three Napoleas – elite schools run by the SS – two were for women. Their function was characteristically gender-specific: to train a female elite as suitable companions for leading Nazis. But attempting to equip young women for polite society completely contradicted the NSDAP's – and especially the SS's – proclaimed attitude to socialites [Doc. 19].

In higher education, during the 1930s, women were still well-represented in subjects considered relevant to their future in 'caring professions' – arts subjects, medicine and pharmacy. But elsewhere there was a massive gender gap, with the technical universities and colleges for mining and forestry continuing to attract few women, while women's numbers in university science, law and economics departments dropped sharply, before reviving slightly in the later 1930s. By then, however, policies based on sexist prejudice were causing alarm, and even before the war women were being encouraged to study science subjects, although their schooling was simultaneously being altered to prevent their preparing for them. The withdrawal of male students into the *Wehrmacht* left universities with a high proportion of women students [Doc. 18].

Changes in girls' school curricula and wartime exigencies disrupted the education of those expected to compensate for wartime losses of young men. Schools were closed because of winter coal shortages, or else they were requisitioned as makeshift hospitals. Girls' and boys' senior schools sometimes used the same buildings in separate shifts. Pupils were sent to help with the harvest, and, eventually, whole classes were evacuated from bombed or bomb-threatened areas to safer havens where the novelty of different surroundings offered diversions from school work. Tired and hungry girls who remained in towns had their nights and sometimes their schooldays disrupted by air-raid alarms. Nevertheless, until the war's last stages, schooling continued in increasingly difficult circumstances, with substantial numbers of girls preparing for the *Abitur* (university entrance) and many proceeding to higher education [Doc. 18]. Yet Szepansky's 'lenient exam' in January 1944 was undoubtedly a sign of falling wartime standards (1986: 35).

Nazi priorities eroded traditional girls' education, through racist and sexist propaganda in class, through attempts to suppress confessional schools, and through the disruption of school life by the demands of BDM activities. If challenging the forces of traditional conservatism was welcome, their replacement by indoctrination and compulsory Nazi youth activities was repellent. Teachers had to attend ideological training courses, including residential camps, and many joined the Nazi women's organizations or the BDM; yet 'only a few were convinced National Socialists' (Focke/Reimer, 1979: 77) [Doc. 15b]. Many in Catholic areas campaigned successfully against the replacement of the crucifix by Hitler's portrait in classrooms. In universities, the *Arbeitsgemeinschaft der nationalsozialistischer Studentinnen* (ANSt – Nazi women students' group) was created for 'the specific tasks of the German woman student in the National Socialist movement' (Weyrather, 1981: 134). It attracted little enthusiasm from its constituency, but it made intrusive demands for commitment and service, especially in vacations. During the war, even some Nazi teachers complained about poor academic standards as a result of extra-mural demands on pupils' time, while complaints about the frivolity manifested by some women students overlooked the damaging effects of contradictory government policies in women's education [Doc. 18]. Hitler's wish that intellectual values should have the lowest priority had been implemented, with a vengeance.

Youth organizations

The Nazi girls' organization, the *Bund Deutscher Mädel*, was, as Dagmar Reese comments, 'an institution created by men for the recruitment of the "German woman"'. It was strictly for 'valuable Aryans' and belonged to the Hitler Youth (HJ), whose four sections included the BDM, for girls aged 14 to 21, and the *Jungmädel* (JM – Young Girls), for those aged 10 to 14 (Reese, 1981: 164, 169). In July 1932, the BDM was assigned a monopoly of Nazi female youth organization, although in 1935 the NSF gained the right to organize six to 10 year-olds in 'children's groups'. From 1938, the BDM's *'Glaube und Schönheit'* ('Faith and Beauty') section provided separate gymnastics and homecraft training for the oldest BDM members. The BDM uniform included a navy skirt and white blouse, with a black scarf awarded after a probationary period.

From 1933, the dissolution of other girls' groups, peer pressure and genuine enthusiasm provided the BDM with an influx of members. Socialist and communist youth groups were banned, and the national federation of Evangelical female youth organizations was dissolved; its members formed a Bible study group which survived for years. Nevertheless, one Evangelical youth leader claimed that the BDM 'undermined and combated our confessional work and got the Gestapo to close down our free time activities and youth camps' (Wiggershaus, 1984: 50–51). Roman Catholic girls' groups were nominally protected by the 1933 Concordat with the Vatican, but encroachments on them began almost immediately. Nevertheless, Catholic groups organized by a school-teacher could prove an obstacle to BDM recruitment [Doc. 15a and d]. Until they were banned in 1937, Catholic youth groups maintained a 'semi-legal existence, although a huge amount of hate-propaganda was directed against them' (Wiggershaus, 1984: 51). Even then, clandestine groups survived; in 1939, confessional youth groups in Württemberg were 'resurgent' and 'intensifying their work' (Source 2).

In December 1936, the Law on the Hitler Youth declared that 'the whole of German youth . . . is organized in the Hitler Youth'. By January 1939, the BDM and JM had altogether 3,425,990 members. But compulsion was not enforced until March 1939, when it was decreed that 'all young people must be registered for admission by the 15 March in the year they reach their 10th birthday' (Noakes/Pridham, 1986: 419–21). In middle schools in 1940, where 49 percent of the pupils were girls, 97 percent of all pupils were HJ members. In girls' senior schools in 1940, 96 percent were BDM members, although at the few private schools this fell to 87 percent (*Statistisches Jahrbuch*, 1941/42: 638–39). The peak age for membership was between 10 and 14; once girls had left school – mostly at 14 – they could let membership lapse. For older teenagers, as Reese shows, the BDM 'lost any attractiveness more quickly in an urban environment' where there were other forms of entertainment (1989: 218). The Nazi prohibition on cosmetics, for example, did not appeal to city girls, many of whom were employed and sought an adult social life.

Some BDM members were unwilling conscripts, and some managed to avoid more than token involvement. During the war, particularly, dissident youth groups with male and female members emerged in explicit opposition to the HJ, which was seen as part of the new establishment. Subversive working-class youths in the Edelweiss Pirates or the Rebels (*Meuten*) harassed HJ members and created an alternative youth culture. Similarly, the middle-class Swing Youth 'rejected the Hitler Youth norms . . . of a rigid demeanour and tidy dress' and embraced American 'hot jazz', which Nazis deplored (Peukert, 1987: 167). Those who were arrested, including some girls, might end their days in a concentration camp. Yet other girls became BDM enthusiasts: one memoir recalls, 'I was needed! The feeling of being essential to the whole, of no longer having to stand on the margins as a spectator – this feeling was for me new and like a drug' (Wiggershaus, 1984: 41). But this sense of belonging explicitly involved believing that those who were excluded, who could not or would not belong, were weak, hostile and decadent outsiders. As a member of the BDM's national leadership, Melita Maschmann, would recall, the 'worship of our own nation, the obverse of which was our contempt for foreign nations, was the central driving force in our training of young people' (1965: 158–59).

The BDM emphasized hierarchy and uniformity, with a stratified leadership corps whose lowest level commanded up to fifteen girls. At the highest level, a BDM leader was responsible for up to 375,000 girls. But the sudden rise in membership in 1933–34 raised a problem: sufficient leaders could not be trained overnight. They had to be young women, close in age to BDM members, because 'everything was done to immunize young people against any influence from the adult world that was not National Socialist' (Wiggershaus, 1984: 38, 57). Many who became BDM leaders were from more prosperous families. With some avenues in the professions restricted, unemployed teachers and those styling themselves as the elite-in-waiting sought opportunities in the new system; the party's women's and girls' organizations offered novel career choices. Jutta Rüdiger, from 1937 BDM national leader, was an example: with her university qualifications and shameless opportunism, she quickly climbed through the hierarchy, remaining leader until 1945. Nevertheless, especially in working-class areas, a shortage of candidates meeting inherently middle-class criteria of suitability meant that 'a lack of commitment, deficient ideological conviction and Social Democratic parents' did not disqualify a girl from selection as a BDM leader if she had 'leadership potential' (Reese, 1989: 76). Not surprisingly, in some areas the BDM struggled. In rural Württemberg in 1939, the SD reported that 'the absence of suitable, and especially of ideologically reliable BDM leaders' was a problem. 'Outside the towns, there is hardly anyone at all to build up a BDM-"Faith and Beauty" group' (Source 3).

BDM girls were to be indoctrinated to aspire to 'strength and steadfastness', to aim to be not merely mothers but 'heroine mothers' (Lück, 1979: 77). At their weekly meetings, sport, cultural work, health care, social work and homecraft training were geared to promoting the characteristics favoured by the regime's leaders: courage, endurance, willingness to serve, readiness to make sacrifices [Doc. 19]. This meant being fit and healthy for both childbearing and physical work, adapting habits and instincts to the demands of the ruling elite, and forgoing cosmetics and popular entertainment. It meant striving to make the German 'ethnic body' pure, and guarding against 'alien' influences, with hiking and camping in the German countryside to strengthen them physically. It meant doing voluntary work with the 'valuable' socially disadvantaged in both town and country, especially helping with children and housework. It meant serving government policies: for example, in the 'campaign against waste' to promote autarky, BDM girls collected used materials for recycling. During the war, the BDM arranged camps for evacuated schoolgirls, helped with the harvest, assisted the victims of bomb damage, and much more. Some went to the occupied east to educate and assist ethnic German settlers, to the extent that 'the BDM became the dominant force in the community'. Almost 10,000 girls were involved in 1941, with a further 16,022 in 1942 (Rempel, 1989: 151–53). Latterly, BDM members operated anti-aircraft batteries, and some served in the SS female auxiliary corps, chiefly in signals duties.

Yet the leadership's aims were frequently not observed in the localities. The extent to which 'political education' figured depended on local leaders; some were well aware that their group's enthusiasm and cohesion improved if activities were more social in character, with political messages soft-pedalled. Where this was the case, the BDM was positively popular, especially when it provided group activity and bonding of a kind that a restrictive upbringing had previously prevented. As one Bavarian woman recalled, 'we learned to dance in the BDM' (Fröhlich, 1981: 267). Nevertheless, 'compulsion resulted in loss of enthusiasm, boredom, apathy', which reached their apogee in wartime, leaving some enthusiasts disillusioned (Reese, 1989: 42).

Service schemes

While BDM membership lasted for years, the service schemes involved a one-off commitment, with young women – like young men – residing for several months in either another household or a purpose-built camp, and serving as cheap labour for domestic and farm work. Both the HJ and the Reich Education Ministry channelled young people into agriculture for a year at a time, through the Land Service (*Landdienst*) and Land Year (*Landjahr*) projects, respectively. Various agencies, including the HJ and the NSF, collaborated in introducing a Household Year (*Hauswirtschaftliches Jahr*) in April 1934, while the *Reichsnährstand* had its Girls' Land Service (*Mädellanddienst*) scheme. The ANSt introduced a compulsory *Frauendienst* (Women's Service) for women students from October 1933. Göring, too, as Four Year Plan supremo, introduced the *Pflichtjahr* in February 1938, which directed teenage girls into agriculture and domestic work. But the most important Nazi service project was the Labour Service (*Arbeitsdienst*).

In these schemes, 'Aryan' men and women were treated separately but equally, with those excluded from the ethnic community barred from these community obligations. There were consistently more men than women involved, particularly in the Labour Service. In Land Service, for example, in 1936 there were 6,800 recruits, of whom merely 'over 1,000' were female (Source 4). Further, the kinds of service which the two sexes performed differed, because service was intended both to benefit the community and to impress on the recruits their essential – and separate – functions. Thus, young men received military training as well as engaging in physically taxing work, while women learned household and childcare skills as well as engaging in less arduous physical work.

In the Labour Service, young men and women – normally aged between 17 and 25 – spent six months working in gender-segregated groups in return for their board and pocket-money. This served various purposes. It occupied some of the young unemployed in 1934–36; it provided cheap labour for agriculture; and it instilled a sense of service in the young. Further, it had a social engineering aspect, bringing together people of the same age but from differing social backgrounds: 'the young women were removed from their familiar environment – parents' home, school, circle of friends, employment – and came, for example, as city girls to a camp for helping settlers' in rural areas (Lück, 1979: 99). This rendered them both accessible and susceptible to collective indoctrination. In wartime, Labour Service provided a useful pool of easily-directed labour.

At first, Labour Service was voluntary for all but some of the young unemployed and prospective students. It became compulsory for the latter – men in 1933, women in 1934 – to delay university entrance, thus relieving the pressure on overcrowded universities and colleges (see Table 4.1). Labour Service was also designed to ensure that young Germans – and especially students – were not exposed to 'the danger of a one-sided academic education' (Stephenson, 1982: 250). While some prospective students undoubtedly resented Labour Service, others seem to have approached it with idealism and there were genuine enthusiasts [Doc. 20]. Labour Service became generally compulsory for men in 1935 and for women in September 1939.

Table 4.1   Numbers in the women's Labour Service in selected months in 1934

February	May	August	November
7,566	9,674	11,314	10,543

(*Statistisches Reichsamt: Statistisches Jahrbuch für das Deutsche Reich*, 1935: 311)

There were limits to how useful Labour Service could be because of both a chronic shortage of trained and reliable leaders and limits to the funds provided for uniforms and housing recruits in camps. This amounted to a significant sum for 50,000 girls, in two six-month cohorts of 25,000 in 1937, and altogether 100,000 girls in 1940. The *Pflichtjahr*, which placed girls in private homes – often in middle-class and/or child-less homes when they were meant to be helping hard-pressed mothers of several children – was cheaper to run and its numbers were larger (see Table 4.2).

Table 4.2   Number of girls starting their *Pflichtjahr* in 1940

Total	335,972
In agriculture	157,728
In domestic service	178,244

(*Statistisches Reichsamt: Statistisches Jahrbuch für das Deutsche Reich*, 1941/42: 420)

In wartime, the women's Labour Service increased dramatically, with 150,000 recruits in December 1943, and the period of service was ex-tended in 1941 to include a further six months' Auxiliary War Service (Stephenson, 1982: 255–56, 260). This second period was spent in cler-ical work, auxiliary nursing, social welfare, public transport, munitions work; increasingly, women were also drawn into work with the *Wehrmacht*. This culminated, in the final phase from autumn 1943, in often danger-ous work supporting military operations, with searchlight batteries and anti-aircraft guns [Doc. 21].

Reactions to the service projects varied. Some women tried everything to avoid being drafted; some recruits regarded their service as purgatory. For example, 'Inge D.' was conscripted into Land Service on leaving school; she felt homesick for Berlin and was terrified of the cows which she had to feed and milk (Szepansky, 1986: 51). Irmgard Lotze deserted from first the *Pflichtjahr* and then the Land Year because the farmers to whom she was allocated expected to have sex with her. She was insti-tutionalized and classed as 'asocial' (Kaminsky, 1999: 330–32). In Würt-temberg, the shortage of 'suitable leaders' for Land Service meant that 'discipline left much to be desired' and some parents felt obliged to with-draw their daughters (Source 5). But Lore Walb regarded Land Service as 'the most wonderful group experience' which 'strengthened my self-esteem' (Bronnen, 1998: 75). Others, like 'Herta P.', conscripted in early 1944, regarded it as an adventure. After Labour Service in agriculture, she was sent, under Auxiliary War Service, to searchlight duty with the *Wehrmacht*.

She 'had great ideals' and recalled that 'at nineteen, there's always something to laugh about' (Szepansky, 1986: 238, 240). Farquharson is probably right in saying that 'even if the individual girls were relatively unskilled they would still perform domestic chores . . . which relieved the hard-pressed [farmer's] wife' (1976: 235), although some farmers' wives found short-term raw recruits a nuisance. For Gersdorff, the Labour Service was, whatever its shortcomings, 'the only exception to the failure to bring women as a group into war service' (1969: 68), and in Heineman's view it made a significant contribution to the war effort.

Non-Nazi women's organizations

By the 1920s, Germans of all classes and conditions had developed various political, professional, vocational, religious, social and charitable organizations. Among women's groups, the major division was between those for working-class women, affiliated to either the SPD or the KPD, and those for middle-class women – including liberal, professional and vocational groups – mostly affiliated to the *Bund Deutscher Frauenvereine* (BDF – Federation of German Women's Organizations), which in the 1920s had *c.* 900,000 members (Kaplan, 1984: 181). Beyond these, politically independent radical feminists campaigned for fully equal rights, while some nationalist and conservative groups developed links with the Nazis, whose views on women were similar to their own. Nancy Reagin's comments about those in Hanover are generally applicable:

> They prepared bourgeois women for the Nazis' message in many ways: in their distaste for women who worked outside the home; in their espousal of a rigidly 'traditional' sexual division of labor; in their hostility toward the SPD; in their aggressive concern for the 'oppression' of ethnic Germans who lived outside of Germany. . . . (1995: 246)

Even closer to the NSDAP stood Guida Diehl's Newland Movement.

Both the Evangelical and Roman Catholic churches had active parish women's groups; there were also Catholic and Evangelical national women's associations – boasting some two million members each *c.* 1930 – with local branches, while the *Jüdischer Frauenbund* (JFB – Jewish Women's Association) had *c.* 50,000 members (Frevert, 1989: 173; Kaiser, 1982: 483; Kaplan, 1979: 90). Both Christian churches had an explicitly conservative outlook on the 'woman question', which Judaism largely shared. Indeed, the attitude of Christian women's groups had, as Kaiser says, 'been reduced to a matter of how they could act to protect family, community and state against the "unhealthy" politicization of women' since about 1900 (1982: 483). Church-based women's groups had charitable branches, like Evangelical Women's Aid, and the JFB was active in welfare work. But, in denominations with an all-male clergy, women were followers, not leaders; charitable and social work was compatible with Judæo-Christian views that women's chief characteristic was 'motherliness'. The confessional teaching organizations saw the teacher as 'born educator of her own sex, embodying in her own occupation that "motherliness" which was conceived as service to young people and ultimately as service to the "whole community"' (Said, 1981: 105).

In 1932, the secession of two large housewives' associations weakened the BDF numerically, making it an easier target for Nazi *Gleichschaltung* (co-ordination) in 1933. Divisions among organized women were accentuated by a generation problem: the non-communist organizations, including the SPD's and the JFB, were dominated by women active before 1914, and were therefore unattractive to younger women, some of whom favoured the KPD's or NSDAP's more vibrant organizations, especially in the depression. Organizational diversity indicated that there was no single 'women's cause', that women from different classes and conditions had differing priorities and interests. Diversity would, however, prove fatal when the Nazis moved to eliminate competitors piecemeal in and after 1933. Nevertheless, at the beginning of 1933, various women's groups were active in associational life and in lobbying political parties at local, *Land* and national level. Hitler's accession to power on 30 January 1933 changed this dramatically.

Nazi women's organizations: growth and 'co-ordination'

During the 1920s, Nazi women's groups emerged in areas where the party was well-organized; some were associated with their local NSDAP branch, while others belonged to Elsbeth Zander's *Deutscher Frauenorden* (German Women's Order), which affiliated to the NSDAP in 1928. These groups provided soup kitchens for needy party members and SA men, collected money and goods, made and mended uniforms, circulated propaganda material, and provided first-aid for injured SA men. These activities were suitably 'womanly'; the 'political struggle' was left strictly to men. In 1931, Gregor Strasser, the NSDAP's organization chief, replaced these support groups with the new *NS-Frauenschaft*. The NSF had a territorial organization matching the NSDAP's, confirming that Nazi women would work under men's authority. In each *Gau* (region), a *Gau* NSF leader was subordinate to the male regional leader, the *Gauleiter*; in the districts, similarly, a district NSF leader was subordinate to the male district leader; and in the local branches a local branch NSF leader was subordinate to the male local branch leader. This structure persisted until 1945, with the addition, in densely Nazified areas, of cell and block NSF leaders who monitored a neighbourhood, informed on dissidents and encouraged the women to fulfil National Socialist demands (Table 4.3).

Table 4.3   The number of NSF functionaries *c.* 1939 (in the *Altreich* – pre-1938 German borders)

32 *Gaufrauenschaftsleiterinnen* (regional NSF leaders)
725 *Kreisfrauenschaftsleiterinnen* (district NSF leaders)
22,593 *Ortsfrauenschaftsleiterinnen* (local branch NSF leaders)
59,802 *Zellenfrauenschaftsleiterinnen* (cell NSF leaders)
223,024 *Blockfrauenschaftsleiterinnen* (block NSF leaders)

(Scholtz-Klink, 1978: 74)

Some *Gauleiter* welcomed their women's group's practical support: for example, Robert Wagner praised the Baden NSF, under Gertrud Scholtz-Klink, the future NSF national leader. Elsewhere, however, the NSF was riven by strife. While Nazi women mostly accepted relegation to 'womanly' roles, some *Gauleiter* allowed enthusiasts latitude for initiative. It is perhaps misleading to call them 'Nazi feminists' (Rupp, 1978: 17–26), or even 'Nazi "feminists"' (Kater, 1983: 228–34), but many clearly expected to have authority and autonomy within their organization, and freedom from control by the NSF's central office in Munich, under Zander, who had status but little power. The depression and the turmoil of 1932, with its many elections, made Nazi women's 'charitable' work and their assistance to Nazi men assets to local branches, as many *Gauleiter* acknowledged.

Once Hitler was Chancellor, the NSDAP acquired decisive influence over German organizational life and, with Zander's retirement as NSF leader in spring 1933, various ambitious women competed for the succession. Eventually, in February 1934, Scholtz-Klink emerged as leader of both the NSF and the DFW (*Deutsches Frauenwerk* – German Women's Enterprise), a new umbrella organization to assemble under Nazi leadership existing organizations which were not objectionable enough to be purged; she was already leader of the new women's Labour Service. In general, she manifested the obedience and conformity required by party leaders, and she proved conciliatory towards leaders of the remaining non-Nazi women's organizations, those conservative/nationalist, occupational and religious/charitable groups which survived the initial purges. As the mother of a large family who could mouth Nazi platitudes without saying much, she seemed the ideal public face of Nazi womanhood [Doc. 22]. Kater's judgement that 'she was colourless enough for a third-rate organization like that of National Socialist women' (1983: 217) is unkind but not unjust. Appointing her *Reichsfrauenführerin* (National Women's Leader) in November 1934 was 'tactically a clever move . . . [and] Scholtz-Klink remained in office as a useful instrument of the party leadership through to the end of the war' (Dammer, 1981: 219).

Gleichschaltung meant first the disbanding of organizations which were considered objectionable, whereas apparent allies – and Catholic groups ostensibly protected by the Concordat – survived, for a time. Socialist and communist organizations were banned and driven underground. By 14 July 1933, when the one-party state was declared, the NSF was the only women's political organization. Further, organizations associated, however mildly, with feminist campaigning were dissolved. The General German Women Teachers' Union, with over 30,000 members and affiliated to the BDF, dissolved itself after its members were absorbed into the NSLB (Hahn, 1981: 78). The BDF, which tried to compromise with the new regime, dissolved itself in May 1933, although most of its leaders remained in Germany and its magazine, *Die Frau* (*Woman*) continued with self-censored publication for several years. Radical feminist leaders, having fearlessly attacked Nazism before 1933, fled abroad and their organization and journal were suppressed. Various professional, vocational, religious, charitable and social women's organizations remained, some clearly sympathetic to Hitler's government, particularly over its implacable hostility to the left. The leadership of conservative groups like the *Bund Königin Luise* (BKL – Queen Luise League) and the *Ring Nationaler Frauenbünde* (Circle of Nationalist Women's Organizations) acclaimed the new regime, despite misgivings about co-ordination.

Because the continued existence of independent organizations, even with attitudes similar to the Nazis' own, was fundamentally intolerable, creeping *Gleichschaltung* increasingly gave Nazi women's organizations a virtual monopoly. After the initial purges, remaining groups were brought under Nazi leadership to ensure unanimity of purpose. Grill shows that Scholtz-Klink was ahead of the game, ordering the dissolution of the Baden Women's League in April 1933 'to allow the NSF to dominate women's activities. . . . In August 1933 Scholtz-Klink formed a new umbrella agency for Baden's women that included the NSF and all other female clubs' (1983: 312). This doubtless commended her to party bosses when they sought a reliable national women's leader.

Gleichschaltung proceeded in two stages. First, surviving organizations became corporate members of the DFW. Those which slotted seamlessly into its activities survived until the DFW's programme was clarified; later, they were dissolved. For example, the two housewives' organizations merged in March 1934, and then agreed to join the DFW's new section for 'National economy/Domestic economy'. In September 1935, the housewives' organization was dissolved, with the DFW retaining its members and assets, including its magazine. Groups which did not fit into the DFW's organization plan, including conservative associations like the BKL, were dissolved. In 1935, the DFW claimed to have eighty-seven constituent groups; by March 1938, thirteen of these remained (Stephenson, 1981: 139). The former members of dissolved groups either joined the DFW as individuals or else abstained from organizational life. Those who tried to revive even the most innocuous group activity might fall under *Gestapo* surveillance. In Hamburg in 1936, former members of the dissolved housewives' organization were prohibited from meeting for 'coffee mornings', presumably because this threatened the DFW's monopoly. And in Württemberg in April 1939, '40–50 women of the former local branches of the Bund-Königin-Luise met together in an organized coffee and knitting circle'. This was reported under the heading 'Illegal Organizations' (Source 6).

Religious associations had the best chance of survival. The Concordat promised protection for Catholic non-political organizations, and many, including women's parochial groups, survived for some years. The Union of Catholic German Women Teachers survived by declaring itself a charitable organization under the Concordat's provisions, and even retained its magazine until 1937. In general, teachers in confessional schools supported the new regime; the Union of German Evangelical Women Teachers welcomed its stance against '"Marxist" poisoning of secular schools' (Said, 1981: 116). Nevertheless, both Evangelical and Catholic organizations were targeted for *Gleichschaltung*. For example, at first, Evangelical and Catholic social and counselling groups were brought into the DFW, forming the core of the Reich Mothers' Service section, founded in May 1934. But, as the DFW's structures were developed, these groups became expendable, with the Evangelical groups' corporate membership of the DFW revoked in 1935.

Evangelical women's groups were handicapped by division, by contrast with the solidarity and relative unity in the Catholic church. The 'German Christians', the pro-Nazi wing of the Evangelical Church, had their own women's groups, which were hostile to those sympathetic to the Confessing Church – Evangelicals who resisted Nazi attempts at control. But Catholic women were under pressure to co-operate with Nazi women, and, where they refused, were forced to focus on purely religious matters. Parochial church women's groups persisted, sometimes reinventing themselves after a zealous local NSDAP leader had dissolved them. For example, in 1938 a priest in Saarburg reportedly revived the former Catholic Women's Union there, under another name.

The JFB survived because Nazi policy was to segregate Jews for racial rather than religious reasons. Jewish women were excluded from Nazi groups, but their own organization survived beyond 1933, trying to mitigate distress within their persecuted community and, increasingly, preparing Jews for emigration. After the atrocity of *Kristallnacht* ('the night of broken glass') in November 1938, the JFB was ordered to dissolve and merge into a single organization representing Jews. In this capacity, its leaders continued with social welfare work within the diminishing Jewish community, until they were deported to their death in 1942.

Nazi 'women's work', 1934–39

Strife in the NSF before and during 1933 led NSDAP leaders to entrust ultimate authority over it to a strong man. Erich Hilgenfeldt, leader of the NSV, became 'Leader of the Office of the *Frauenschaft* in the Supreme Leadership of the Party's Organization' (Böltken, 1995: 33). He forcibly solved the NSF's leadership crisis, appointing Scholtz-Klink as his deputy and leader of the NSF and DFW. But whereas previously the NSF had provided most Nazi welfare assistance, Hitler assigned to the NSV a monopoly of party welfare work in May 1933, depriving the NSF of its key function. Thereafter, NSF/DFW volunteers served in projects organized by the NSV, whatever propaganda boasted about the NSF's role [Doc. 24]. Hilgenfeldt was formally NSF/DFW superintendent for several years, but his direct involvement ceased once order was established under Scholtz-Klink's leadership, from 1934. She quickly appointed loyal female staff and developed 'the women's work of the nation'.

The nature of this work demonstrated the party's views on women even more clearly than leading Nazis' prescriptions. In her first speech at a Nuremberg Party Rally, in September 1934, Scholtz-Klink described her organizations' aim as being to show women how their small individual actions could affect the destiny of the entire nation, and how, therefore, they must learn to subordinate their individual desires and aspirations to the greater good, as defined by Nazi leaders. The emphasis was strongly on service to, and personal sacrifice for, the community; to achieve this, the DFW, under the NSF's 'politically reliable' supervision, ran training courses to try to imbue 'valuable' women with their message. Participation in the DFW's activities was, while full of duties, also portrayed as a privilege; it was therefore restricted to 'valuable Aryans'. But participation did not necessarily indicate enthusiasm for the regime, the party or its women's organizations. After *Gleichschaltung*, if women wanted any associational life, there was little alternative to accepting Nazi structures and leadership. The major exception was religion, because, even where women's guilds or church youth clubs were dissolved, church services continued.

From 1934, the DFW – led by the NSF, at every level – ordered its work according to the administrative divisions within Scholtz-Klink's Berlin central office, the *Reichsfrauenführung* (RFF – National Women's Leadership). The 'working sections' were: National Mothers' Service; National Economy/Domestic Economy; Border/Foreign; Auxiliary Service; and Culture/Education/Training. Purely administrative sections included Press and Propaganda, Organization/Personnel, Law and Arbitration, and Finance. Through the sections' practical work and through courses in Culture/Education/Training, the NSF/DFW leadership aimed to instil in 'valuable' women from all social, political, regional and religious traditions an awareness of their responsibilities and pride in their racial identity. The NSF/DFW promoted 'politicization', which, in a dictatorship with multi-party politics outlawed, effectively meant indoctrination. Yet the regime's aim was not simply to suppress opposition and dissent: for 'valuable' women, 'politicization' meant active acceptance of the regime's policies and their implementation in daily life, under the NSF/DFW's guidance. Thus women should attend the National Economy/Domestic Economy section's courses in housekeeping and cooking, to absorb Nazi notions of cleanliness, efficiency and thrift – or else risk being branded 'asocial' – and to serve the policy of autarky, by, for example, using seasonal produce and eschewing expensive labour-saving devices. As Nancy Reagin says, 'in Nazi programmes . . . almost all attempts to be thrifty . . . entailed additional labour' (2001: 167–68).

The DFW's top priority was work in the home and with children. Through the Reich Mothers' Service, women would learn about childcare within the context of 'hereditary health' and the new racist legislation. The Border/Foreign section would raise their consciousness about allegedly oppressed German minorities abroad, while Auxiliary Service would train and deploy them in the social welfare projects of the NSV or the Red Cross, as well as in air-raid protection. Culture/Education/Training provided courses in ideology, as well as instruction about Germany's cultural traditions; its offerings attracted far fewer women than the practical courses of the Reich Mothers' Service and National Economy/Domestic Economy.

In some ways, the NSF/DFW's activities differed little from those of the old housewives' organizations and the churches' mothers' welfare groups, and some opportunists from these older groups joined the DFW, hoping for influence and authority. But issues of race and 'value' permeated Nazi women's activities, even where they were not explicit. NSF/DFW leaders repetitively reminded women not only to cherish existing children and to educate them to 'think in the National Socialist way', but also to bear more children. Crucially, they were to safeguard the future of the 'Aryan race', by ostracizing the 'worthless' and ensuring that their children did the same. Thus warmth, generosity and comradeship – the organizations' boasted qualities – were built squarely on the exclusion of all who failed the tests of 'value' dictated by the male political leadership. In this way, Nazi women contributed to the marginalization and persecution of individuals whose conduct would have transgressed no law in a state where human rights were protected and the rule of law prevailed.

Gertrud Scholtz-Klink received many distinctions; she was an honoured guest at functions at home and abroad, and she was nominally a member of various committees and leadership groups. She was nominally leader of the women's section of the DAF – with Robert Ley her superior – and, until 1936, leader of the women's Labour Service. Her high profile was, however, cosmetic: NSF/DFW leaders had no powerbase within the NSDAP itself and no input into general party affairs. Women's membership of the party was tiny in the Third Reich's formative years, at 5.5 percent in December 1934, falling to four percent in the two following years, although it rose sharply from 1937 (Kater, 1983: 206–7). But many women party members shunned the NSF/DFW, while in Scholtz-Klink's home *Land*, Baden, for example, even some NSF district leaders did not join the NSDAP until 1937. The party was and remained a male-dominated, male chauvinist concern, with members' wives – apart from tokens like Magda Goebbels – kept firmly in the background. Women leaders' authority was confined to the NSF/DFW, while they themselves remained subordinate to the party's male territorial leaders.

The NSF/DFW did not even have a true monopoly once non-Nazi groups were suppressed. Urban working women joined the DAF, while rural women's interests were the concern of the *Reichsnährstand*. The Hitler Youth claimed the right to organize young women, even if the NSF for long contested that. But, like the pre-1933 women's organizations, the NSF/DFW had a generation problem: young women experienced the virtually paramilitary organizations of the BDM and Labour Service, but then were expected to accommodate to the 'womanly' NSF/DFW, whose leaders had a very different outlook; this became increasingly obvious, particularly in wartime.

The NSF/DFW's leaders tended to be middle-class, and often lower middle-class. When Scholtz-Klink said 'all working German women are gathered together [in the DFW] regardless of which position they are working in' [Doc. 22], she was referring to neither employed women nor working-class women, but to DFW members who 'worked' in its sections as volunteers, in the tradition of leisured middle-class women. The RFF patronized its local leaders and members, gearing their activities to women with little education and less intellect. Every detail of a local branch's work and courses was prescribed, 'down to the details of table decorations' (Dammer, 1981: 227–28). A centrally-dictated text left no room for individual discretion among even 'politically reliable' leaders who had attended training courses. Most were volunteers; even in the elite NSF, salaried officials were rare. In Württemberg, many NSF functionaries came from sufficiently affluent households to allow them to serve unpaid, but, even in 1939, some local branches had no NSF because nobody would organize one without pay. There were even districts, like Öhringen, where in '1937 the district *Frauenschaft* leadership [was] "currently unoccupied"' contrary to party instructions (Arbogast, 1998: 85). In Baden, while Karlsruhe district had a comprehensive NSF organization in May 1934, still in 1936 there was no NSF in 35 percent of all districts (Michel, 1999: 239). Elsewhere, one woman might serve as NSF leader for several districts. In the DFW, 'there was a lack of suitably skilled women' to run training courses, 'and so it was obliged to work with personnel from the old women's associations' (Dammer, 1981: 225).

Further, Nazi women exerted little direct influence on their own constituency, 'valuable' German women, unless these joined the DFW. While a few hundred thousand initially became corporate members, through a co-ordinated organization, in 1936 a mere 23,000 women were individual DFW members. By the end of 1938, this had risen to a million and a half, after recruiting drives and the acquisition of Austria, whose women – like Sudetenlanders – showed disproportionate enthusiasm for the DFW [Map 2]. But in early 1939, only six percent of women over the age of 20 in the '*Altreich*' were DFW members. The NSF, with around two million members – not the '11 million' quoted by Saldern (1994: 151) – was an elite group whose individual followers were less numerous than itself. By contrast, the women's section of the DAF – not part of the *Reichsfrauenführung* – had some four million members (Stephenson, 1981: 131, 141–42, 148). The 'women's organizations', then, were directly relevant to only a few 'valuable' women, although their public events were well-attended 'because they were often the only chance [a woman] had to leave the house without her husband' (Dammer, 1981: 225). As Winkler says, the NSF 'was relegated to an unpolitical and relatively unimportant corner in the Third Reich' (1977: 41). Yet local NSF busybodies – in the block or cell – might irritate the uninterested by trying to mobilize them or they might prove dangerous by spying and informing on individuals. Where their networks were patchy, however, as in many rural areas, this was hardly an issue.

Other ways of reaching women were tried, through control of women's media. The Mothers' Service section's magazine, *Mutter und Volk* (*Mother and People*), had 150,000 subscribers in 1938, but the DFW's glossy magazine, *Frauenkultur im Deutschen Frauenwerk* (*Women's Culture in the DFW*), had a mere 23,000. The NSF's magazine, *NS-Frauenwarte* (*NS Women's Viewpoint*), had a circulation of 1.2 million in 1938; thus, almost half of NSF members did not subscribe to it. Non-Nazi publications were transformed into organs of the DFW's sections: for example, *Deutsche Hauswirtschaft* (*German Housekeeping*), the magazine of the dissolved housewives' association, became the magazine of the National Economy/Domestic Economy section, dispensing household hints and recipes to its 140,000 subscribers in 1938 (Stephenson, 1981: 155, 168).

There was more success in reaching women via the new medium of radio, which from 1933 was under strict government control. By 1939, there were 12.5 million radio sets in Germany, and housebound housewives comprised much of the daytime audience (Lacey, 1996: 102). The RFF's Press and Propaganda department collaborated with the state broadcasting authorities to produce programmes directed at women in the home, to try to order their attitudes and patterns of consumption. Other organizations, like the RdK and the DAF's women's section, broadcast their own programmes, and government policies regarding women were

1. The Nazi ideal: a 'German mother' happily feeding her large family of young, blond children (1938)
Source: Ullsteinbild

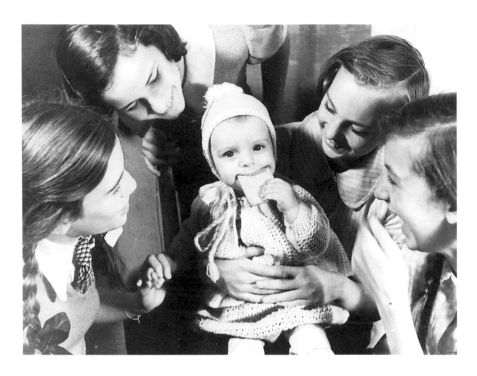

2. Education for motherhood: pupils at a girls' senior school in Berlin adopt a 'class baby' (1936)
Source: Ullsteinbild

3. 'Womanly work': NSV nursery nurses bathing children (1939)
Source: Ullsteinbild

4. 'Married women return to factory work in wartime': a newspaper photograph encourages recruitment (*Deutsche Allgemeine Zeitung*, 4 August 1940)

Source: Ullsteinbild

6. Trainee tram conductresses learning to pull the bogie (second car) out of its shed (c. 1940)
Source: Ullsteinbild

5. Women workers making parts for water hoses for use by the fire service after air raids (1940)
Source: Ullsteinbild

7. 'Enemy alien': a woman from the Ukraine at work in Stuttgart. On her right
breast is a badge marked 'OST' to indicate that she is an 'eastern worker'
(i.e. from the USSR) (1943)
Source: Ullsteinbild

8. The image: models demonstrating fashionable suits (1943)

Source: Ullsteinbild

9. The reality: women at a shop window viewing shoes made partly or entirely from straw, which could be purchased without ration tokens (1941)

Source: Ullsteinbild

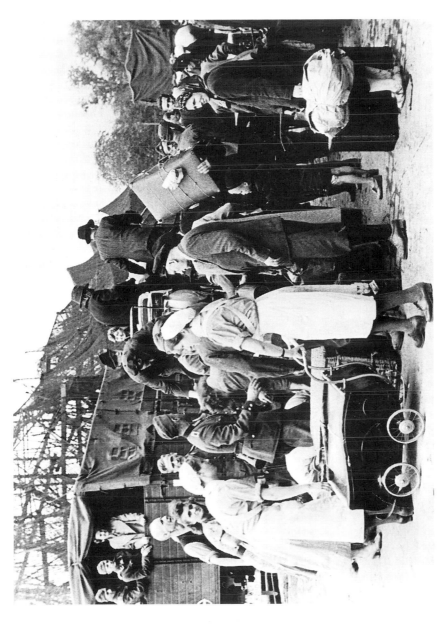

10. NSV nurses helping Hamburg citizens to evacuate the city after the fire-bombing of 'Operation Gomorrha' in summer 1943

Source: Landesmedienzentrum

11. The persecuted: newly-arrived Jewish women and children as prisoners on the ramp at Auschwitz-Birkenau concentration camp (c. 1944)
Source: Ullsteinbild

12. The persecuted: women prisoners, in striped uniforms, at work in Ravensbrück concentration camp during the Second World War
Source: Ullsteinbild

publicized on air. For example, 'the *Pflichtjahr* was given a high media profile . . . [while] only careers considered "useful to the nation" and befitting the maternal spirit . . . were given airtime (at least in the early years of the regime)' (Lacey, 1996: 119). The NSF/DFW enjoyed some influence over women's programme-making, and even made programmes itself. This enabled them to reach women who shunned their activities, bombarding them with advice about health, childcare, recipes, house-keeping. This truly was an invasion of the private sphere, which was consistent with Nazi attempts to permeate family life and to politicize women.

Overall, the Nazi women's organizations had negative success, destroy-ing the rich variety of German women's associational life. Yet in a sys-tem allegedly aiming to return a woman to her family circle and limit her options in the public sphere, the existence of a nationwide Nazi women's organization was perhaps a contradiction in terms. It provided career opportunities for several, including mothers like Scholtz-Klink, and plentiful scope for voluntary work outside the home. It manifested the Nazi managerialist obsession with 'training courses' for everything from mothercare and cookery to ideological awareness and air-raid pro-tection, while accepting party leaders' emphasis on women's instinct and emotion. It aimed to turn women's leisure time into productive service, yet the activities which women favoured most were those with a low service and/or ideological content and a high degree of sociability. For example, the *Frauenhilfsdienst* (Women's Auxiliary Service) of the NSF/DFW, introduced in May 1938 to provide volunteer welfare workers, in practice depended overwhelmingly on young, single women. The war would only extend Nazi women's 'public sphere' activities, with the absence of men, the effects of bombing, and territorial conquests creat-ing new roles for them outside their home.

5

The crisis of war

War on the home front

Ostensibly, Germany should have been well-prepared for war in 1939, with the introduction of rearmament and conscription in 1935 and a Four Year Plan for the economy in 1936, and with plans for mobilizing civilians to prepare for a 'total war' in which the nation's entire resources would be concentrated on achieving victory as quickly as possible. Hitler was haunted by both memories of and myths about the First World War, when, he and many others believed, a strong and successful German army had been 'stabbed in the back' by Jews and socialists (and perhaps also women) at home, in a protracted conflict. In *his* war to overturn the remnants of the hated Versailles Treaty and give Germany hegemony in central and eastern Europe, the home front would be geared, as never before, to war production. A successful Germany would dictate the pace of aggression, and would therefore be able to avoid the mistakes of 1914–18, when a long two-front war with unsatisfactory allies and against a coalition of enemies had sapped Germany's strength on the home front.

While 'total war' was strategically desirable, however, attempts to implement it would collide with Hitler's main domestic preoccupation: preventing another 'stab-in-the-back'. Policies which risked generating serious discontent among the 'valuable' population were to be avoided, and every effort made to maintain civilian morale. In wartime, there were three crucial issues which affected morale. Firstly, the question of compelling inactive German women to work for the war effort was debated at great length before the nettle was tentatively grasped in January 1943 (see Chapter 3). Hitler was anxious not to antagonize women who were reluctant to enter employment, and even more anxious not to cause discontent and defeatism among husbands, brothers and fathers who, at the fighting front, might receive distressing letters from home. Secondly, the diminishing domestic supply of foodstuffs and other goods and services could be mitigated by plundering vanquished countries of food, raw materials and people, but only up to a point. Thirdly, especially from 1942, enemy bombing and, from late 1944, invasion inflicted damage and terror. Censorship and propaganda could disguise the nationwide effects of bombing and strengthen Germans' hatred of the enemy, but they could not camouflage the increasingly desperate situation experienced on a daily basis in many German cities. Individuals could see that official propaganda diverged sharply from their own reality, and they turned in on themselves, insensitive to the suffering of others and sceptical about officially-managed news media [Doc. 25].

At first, while not welcoming a second twentieth-century war, many did applaud the expansion of Germany's power and the overturning of Versailles. As Szepansky says, in Berlin, 'news of the outbreak of war . . . was received with mute horror. . . . But the victorious [campaigns] were not without effect, impressing a large section of the female population and altering attitudes' (1986: 13). In the western town of Marburg (Baden), there was manifest enthusiasm on the fall of France in June 1940. By contrast, in the nearby village of Oberschopfheim, 'such euphoria did not exist at any time during the war. On the home front the conflict was essentially a repetition of World War I, and, like the first war, it was especially arduous for women' (Rinderle/Norling, 1993: 166). As in 1914–18, the conscription of millions of men into the *Wehrmacht* distorted the balance of the civilian population. Able-bodied men were increasingly withdrawn from their peacetime occupations, leaving adolescents, old men and, above all, women to try both to replace them and to make increasingly desperate attempts to fuel a gigantic war machine. Over three million German men were killed, and millions of others were either wounded, missing, or POWs in Allied hands. Nevertheless, although Hitler approved in February 1945 Bormann's scheme for a 'women's battalion' to join the fighting forces, 'it is unlikely that these women ever saw active service' (Willmot, 1985: 18). Although women were utilized in work with the *Wehrmacht* towards the end of the war, and sustained casualties in this role, it was men who fought at the front in their millions [Doc. 21]. And while some Nazi and professional women were deployed in civilian tasks in occupied countries, women's arduous effort was overwhelmingly confined to the home front, in a war in which aerial bombardment increasingly put urban civilians, too, in the front line [Doc. 27a and b].

From being victors over various European countries in east and west from 1939 into 1942, albeit with tenacious resistance in Yugoslavia and the USSR, Germans found themselves on the defensive in 1943–45, with their armies in retreat and their cities devastated by bombing. In 1945, Germany itself was progressively invaded by enemy forces, yet the war continued until the entire country was under foreign control. Even if the Allies had not formulated a policy of 'unconditional surrender' in January 1943, Hitler would not have contemplated a loser's negotiated peace: he preferred to see Germany devastated and humbled. And as defeat loomed, the Nazi state unleashed brutality and terror on its 'valuable' citizens: particularly in 1944–45, men and women were incarcerated and, increasingly, executed for the most trivial kinds of 'defeatism'. The persecution and murder of Hitler's perceived 'enemies', especially Jews, continued until the end, with extermination camps abandoned to the advancing Red Army, their inmates forced westwards in the appalling death marches, and concentration camps liberated by foreign troops, in time to rescue some, but too late for many, of their prisoners.

Bombing of towns

The Spanish Civil War of 1936–39 demonstrated the destruction and carnage that aerial bombardment could inflict. Like other governments, Hitler's issued gas masks because of the possibility of gas attacks from the air in a future war, while its organizations had in peacetime mounted air-raid protection courses. Both the ANSt and the DFW's Auxiliary Service section, among others, had actively promoted awareness of and competence in air-raid protection. From as early as 1940, the British RAF bombed northern and western German cities, but a qualitative change occurred in 1942, with the use of large phosphorous incendiary bombs. The northern city of Lübeck was severely attacked on 28 March 1942, with the loss of 320 lives. Two months later, the first thousand-bomber raid inflicted devastation on Cologne, with the loss of 469 lives. In both cases, many more were injured and tens of thousands rendered homeless (Sorge, 1986: 90–91). From this point onwards, the frequency and severity of Allied bombing raids steadily increased, with catastrophic effects on German cities. Hamburg endured a 'fire-storm' for ten days in summer 1943, with 34,000 people killed and '255,691 homes completely destroyed' (Büttner, 1993: 25–26) [Doc. 27a]. The razing of Dresden in February 1945 is a particularly well-known disaster; there were many others.

For those on the ground, bombing meant terror and disruption. Survivors tried to continue with normal life, perhaps with little sleep for nights on end, as the air-raid sirens summoned them to cold and crowded shelters. Mothers remaining in towns had to shepherd children and carry babies, first to a shelter and later back to see if their home was still standing [Doc. 27b]. If it was not, they might go to relatives in less vulnerable areas, or they might be more or less forcibly evacuated from towns to the countryside by the NSV [Plate 10]. Employers complained about absenteeism or poor productivity on the part of women who had perhaps always been unwilling workers. But if they had had little sleep, if they could not find food because their local shops had been bombed, if their water, gas and electricity supplies and their transport to work had been disrupted by bombing, it was hardly surprising if they were late for or absent from work – or preoccupied while they were there. If their own or a neighbour's home had been damaged, they had more immediate concerns. It was, indeed, 'amazing that the number of employed women remained constant or even rose slightly, right up to the end of the war' (Schupetta, 1981: 297).

Consumers and the 'black market'

Even before the war, there had been food shortages, especially in 1934–36, as Hitler's government gave priority to rearmament at the expense of foreign imports. The drive for autarky in the 1930s, especially under the 1936 Four Year Plan, included a 'campaign against waste', as part of which the NSF/DFW launched a massive propaganda campaign to try to persuade women to 'cook cheaply, thriftily, responsibly and healthily', as well as to 'mend well – darn well' (Stephenson, 1983: 131). Women were exhorted to minimize their demands on industry and to utilize German produce in season, preserving any surplus for later. The DFW's National Economy/Domestic Economy apparatus of advice centres, dispensing leaflets and giving demonstrations of and courses in new cooking techniques, was already in place before 1939 [Doc. 23]. During the war, many goods became scarce or unobtainable, and the German diet was increasingly restricted in both size and variety: by the last two years of the war, it consisted overwhelmingly of bread, potatoes and other vegetables. But German 'Aryans' did not starve in this war, as civilians in some occupied countries, like Greece and The Netherlands, did. At no time during the war did 'Aryans' suffer the disastrous shortages of the years 1916–18, although Jews and other 'enemies' did. Thus Hitler's aim of avoiding another 'stab-in-the-back' by aggrieved and starving urban consumers – the majority of them women, as in 1914–18 – was successful, even if consumers were far from contented [Doc. 26a and b].

To conserve goods that were in short supply, by pacing their release to consumers, consumption was controlled. Even before German forces attacked Poland, the rationing of some foodstuffs and other essentials was introduced, on 27 August 1939. Further controls complemented rationing: for example, the prices of non-rationed goods were controlled, to prevent their being bought up by the wealthiest. Hoarding and bartering became punishable offences, along with profiteering, black-marketeering and the illicit slaughtering of livestock. By their universal application, the controls were intended to create a sense of national solidarity, with everyone, regardless of class or station in life – with the major proviso that they were 'Aryan' and 'valuable' – making the same, limited sacrifices. But the controls also facilitated discrimination between different categories of inhabitant, in favour particularly of industry's 'heaviest workers' and pregnant and nursing mothers, for example, and also to favour 'Aryan' Germans at the expense of Jews, foreign workers and POWs. 'For Jews . . . caloric intake plummeted immediately [in 1939]' (Kaplan, 1998: 151). Jewish women had dreadful difficulty in shopping when they were restricted to an hour or two each day at designated shops, obliged to wait until 'Aryans' had been served, and forbidden to buy a wide range of goods.

Where there were controls, there was evasion of them, and a comprehensive 'black market' developed. Women would buy up available non-perishable commodities and hoard them for use in bartering. For example, women might hoard detergent or glass jars which they could exchange with farmers for otherwise unobtainable foodstuffs, in flagrant violation of rationing controls. Urban women travelled to the countryside by train to barter, and rural women, who had no time to shop, were glad to obtain otherwise elusive items in this way. Ration cards were a prized commodity, particularly as more goods were controlled, and they could be used to prevent people from leaving their area without permission [Doc. 27a]. But some people obtained additional cards illegally. For example, in January 1943, a cleaner in the Stuttgart Food Office was jailed for over two years for stealing and using masses of ration cards, and her friend, who had used some of them, was jailed for two years. Groups of friends and clients worked together to breach the controls. In Württemberg, a Roman Catholic convent claimed ration cards for far more nuns than it housed, from 1939–41, and failed to deliver its own food produce to the official collecting depot, in conformity with the controls. The convent's leaders and their neighbouring accomplices were jailed for this offence.

Even from the start of the war, women complained about the unavailability of goods, and working women complained about difficulties in shopping before or after work [Doc. 26a and b]. Undoubtedly, part of the anger about women who refused to take employment resulted from their freedom to shop when goods were available; part of the reluctance of those who refused employment perhaps derived from fear of being disadvantaged as shoppers if they worked all day. Standing for hours in queues after a day's work generated complaints and was not an attractive prospect for the non-employed. Especially from 1943, with rations cut repeatedly and shops closed on some days each week, many women 'had sleepless nights because they did not know what they would put on the table the next day' (Beck, 1986: 103). Some saved ration tokens to spend on a Christmas treat, but this meant going without beforehand. Yet if urban 'Aryan' Germans faced shortages, they received the lion's share of supplies. As Kaplan says, 'many Jews feared starvation almost as much as they feared the Gestapo' (1998: 151). By the end of the war, foreign workers in industry, especially eastern Europeans, were often living at or near starvation level. Both Germany's remaining Jews and some foreign workers had to resort to begging from sympathetic 'Aryans', or stealing food or ration cards, in order to survive.

Clothing, too, was rationed, and from March 1942 clothing stamps were issued only for the purchase of mourning dress; even so, women were encouraged, instead, simply to add black crepe to their existing clothes. Any available material was required for surviving victims of bombing who had lost everything, although small squares of material could be bought for mending. To those who complained about women wearing trousers in public, the SS newspaper replied in 1944 that 'they are doing us a good turn when they utilize textiles which have been used for men's trousers' (Noakes, 1998: 358). The requirement by some occupation forces in 1945 that German households provide liberated foreign workers with a full outfit of clothing was regarded as particularly harsh after years of recycling and mending existing clothes.

While food was plentiful in the countryside, in the towns the increasing shortages of food, clothing, shoes and fuel – quite apart from non-essentials – bore particularly heavily on women with families. Growing children needed not only abundant food but also larger sizes of clothing. Particularly with men away from home, it was women's responsibility to provide these, and trying to do so was time-consuming, worrying and exhausting. Some urban women tried to maintain 'war gardens' to supplement their rations: 'the small amount of extra vegetables was very important to us' (Szepansky, 1986: 66). Some families received the occasional food parcel from rural relatives. Women who had lost their possessions through bombing could obtain replacements – if they had the tenacity to go from one office to another to find someone to authorize this. By the last months of the war, with utilities and communications disrupted and the country increasingly invaded by enemy forces, merely surviving was enough of a struggle.

Migrants, evacuees and refugees

As never before, between 1939 and 1945 vast numbers of people were on the move, whether voluntarily or not. In autumn 1939, for example, families living in Baden near the French border moved to Württemberg, returning home once the threat of bombing had passed. From 1940, there were also social migrants, women who were wealthy enough to move to south German resorts which were still safe from bombing and had smart hotels which were, at first, unaffected by rationing. Other women who feared the bombing of towns in the north and west migrated to safer rural areas even before mass government-sponsored evacuation began in earnest from 1942, once Allied area bombing began to devastate towns and cities in industrial and port areas. Places like Berlin, Hamburg and the Ruhr cities were particularly hard and repeatedly hit, with the result that mothers and children, and even teachers and whole school classes, were relocated to rural areas in the south and east. By December 1942, almost a million mothers and children had been evacuated from cities to the countryside, and the numbers would only increase (Beck, 1986: 24–25). But southern cities, too, were bombing targets from 1943, with heavy raids on Munich and Stuttgart, particularly, in 1944. Many of their women and children moved to the nearby countryside, although women working in cities had to remain there.

Evacuation was intended to protect non-combatants who were not involved in essential industries and services; it also involved social engineering which demonstrated that there was often little fellow-feeling between urban and rural women. Their shared membership of the *Volksgemeinschaft* had little meaning for people who were often as alien to each other as foreigners. Rural women complained about the ingratitude of those billeted on them, who believed that, 'as "guests of the *Führer*" they had a right to special respect and attention' (Source 7). Urban women were aghast at rural living conditions: if they were used to homes with electricity and piped water from taps, they were quite unprepared for the absence of these facilities in far-flung villages, complaining: 'I'm used to something better than this. At home I have central heating and hot and cold running water' (Stephenson, 1987: 358). They were accustomed to the rhythms and noises of a town and complained about the squawking of farm animals at daybreak. Leaving their familiar environment was traumatic enough without being expected to undertake farm work. The NSV paid host families for their bed and board, which seemed to many evacuees recompense enough. Yet worn-out farmers' wives regarded them as lazy and snooty – 'expecting to be waited on as if they were in a hotel' (Source 8) – and as promiscuous as well. The urban women complained about squalor and boredom in the countryside, but brightened up if a German military unit was stationed nearby.

Evacuees were denied the little luxuries of their home environment. Small villages might be safe from bombing, but they lacked entertainment like a cinema or even a café. Many village homes had no radio, and the shops and services of the towns were far away. In Berlin, Szepansky's German teacher had 'pitch-black hair parted in the middle', but, after the school's evacuation eastwards to Upper Silesia, the parting showed white at the roots, ' "because she couldn't bring her hairdresser with her", as the malicious among us remarked' (1986: 34). Sometimes the incomers were made to feel so unwelcome that, after a few weeks, they and their children returned home, contrary to social workers' advice to remain in the safer countryside. Some said that they 'would rather go back to where the bombs are than live here in a village where nothing ever happens' (Source 9). Others worried about their homes and about husbands who had been left to fend for themselves. The DFW organized cookery courses for the men, and its 'Neighbourhood Aid' scheme sent women volunteers to ensure that they were cared for [Docs 23 and 24]. But this was anything but comforting for evacuated women, and many returned home in spite of official threats to withdraw their ration cards if they did so.

Not all evacuees' experiences were bad: 'The children and I lived with a very nice family in [East Prussia]. . . . We mostly cooked together. . . . I didn't have to work, but I did a bit of sewing or helped in the fields' (Szepansky, 1986: 67). Many women stayed with relatives, but this could mean splitting up their own family for months at a time between different relations in separate locations, when their husband or sons were already absent in the *Wehrmacht*. Nevertheless, the major difference between town and country – apart from bombing – was that the rural population had food supplies of a kind increasingly unavailable in the towns. Some women evacuees were able, at least in 1941, to send food parcels to urban relatives. Even if traditional rural dishes were sometimes unpalatable to urban families, the greater availability of food was attractive. Some of the children learned to assist on farms, and some evacuees kept in touch with their former hosts for years afterwards. By the time they had returned home, a new wave of refugees had reached rural areas,

as families from Germany's eastern territories fled westwards ahead of
the advancing Red Army in 1945. Once again, there were cultural differences between incomers and hosts; once again women sharing a small
kitchen often worked in less than harmony.

Nazi women at war

The NSF/DFW had the unenviable tasks of trying to ensure that German
women complied with government demands in wartime and of maintaining women's faith in a German victory, even – and especially – when
that looked increasingly impossible [Doc. 23]. Encouraging women to
take paid employment or to work as volunteers was the subject of a
massive campaign in the *NS-Frauenwarte*, with its limited readership, in
1939–40. It was also the thankless task assigned to NSF cell and block
leaders in the localities. Propaganda boasted of women's 'readiness for
service' [Doc. 24], but most of those involved in voluntary work were
young unmarried women who were either enthusiasts or else could be
pressured into it. When older and married women did exert themselves,
it was less to support NSF/DFW projects than to deal with desperate
conditions in their neighbourhood – for example, after a bombing raid.
The *Reichsfrauenführung* – removed from reality – busied itself with plans
for a victorious postwar era and the NSF continued to hold 'ideological
training courses' to ensure that its functionaries were purveying up-to-
date details of Nazi orthodoxy within the NSF/DFW and to women in
their locality. Scholtz-Klink still regarded 'political education' as vital in
the desperate winter of 1944–45, when for most it was an irrelevance.

At local level, NSF/DFW officials monitored shops to try to prevent
fraud. For example, in August 1940 in Stuttgart, a DFW official reported a
shopkeeper who had not stamped the tokens on his customers' butter
ration cards, allowing them to be used again. The DFW urged housewives to shop early in the day so that working women did not face long
queues in the evening; this open invitation to the non-employed to buy
up scarce goods while overburdened women worked only added to working women's discontent. The NSF helped to organize bomb shelter places
for expectant mothers. In Berlin, for example, 'there was a delivery room,
a midwife and a couple of nurses. About 30 women stayed there' in 1940

(Szepansky, 1986: 66). The 'Neighbourhood Aid' section – under the direction of the NSV and mostly staffed by the BDM – performed various tasks, from clearing up after bombing raids to darning socks [Doc. 24]. For the most part, NSF/DFW women worked at arm's length from the major Nazi atrocities. But in a host of small ways they reinforced the regime's demands and helped to marginalize and persecute anathematized groups. They might, as local officials, inform on those in their block, cell or local branch who contravened laws or Nazi norms. They might ensure that Jewish women were not shopping outside their prescribed hours or purchasing forbidden goods. Scholtz-Klink's postwar claim that Nazi racial policies 'were nothing to do with me and equally nothing to do with the *Reichsfrauenführung*' was patently false (Zentner, 1975: 262).

Germany's victories created pastures new for the NSF/DFW. Ethnic German women in both eastern and western Europe had to be cared for, taught how to 'become German again', and have their attitudes Nazified. They included immigrants from Soviet eastern Poland, Romania and the Baltic States. The NSF/DFW sent members to look after them: in 1940, 1,265 of them worked in reception camps and with the NSV, finding accommodation and furniture for the immigrants (Stephenson, 1981: 191). This property had usually been seized from Poles and Jews. BDM groups and Labour Service recruits directly participated in the evictions and also helped ethnic Germans from eastern Europe to settle into properties which Polish families had, in their view, 'forfeited . . . through untidiness and lethargy' (Harvey, 1998: 198). There can be little doubt about the enthusiasm of some young women, especially the leaders, for this heartless task: 'I was filled with a cold, almost intoxicating feeling of superiority', was Maschmann's attitude to the Poles (1965: 106). With similar attitudes, including an utterly patronizing approach to ethnic German settlers, the NSF/DFW ran both practical courses in childcare and homecraft, and ideological training courses to 'educate' them. NSF members from the '*Altreich*' were encouraged to visit the new territories to learn about the NSF's work there, so that they could return home and enlist volunteers for it.

One priority was to create branches of the NSF/DFW in the new territories and to win members for them. In the new *Gau* Wartheland, on former Polish territory [Map 3], there was a virtually captive constituency among immigrants who were either in transit camps or in sequestrated accommodation. Disoriented and deprived of free choice, they had to submit to training in childcare, cooking, sewing and – above all, in more primitive eastern Europe – health and hygiene. In western areas like Alsace and Lorraine, each annexed to a Nazi *Gau*, organizational structures could be built at speed, and some local women rushed to join. The Strasbourg district of *Gau* Baden was able to found seventeen new NSF local branches between October 1941 and April 1942, and these mounted the usual round of courses and events (Stephenson, 1981: 195). But, although the tireless district NSF leader, Rosel Reysz, tried to pressure unwilling Alsatians into her organization, she found that even the NSDAP's district leader could not force his subordinates to ensure that their wives joined the DFW. When unwilling women were prevailed on to join, they often merely paid a subscription and remained inactive. As in the '*Altreich*', the enthusiasts faced an uphill struggle against the apathy or hostility of the majority.

The exigencies of war at once expanded and restricted the NSF/DFW's activities. Its missionary work in occupied territories gave its activists a new sense of purpose. There was work to do at home, usually under NSV direction, with evacuees and victims of bombing. Comforts were knitted for the troops, and injured soldiers were visited. Shortages of food and clothing kept the National Economy/Domestic Economy section busy, especially in dispensing advice over the radio. Its local offices sold leaflets about repairing and conserving furniture, clothes, appliances and encouraging the consumption of wholemeal bread and the conservation of energy. The Mothers' Service section gave advice about children's diets and launched a campaign against smoking and alcohol abuse in women. Increasingly uncomfortably, NSF women were in the front line in confronting angry shoppers or factory workers complaining about increased working hours for poor rates of pay.

But while NSF/DFW officials busied themselves with 'womanly' activities, the organizations themselves withered: wartime problems made increasing demands, so that even non-employed women had little time for unpaid NSF/DFW activities. If they were not standing in queues or mending clothes, they might be volunteers with the Red Cross or in air-raid protection. Yet the NSF/DFW always had a false prospectus: the elite NSF had not constructed a truly mass following in the DFW. In 1940, 'the ratio of footsoldiers to functionaries was three to one' (Kater, 1983: 223). The final admission of failure came in 1942 when Scholtz-Klink – frequently absent from her office for long periods – sought to have the NSF and DFW merged. As the war disrupted communications, NSF/DFW activities became increasingly localized, dependent on a depleted number of activists as young women were drafted into service schemes and older women were either working long hours or perhaps had been evacuated elsewhere. The propaganda continued to the end, in areas still under German control, but the realities of bombing, casualties and floods of refugees from the east meant that remaining NSF stalwarts were reduced to the kind of local welfare work that Nazi women had performed in pre-1933 days.

The last days of the war

Fighting ended at different times in different places in late 1944 and early 1945 because of Hitler's insistence that Germans defend every village and every house. Most obeyed, not out of loyalty but because in the east they were terrified of the Red Army and in the west they were dragooned – on pain of death for 'defeatism' – by NSDAP officers or army or SS forces into destroying bridges and digging anti-tank ditches, in a pathetic attempt to block a well-equipped invader. By this time, remaining civilian men under the age of 65 had been drafted into the *Volkssturm* (home guard), and women were left either to prepare their families for flight into the diminishing core of Germany or to await enemy attack and occupation. Some 4.5 million Germans fled westwards in 1945–46, 'belong[ing] mainly to female-headed families' (Heineman, 1999: 81). For those who stayed, 'the few remaining men, and in some areas even the strongest women, disappeared to do slave labor in the Soviet Union. . . . Many thousands never returned' (Botwinick, 1992: 106). In the west and south, women, like men, protested against the senseless struggle to the finish which Hitler decreed. 'In Bad Windesheim [in Bavaria], the women of the town engaged in open mutiny against the move to make it part of a defensive area for the retreat of a German division' (Beck, 1986: 191). As a reprisal, one woman was singled out and shot. Many women and old men helplessly obeyed orders to build defences, but they resisted attempts to try to enlist young boys for a last-ditch military effort, occasionally with success.

In both east and west, invading armies were accompanied by women 'camp followers', but this did not prevent mass and multiple rapes. Foreign troops sometimes regarded Germany's women as part of the spoils of war. The western allies were not above this: 'they *stole, robbed, raped women.* It was indescribable. The English, the Canadians, and the Americans. Indescribable' (Owings, 1994: 97, her emphasis). French soldiers invading south-western Germany also raped German women [Doc. 28]. But the mass rapes perpetrated by Red Army soldiers in eastern Germany were of a different order. In villages and towns, Soviet soldiers sought out German women:

> women were raped without concern or consideration for age or appearance. Many victims felt that the Soviet troops treated such sexual abuse as a victor's justly earned prerogative. In Winzig, three women who sought refuge in the ruins of [a] house . . . lived through months of sexual terror. Their experiences were repeated thousands of times from the [eastern] border to Berlin. (Botwinick, 1992: 106)

After multiple rapes, some women were seriously injured and many were diseased [Doc. 28]. Others, seeking release from the seemingly inescapable, committed suicide, hanging or drowning themselves, or taking poison. The Soviet soldiers were undoubtedly partly motivated by revenge for the atrocities inflicted on Soviet citizens by Germans. This was also why they killed and mutilated civilians in their path, sometimes after raping them.

As news of these atrocities spread, women hid in cellars or cupboards [Doc. 27b]. But in the south and west, news of the western Allies' conduct in occupied areas was more positive: in Württemberg, it was said, 'it isn't the Russians who are coming, but, on the contrary, civilized people, and it's clear from areas already under Allied control that the inhabitants are finding the occupation tolerable' (Stephenson, 1990: 355–56). 'Tolerable' meant that it was appreciably better than either occupation in the east or the continuation of war.

With many men killed or taken prisoner, women were left to try to rebuild shattered lives in the towns or to maintain farms. Some evacuees

stayed in the countryside for several months because of the urban housing shortage. The plight of urban women was particularly acute, with
utilities disrupted or destroyed and food barely obtainable. Some formed
relationships with Allied – particularly American – soldiers to gain access
to illicit rations or little luxuries like chocolate or silk stockings. The Americans in Heilbronn district (Württemberg), it was sourly observed, 'soon
had their "lady friends", particularly among loose women [evacuees]
from Duisburg but also among chocolate-hungry Swabians [locals]'
(Source 10). In these instances, the vanquished could hope for material
gain in return for sexual favours.

6

Opponents, perpetrators and the persecuted

Opposition and reprisals

While most Germans accepted Hitler's regime as a fact of life and some
enthused about it, there were many varieties of dissent, disaffection and
opposition, among women as well as men. At its simplest, there were
'women who only reluctantly hung out the Nazi flag, [and] women who
carried two shopping bags so as not to have to raise their hand in the
so-called German greeting' (Wiggershaus, 1984: 106). At its most dangerous, there were those who demonstrated, by word or deed, their contempt
for Nazism and Nazis. Describing the entire spectrum of dissenting or
oppositional activity as 'resistance' is controversial. Yet if people could
be executed for distributing anti-regime leaflets – as members of the 'White
Rose' group were in 1943 – or for listening to enemy radio during the
war, then these activities were perhaps 'resistance', even if they posed
no physical threat to the regime. The ferocity of the Nazi leadership's
reaction to mere disobedience or dissent, especially in later wartime
Germany, was compounded by its arbitrariness: as Hans Mommsen says,
'the highly fragmented nature of the Nazi political system resulted in a
wide-ranging variety of opposition and . . . ultimately it was primarily
the Gestapo that decided what resistance was' (1991: 161).

The regime's officers were ever-vigilant, but their numbers were limited.
Thus they targeted as a priority those designated as their opponents, in
particular Jews, socialists, communists. With political opponents, 'the

persecuting authorities were more likely to train their sights on men than on women' because of their own prejudices (Kaminsky, 1999: 208). Often, women took over tasks in the illegal SPD and KPD after men had been arrested. They acted as couriers and instructors, and, in the absence of men, sometimes assumed leadership functions from which they had previously been excluded. Under hazardous circumstances, they bought paper and typed illegal leaflets or pamphlets which they transported in a shopping bag or pram. At even greater risk, they harboured printing presses, and offered their homes for illegal meetings or as havens for fugitives. The *Gestapo* did not refrain from using torture on women who took these risks and were detected; some women died as a result and others were convicted and executed. Further, the regime's exploitation of 'collective responsibility' – seizing as hostages those closest to a known or suspected opponent (Bennett, 1998: 3–5) – was particularly effective with women when their children were involved.

Those involved in high-profile resistance were mostly men, although Sophie Scholl was one of the leading figures in the 'White Rose' group in Munich in 1943; she was executed. Nevertheless, female relatives of prominent male resisters fell under suspicion or were arrested for refusing to divulge their man's whereabouts [Doc. 29b]. The wives of the 1944 July Plot conspirators were arrested, but none was executed. Even in some KPD groups the traditional division of labour prevailed, with men performing most of the political work and depending on women for food and shelter. When the Knöchel organization in Düsseldorf was uncovered by the *Gestapo* in 1943, twenty-three women and twenty-five men were indicted, of whom twenty men and two women were sentenced to death. One of these two, Berta Fuchs, told her daughter and sisters that she had only 'done her duty by helping human beings'. It was perhaps disingenuous to regard providing refuge for KPD functionaries as 'unpolitical' (Wickert, 1994: 418).

Opposition was, then, highly dangerous. An SPD activist, Minna Cammens, who was arrested in March 1933 for distributing leaflets, was one of the earliest women to be killed after incarceration. Yet, 'although it was particularly risky for her as a Jew', a former trade unionist, Aenne Heymann, 'engaged in illegal opposition activity after 1933. She was murdered in the Auschwitz extermination camp' (Schmitt-Linsenhoff et al., 1981: 109). Johanna Kirchner, another socialist activist, sought safety in France, where she prepared illegal leaflets, gathered information and helped fugitives. In 1942 the French authorities arrested her and handed her over to the Germans. She was put to death in Berlin's Plötzensee prison in June 1944. In Plötzensee alone, 269 women prisoners were executed, including very young women; one 17-year-old was executed for compiling and distributing anti-Nazi leaflets. A 21-year-old woman was hanged in 1943 (Wiggershaus, 1984: 47).

Women belonged to resistance organizations like the Baum Group, which mostly consisted of Jewish members of former communist and socialist organizations. Twelve of the eighteen members who were arrested and executed were women. In the communist '*Rote Kapelle*' (Red Band) there were disproportionately many women who affixed posters in public places at night and typed leaflets. Of the forty-nine group members who were arrested from August 1942 and hanged in Plötzensee prison, eighteen were women (Schefer, 1981: 279). Women were also disproportionately represented in another communist group, the Saefkow group. Several of them were condemned to death or long prison terms. Women who had acted as couriers, gathered money for fugitives, or acted as a liaison between different cells of the group, were hanged. Arnold Paucker suggests that 'women were particularly suited to underground work' (1999: 20). Certainly, while young Jewish women were prominent in several communist resistance groups, they figured also in the Berlin anti-fascist girls' group, whose members were denounced in 1941 for anti-war propaganda and condemned to death.

Being arrested could act as a deterrent. An Evangelical youth leader who persisted with illegal group activity was arrested, interrogated and imprisoned for two months to await transfer to Ravensbrück concentration camp as a 'stubborn case'. She was held with more than twenty people in one room: 'very decent women and girls, who had been incarcerated because of a political joke or listening to an English broadcasting station. . . . Jehovah's Witnesses, fortune-tellers and all kinds of criminals, thieves, procuresses, robbers and murderers' (Wiggershaus, 1984: 51). One of her relatives knew Gertrud Scholtz-Klink and managed to achieve her release. She spent the rest of the war – from July 1942 – quietly in her parents' house, refraining from youth work until after 1945. Nevertheless, some women, particularly in socialist or communist groups, were arrested and imprisoned several times for repeated 'illegal' activity.

In the later war years, women especially demonstrated a dissident attitude – chiefly a matter of grumbling that was difficult to prosecute without denunciations. There were even some demonstrations, as in November 1943 in Witten and elsewhere, when women evacuees from the Ruhr and Rhineland publicly protested about the confiscation of their ration cards, and the police refused to stop them. But someone reported Margarete Schäffer, who had been drafted as an interpreter with the air force. She asserted, 'in a group of comrades', that Hitler was 'the greatest criminal of all time', and called his government 'a rabble', among other things (Szepansky, 1986: 63). For this, she was sentenced to death and executed on 20 July 1944.

Perpetrators: warders, professionals, denunciators

One of the 'opportunities' which the male-dominated Nazi system permitted women was the chance to participate in perpetrating its worst crimes. The apparatus of Nazi oppression became so vast and well-organized that large numbers of people, including thousands of women, assisted in its operation. Some used their initiative in torture and other forms of abuse. The policies and the apparatus – for example, in the 'euthanasia' programme – were, however, devised by men; patriarchal society survived intact, reinforced by female as well as male executors. The most obvious female perpetrators were warders in concentration camps like Ravensbrück, but some women doctors, nurses and social workers collaborated in the regime's policies of racial harassment, identifying, segregating and persecuting individuals who were 'hereditarily diseased', 'asocial' or non-'Aryan'. Teachers who pilloried and bullied Jewish children were despicable. Leaders in the youth and service organizations who instilled in their impressionable charges a doctrine of xenophobic hatred, and took the initiative in bullying foreign families and dispossessing them of their homes, reinforced the oppressive dictatorship.

Certainly, most of the 3,000 or so women warders often behaved in a gratuitously brutal manner, contradicting both the traditional stereotypical view of women as gentle nurturers and the NSF's view of women as warm, comradely, generous (Milton, 1984: 308). As Wiggershaus says, 'in terms of arrogance and self-righteousness, inventiveness in kinds of torment and unbounded sadism, there was no gender-specific difference in women's favour' (1984: 96). Women victims were shocked by the pleasure some female warders took in inflicting cruelty from a position of power. For Goldhagen, 'German women [camp] personnel sought to strip the Jews of all vestiges of humanity' (1996: 343). Some showed a pitilessness defying belief in their brutality towards women and children. They personally beat and kicked the defenceless to a pulp, unleashed savage dogs on them, drowned them in latrines. In extermination camps, they whipped victims towards the gas chambers. Wives of SS men and camp commandants sometimes made a sport of tormenting inmates or 'selecting' them for death. The most notorious of these was Ilse Koch, at Buchenwald, but there were others.

Some have tried to explain warders' inhuman behaviour. For Wiggershaus, they often came from a deprived background or dysfunctional family, and welcomed a better-paid job with the SS. They 'wielded power over defenceless people deprived of their rights, whom they abused dreadfully, like, for example, the warders at the Majdanek concentration camp. . . . They functioned as small cogs in the huge NS machine' (1984: 64). Doing the job was bad enough; using initiative in torture and abuse was unpardonable. Rita Thalmann argues that 'the warders – with a few exceptions – compensated for their own enslavement, by picking on those who were more severely oppressed than they were themselves' (1984: 270). That sounds dangerously like pleading in mitigation. These women clearly knew what they were doing: some belatedly tried to make amends when the balance of power changed in 1944–45. Others even tried to disguise themselves as camp inmates.

Besides warders, there were various minor officials in the penal system who had contact with prisoners or performed clerical work for commandants, the SS or the *Gestapo*. Some prison staff were brutal, but others could show humanity. Franziska Haenel, a brewery worker imprisoned in 1944 for saying that German bombers were 'scarcely better' than the enemy, became well-acquainted with women officers in a Hamburg jail and was allowed 'even to do gardening for one of the warders'. Hella Rüthers, repeatedly imprisoned for communist activity, won some sympathy from 'a warder, an old Social Democrat woman' (Kaminsky, 1999: 271, 237). Women employed as *Gestapo* spies and informers had direct contact with repression: 'they delivered their victims to the system, as employees they worked at the very centre of the terror, typing death lists and interrogation records, and they were aware of how the prisoners were tortured' (Wolters, 1996: 113). They perhaps complained about 'excesses', but still continued with their work. One clerical worker, Inge Viermetz, rose to become a leading figure in the SS '*Lebensborn*' organization, deeply implicated in the seizure of foreign 'Aryan' children for 'Germanization', and also in the 'euthanasia' of a child (Böltken, 1995: 109).

Professionally-qualified people of various kinds, including some women, oiled the wheels of the machinery of persecution. History graduates worked in genealogical records offices, categorizing the 'valuable' and the 'worthless'. Social workers, who were overwhelmingly female, identified candidates for sterilization [Doc. 7]: as Rosenhaft says, 'women [in] the welfare service . . . stood at the cutting edge of Nazism's most inhumane policies' (1992: 154). Nurses in psychiatric institutions participated in the murder ('euthanasia') of their charges, or knowingly assisted those who did by moving patients to rooms where the killing took place or preparing lethal medicines. Burleigh mentions 'Pauline K., whose bluff charm was accompanied by a frighteningly matter-of-fact attitude to murder' (2000: 388–89). A few nurses and women doctors experimented on concentration camp inmates and, when they had ruined their health, dispatched them to a lingering and painful death. One paediatrician, 'surpassed them all. . . . She participated in cruel experiments, and helped to cause the death of many a victim' (Kater, 1989: 109–10).

One of the paradoxes of Nazi Germany is that, while the *Gestapo* was rather thin on the ground, 'no one felt far from the scrutiny of the Nazi state whether in public, at work or even at home' (Gellately, 1990a: 186). The reason was that 'there were many professional and amateur helpers on whom they could rely' (Gellately, 1990: 72). There were networks of official informers, and, beyond them, there were thousands of individuals who denounced neighbours, lodgers, acquaintances and even spouses to the police. Franziska Haenel, a clandestine socialist and pacifist, was denounced by a female neighbour in a close-knit community. Her reaction was: 'I just couldn't believe such people existed' (Kaminsky, 1999:

270). While for the state's purposes denunciation served political ends, by uncovering nonconformists and dissidents, for the denunciator it was often a means of settling a personal score. Thus wives informed on husbands who were unfaithful or drunken or violent, in the hope of being rid of them for a while. Alternatively, a long-standing grudge against a former husband might be the motive [Doc. 29b]. Women who were not Nazis might exploit state repression to solve their personal problems.

The accusations varied. Women receiving male visitors might be denounced as sexually promiscuous by neighbours. A slighted wife might denounce her husband's lover. Although the *Gestapo* often recognized personal grudges for what they were, if the woman denounced was a Jew or had dealings – particularly sexual relations – with Jews, its officers took a strong interest. As Wolters says, 'denunciation was indispensable for carrying through state measures of persecution against particular groups of the population and for the control and monitoring of social attitudes. Thus it played a major role in the terror system' (1996: 26). 'Aryans' convicted on the basis of denunciation generally received a prison sentence, but Jews would be sent to a concentration camp; they would be lucky to survive. Denunciation of one 'Aryan' by another tended to be of the stronger by the weaker, 'with both sexes evenly distributed' (Burleigh, 2000: 304). Thus lower-class women denounced middle or upper-class women, and, within the family, wives denounced husbands, but not vice versa. This might involve accusations of friendliness towards Jews or other non-'Aryans', or it might simply relate to 'utterances hostile to the state' [Docs 29a and b]. Some of those who were denounced and tried were executed, but many were not.

Denunciation brought Nazi terror into the private sphere, and women, by participating in it, were partly responsible. As Wolters says, 'denunciation has the status of indirect perpetration, because denunciators did not directly kill their victims, but they delivered them to the state's machinery of persecution' (1996: 8). During the war, women were increasingly brought into traditional 'male' environments, as professionals, as bureaucrats and clerical officers, and in prisons and concentration camps, and they often used their new opportunities for personal gain or to exert unaccustomed authority. In exercising agency, they, like men in Nazi Germany, often abused their power.

The persecuted: non-'Aryan' women

Whatever threats the Nazi leadership had made before 1933, the speed with which legislation and pressure marginalized non-'Aryans', progressively disaggregating them from German society and targeting them with discriminatory measures, caught many unawares. Some, like the 30,000 Sinti and Roma 'Gypsies', were easy targets because they had previously faced discrimination and were often not integrated into society – although some were (Noakes, 1987: 91). From 1933, they were mostly classed as 'racially worthless', and many 'Gypsy' women were summarily sterilized. This was 'a catastrophe' because, for Roma and Sinti, 'a large number of children guaranteed good fortune and respect' (Zimmermann, 1998: 258). The 'asocial', too, often lived on the margins of society. The few Black Germans, the 'Rhineland Bastards', were sterilized in 1937 and later incarcerated. Leaders of the Slav Sorbian minority were sent to concentration camps. But disentangling the bonds that tied many German Jews into their community's commercial, professional or social life was a greater challenge, one to which Nazis were diabolically equal. Part of their strategy involved threatening, pillorying and punishing 'Aryans' who persisted in having contact with Jews, a strategy which produced overwhelming compliance and hastened Jews' isolation.

For Jewish women, the loss of a husband's job through discrimination increased the burdens of caring for increasingly impoverished families, even before the Draconian restrictions on what they could buy in wartime. Sometimes this 'led to an enforced equality between men and women' (Pine, 1997: 154), as women took the day-to-day decisions that helped families to survive. They comforted children who were ostracized by former friends and humiliated at school, insults that they could not prevent [Docs 17a and b]. They made a home wherever they could find one, with some landlords evicting Jewish families and others harassing them. Because 'women's identities were less easily ascertained . . . since fewer Jewish women than men worked outside the home', they managed to obtain food (Kaplan, 1998: 36). If a husband was arrested and incarcerated, as many were after the pogrom of November 1938, the wife, while desperately anxious, had to sustain her family and try to obtain his release. From May 1940, Jewish women under the age of 45 were conscripted for manual labour, adding to their difficulties. Sudden changes, like the order in Berlin in March 1941 for over 1,000 Jews to leave their homes within five days, magnified the nightmare. As one woman said, 'I am so despondent, I really don't know how I can stand it' (Bronnen, 1998: 96).

The continued existence of the JFB until 1938, especially in large cities, helped to maintain Jewish women's morale by providing solidarity and offering cultural activities of the kind from which Jews were increasingly barred. As 'Aryan' friends melted away, it provided society. The JFB's tireless welfare work helped to sustain women and families as conditions worsened. In the end, it provided advice and support for those planning to emigrate. Younger women were more likely to consider emigration; elderly women often feared the unknown abroad more than torments within Germany. If an entire family could not emigrate, the mother might send her children to safety abroad. However difficult that was, 'I was thankful that I had had the strength to send the children away' (Pine, 1997: 166). By 1939, more than half of the 1933 German Jewish population had emigrated, including proportionately more men than women. Thus more Jewish women than men – in a ratio of 1,366 to 1,000 – remained as potential victims of Nazi persecution when their deportation and murder began in 1941 (Milton, 1984: 301).

The terrible logic of Nazi racist policy was evident during the war. Marginalization, sterilization, expropriation and persecution were utilized incrementally from 1933 to reduce both the numbers of non-'Aryans' and other 'undesirables' and their participation in economic and social life. Between 1939 and 1941, 'euthanasia' extinguished 70,000 'lives unworthy of life', with a further 30,000 to follow (Wippermann, 1998: 213). Some of the victims had previously been sterilized; both 'Aryans' and non-'Aryans' were affected. But the only sure way of eradicating the 'worthless' was to destroy fertile women and their children. Extermination camps were not 'even for women and children', as the compassionate say: they were *especially* for women and children, because men could not propagate their genetic identity without women, and surviving children would eventually reproduce. For this reason, quite apart from considerations of fitness for being worked to death, women, especially those with children, were often 'selected' for death on arrival at a camp [Plate 11].

This applied particularly to Jewish women, who were numerically by far the greatest female victims of Nazi annihilation policies; it applied also to others, including Roma and Sinti women, many of whom were deported to Auschwitz in 1943 and murdered, including those in 'mixed' marriages. Jewish women watched and waited as friends and relatives were seized and deported; some became 'submarines', going into hiding if they could find shelter and food. Some were protected by marriage to an 'Aryan', although that protection ceased on divorce – which was not infrequent because many 'Aryans' in 'mixed' marriages resented the hardship they experienced – or on the husband's death [Doc. 30]. While Jewish women in 'mixed' marriages were 'privileged' by being exempted from some of the disabilities imposed on Jews, they increasingly became targets for harassment, unless they had '*Mischling*' sons in the *Wehrmacht*. Familial ties could also help in an 'unprivileged' mixed marriage, where the man was a Jew. In the Rosenstrasse protest in Berlin in early 1943, several hundred 'Aryans' – wives, relatives and even strangers – facing 'savage threats by the Gestapo and the SS', prevented the deportation of 1,500 Jewish men who had been seized (Kaplan, 1998: 193). This was, however, a virtually unique occurrence.

Some individual non-Jews provided shelter or food for Jews who, their possessions confiscated and their access to rations minimal, went into hiding, often moving from place to place. Many Jewish women, like Resi Weglein, 'lived in constant anxiety' until 'the bitter hours arrived for ourselves' (Bronnen, 1998: 110). She and her husband were transported to Theresienstadt – Terezin in Bohemia – nominally a ghetto but in reality a concentration camp, in 1942. They were privileged in not being sent immediately to an extermination camp. But, as Weglein describes, eventually most of the inmates of Theresienstadt were transported to Auschwitz where they perished [Doc. 31].

The persecuted: inmates of prisons and the camps

Many women were sent to jail in Nazi Germany, whether for violations of the criminal law – thieving, fraud, prostitution, for example – or for political or racial 'crimes', or as 'subversives ... includ[ing] female Jehovah's Witnesses and Gypsies' (Milton, 1984: 300). Some were incarcerated as hostages for male opponents who had fled Germany. A jail was bad enough, with poor food, primitive toilet and washing facilities, rigorous discipline and hard work. Living and working in a cramped cell with other women could, however, breed supportive friendships, while evacuation to a basement during an air-raid provided association with other women in the jail. But the teenage communist Hella Rüthers was shocked at being imprisoned with 'prostitutes and thieves' in 1934 and she survived lengthy solitary confinement in a *Gestapo* prison before once again being jailed with 'prostitutes and child-murderers' (Kaminsky, 1999: 234, 237). As a political prisoner, she felt superior to convicted criminals.

Prison was sometimes a staging-post on the way to a concentration camp. But women activists in the SPD, KPD or trade unions were taken into 'protective custody' in a camp soon after 30 January 1933. If they had children, they were told that these would be removed and brought up as Nazis. The first women's camp was established at Moringen in October 1933; before that, women were held separately in improvised camps. When more women had been arrested, for opposition or for being 'asocial', women's concentration camps were established at Lichtenberg in Saxony, and then, most notoriously, at Ravensbrück in Mecklenburg in 1939 [Plate 12]. In June 1939, 440 Austrian 'Gypsy' women, who were 'allegedly workshy and asocial', were sent to Ravensbrück (Lewy, 2000: 175). 'Paula S.' spent six months there in 1941 'for possessing a copy of Bishop Galen's sermon condemning the "euthanasia" programme.... Today, she still cannot describe what she experienced... in the camp' (Burleigh, 1994: 179–80). In 1939, Ravensbrück had 2,500 inmates; by April 1942, this had risen to 7,500 (Noakes, 1998: 174). But women, and especially Jewish women, were also incarcerated in other camps, like Theresienstadt and Auschwitz [Doc. 31]. 'Many of the German-Jewish women were of middle-class origin; others came from small, close-knit rural communities; all were stunned by the noise of the overcrowded ghettos and camps' (Milton, 1984: 313). Added to that were the ritualistic humiliation of inmates – with women often forced to strip naked in freezing temperatures in front of SS men – and the unbridled brutality, with beatings or other physical violence inflicted for little or no reason.

In early 1942, the SS leadership ordered that concentration camp prisoners should labour for the war effort. New camps were built near armaments works while some firms opened branches near existing camps, including a branch of Siemens near Ravensbrück. In March 1942, in Ravensbrück, 'roughly 6,000 [women were] capable of work . . . in the armaments industry' (Noakes, 1998: 174). Rita Sprengel, an economist who, as a prisoner there, did clerical work, remembers calculating piece-rate wages for women working eleven hours a day – 'wage calculations for prisoners who didn't get a penny in wages!'. This was done to measure productivity so that prisoners' treatment – especially their food rations – could be adjusted accordingly. The slightest deviation from strict working patterns resulted in beatings and perhaps death, and the prisoners reached extraordinarily high levels of productivity. They were, after all, 'practically the property of the SS . . . , working for their lives' (Szepansky, 1986: 153–54).

Living conditions in the camps were insanitary and primitive, food was unpalatable and inadequate, and discipline was exceedingly harsh. One 'asocial' teenage girl, who served a short but terrifying punishment spell in a concentration camp, was determined not to repeat the experience. Those consigned for longer had no such choice. As the demands of war industry intensified, conditions increasingly deteriorated, with filth and malnutrition breeding diseases like typhus and tuberculosis which, with cold, hunger and brutality, claimed many lives. But prisoners sometimes formed 'families' whose solidarity helped them to survive the cruelty and hazards of the camps. In Auschwitz, 'families' of three or more Jewish women 'tried to stay together, and identified with a shared group identity . . . [and] helped their members survive by pooling resources and energies' (Neiberger, 1998: 133). Thus the stronger helped the weaker, food was shared, and morale was maintained by, for example, 'family' pressure to attend to personal hygiene and appearance. In Ravensbrück, too, 'families' provided mutual support and food was shared. Those who were punished for poor work by having their rations withdrawn received food from fellow-inmates.

In the 'Final Solution' from 1942, Jewish women perished in huge numbers, with those who arrived at camps either pregnant or with small children immediately 'selected' for death. The old and weak, too, were murdered at once. The remainder were put to work in dreadful conditions which claimed many more lives. The extremes of cruelty, violence, hunger, humiliation and dehumanization inflicted on inmates accounted for many lives. Goldhagen contends that Jewish women at Helmbrechts camp 'were discriminated against in every conceivable manner' and treated much worse than other prisoners (1996: 341). In August 1943, the separate 'Gypsy camp' within Auschwitz was liquidated: 'There were terrible scenes. Women and children were kneeling . . . and calling out: "Mercy! Have mercy!" It was all to no avail. They were brutally beaten and kicked and pushed onto the lorries. It was a terrible, cruel night' (Benz, 2000: 129). Some survived all of this, and more. Resi Weglein stayed on in Theresienstadt largely because, as a nurse, she was useful. It was undoubtedly something of a lottery: Jewish women who were accomplished musicians survived in Auschwitz because the commandant wanted an orchestra.

While many inmates were murdered, either through organized slaughter in gas chambers in extermination camps or through arbitrary, often random, brutality on the part of warders or SS men, others remained in concentration camps until the end of the war. Camps in the path of the advancing Red Army were abandoned, and their remaining inmates forced to flee westwards under the supervision and extreme brutality of their warders. Without adequate food, water or rest, they were forced on. Many died along the way; those who failed to keep up with these 'death marches' were bludgeoned or shot.

The persecuted: non-German women workers

Victories over Poland in 1939 and western European countries in 1940 allowed Hitler's regime to encourage or force foreigners to work in Germany, but the major influx came from late 1941 with the deportation to Germany of masses of Soviet civilians. Altogether 'some 10 to 12 million people were deported from their German-occupied homeland' (Kaminsky, 1999: 348). Some died in transit, and others perished in Germany as a result of ill-treatment, malnutrition, work in hazardous conditions, or bombing. In September 1941, there were 3.5 million foreigners working in Germany, for the German war effort; in November 1942, there were 4.7 million; the largest annual total was 7.6 million in 1944. Some were male POWs, but of the 5.7 million registered civilian foreign workers in August 1944, 1.9 million – one-third – were women (Herbert, 1997: 194, 296–98) [Plate 7]. With over eleven million German men conscripted into the *Wehrmacht* during the war, and with Germany's enemies from 1941 numerically much superior, even millions of foreign workers did not suffice. Wippermann argues that there was a 'gender-specific component' in that 'the "protection" of German women came at the expense of the foreign worker' because otherwise German women would have had to perform the jobs done by foreigners (1998: 185). This is debatable: given the government's reluctance to force 'Aryan' women into arduous work, and given women's reluctance to be drafted, it seems probable that many jobs done by foreigners would simply not have been done without them. Schupetta is hardly exaggerating in saying, 'without the exploitation of foreign workers, as early as 1942 the German economy would have collapsed' (1981: 306).

The manner of recruitment and treatment of foreign workers depended on their ethnic origin. Generally, workers from western Europe had better living and working conditions, better wages and better rations than eastern Europeans – and especially the *'Ostarbeiter* ('eastern workers' – from the USSR). Women were not normally forcibly recruited from western Europe, but in the east they were. Herbert points out that

The foreign female laborers were predominantly from the East (87 percent), contrasted with 62 percent of the men. The lower a given group in the Nazi political and racial pecking order, the higher the percentage of women, ranging from three percent among the Hungarians (allied with Germany) to 51.1 percent of the civilian workers from the Soviet Union. . . . In the summer of 1944, there were more female Eastern workers in Germany than civilian male and female workers from Belgium, France and Holland combined! (1997: 296–97)

Women migrant workers from occupied western Europe sometimes lived in barracks, but sometimes they were able to rent a room because they earned a wage. Complaints were made about the conduct of French and Belgian women, of whom there were almost 15,000 each in Germany in 1941 (Homze, 1967: 57). They were said to be poor workers, and, removed from their home environment, they sought and often found entertainment. German authorities were appalled that both German soldiers and teenage boys found foreign women exotic, and sometimes also sexually available. Western European women were not recruited if they were pregnant, and, if they conceived while in Germany, they received some rudimentary maternity care. They could request that the child be removed to an institution, but their consent was necessary for this.

By contrast, Polish and Soviet women were officially regarded both as purely economic assets and as 'subhumans' whose reproduction was not desirable. At first, if they became pregnant, they were sent home, but, with a massive increase in pregnancies, deportations were stopped from late 1942, and pregnant Polish and Soviet women were either encouraged or compelled to have an abortion, in primitive conditions which sometimes caused the woman's death. Soviet women, particularly, were likely to be sterilized. Rural doctors, however, often refused to carry out abortions – especially in Catholic areas – raising the question of what to do with foreigners' children. The priority was not to lose the woman as a worker, and one Bavarian official told a farmer's wife – to her annoyance and in violation of official policy – that she should treat her Polish worker's child 'as if she had an extra one of her own' (Bauer, 1996: 179). For women in industry, if the pregnancy continued, no concession was made in the hope that arduous work might trigger a miscarriage. Children born to eastern European women could be removed and the women sent back to work immediately. Children showing signs of 'racial value' were sent to an institution like *Lebensborn* for Germanization and adoption. The others were sent to 'foreign children's care units' where 'the babies are given insufficient nourishment, as a result of which . . . after a few months they inevitably die' (Noakes, 1998: 330).

While that was – quite intentionally – the cruel fate of many, some eastern women fared slightly better. For example, a German barracks supervisor at a Krupp concern, who locked Russian women in a metal cabinet for spending the night with Russian men, 'himself delivered six pregnant Russian women, as they lay on the desk in the guard room. He allowed them to keep their babies with them in the camp, and procured extra food for the infants' (Herbert, 1997: 235). A Polish woman worker in Württemberg, impregnated in 1944 by a German, was cared for by the young man's mother. Most remarkably, given the Pole's 'racial worthlessness', the German mother, 'whose husband was one of the best-known Nazis in the area', was a district leader of the NSF; yet she harboured her son's foreign lover and their child (Arbogast, 1998: 182–83).

Perhaps almost as great a determinant of foreigners' treatment as their ethnic origin was whether they were employed in industry or in agriculture. In urban areas and in colonies beside huge industrial concerns, foreign workers mostly lived and worked under oppressively segregated and policed control, and the women faced multiple hazards. They might be forced into prostitution, with bordellos for male foreigners established from 1941 wherever there was a concentration of them. By late 1943, there were sixty 'foreign' bordellos with some 600 prostitutes, and more were planned. As Herbert says, 'a truly mammoth system of pimping was established among the foreign workers' (1997: 131). There were also illegal sexual relationships, between German men in a position of power and foreign women, which amounted to abuse. Sometimes there was outright rape, and sometimes physical violence or the threat of it; alternatively, 'incentives' like presents or privileges were offered to achieve compliance. The victims were usually eastern European women 'who were mostly very young . . . [and] often considered fair game' (Herbert, 1997: 219). If they were found out, they would be sent to a concentration camp.

In south German agriculture, by contrast, where many eastern Europeans worked, Theresia Bauer argues, 'agricultural forced workers broke through a National Socialist "nutritional hierarchy" which was strictly determined by racist principles' (1996: 165). It was virtually impossible to enforce the 'nutritional hierarchy' in the countryside, and Senta Zielinski recalled in the 1990s how well she had been fed when, as a Polish teenage girl, she became a forced worker on a German peasant farm that was 'rich' compared with the 'poor' family from which she had been brutally seized (Kaminsky, 1999: 348). She did not return home after the war, but most foreigners did – if they survived the hazards and abuse of their enforced serfdom during it.

Can women be classed as either victims or perpetrators?

To categorize women as either victims or perpetrators in Nazi Germany – as some women historians did in the 1980s and 1990s – is to use a blunt instrument. Certainly, women have long been regarded as particular victims of Nazism. Contemporary Marxists saw women as victims of capitalism and its ultimate political expression, fascism. In 'Women under Hitler's Yoke', the message was clear: 'Under Fascism, women have no rights at all but only duties, duties and still more duties. . . . Do not the German women sacrifice enough?' (Lode, 1938: 45). Some women undoubtedly were exploited in factories and offices, but others belonged to the families of capitalist bosses, and still others belonged in neither category. Then, in the mid-1960s, David Schoenbaum coined the term 'secondary racism' to describe the Nazi regime's discriminatory attitudes and policies towards women *as women* (1967: 187). There was apparent merit in this, given that women were judged by Nazi leaders on the basis of their reproductive 'value', which – like their 'race' – was involuntary. Yet, invalidating Schoenbaum's neat formula, the treatment of most 'Aryan' women did not approach that of genuine victims of Nazi racism.

More recently, some feminists have regarded Nazism as 'both the highest stage of development, and at the same time the most brutal form of patriarchy' (Wippermann, 1998: 193). Thus women are seen as victims of a patriarchal system which denied them political and employment rights, and relegated them to home and children, the private sphere. Yet, as we have seen, women were not restricted to the private sphere, and there was neither a united female cause nor a uniform female experience. There were certainly women, like men, who were indisputably victims of Nazism, but to extrapolate from that to suggest that 'women' as a gender were victims is to deny the extent to which, at least before the war, some groups of 'Aryan' women either benefited from the regime's policies or else continued with their lives much as before 1933.

Nevertheless, Gisela Bock has argued that women suffered disproportionately highly from Nazi racial policies, especially the compulsory sterilization of those breaching the Nazis' discriminatory racial and biological criteria. Women as a gender, she says, were actual or potential victims in the Third Reich, with 'compulsory motherhood' for 'valuable' women and sterilization for the 'worthless'. However, there was not, as we saw in Chapter 2, 'compulsory motherhood', although there were hundreds of thousands of men and women who were victims of Nazi racial and reproductive policies even before the war, including those who were forcibly sterilized. Adelheid von Saldern gives an astute critique of Bock's claim that sterilization was more traumatic for women than for men because depriving women of motherhood robbed them of their 'social identity' (1994: 144). Did women, do women, have an identity solely if they are or can be mothers? Surely not.

The idea of women, as an undifferentiated category, as 'victims' leads to the strange conclusion identified by Andrea Böltken: 'The premise of women's history is primarily patriarchy and its subordination of the female half of humanity. . . . If every woman is by definition a victim, then "female perpetrators" are also fundamentally victims who were exploited and functionalized simply in the interests of the patriarchal system' (1995: 16–17). Similarly, Rita Wolters exposes how, under theories of 'patriarchy', women's lack of opportunity for initiative could be used to exculpate them, even if they perpetrated evil deeds (1996: 12). Thalmann's excuse that women warders 'compensated for their own enslavement, by picking on those who were more severely oppressed than they were themselves' is an example of this deeply unconvincing argument (1984: 270).

Racial 'enemies' and other earmarked targets of Nazi racist and eugenic policies can properly be called 'victims', without qualification. The women in these groups were clearly distinctive victims of abuse and torture directed at their sexual and reproductive identities. As well as those – 'Aryans' and non-'Aryans' – who were sterilized, many of whom suffered unwanted abortion also, there were others on whose reproductive organs agonizing and destructive experiments were performed. Those forced into prostitution in concentration camps and near army barracks, or in bordellos for foreign workers, were, too, gender-specific victims. The suffering of German women in the last stages of the war, both as pawns of a vindictive regime in defeat and at the hands of avenging foreign soldiers, particularly but not only those of the Red Army, was appalling. To deny that is to support German complaints that it did not seem to matter 'because it was only *German* women' [Doc. 28]. In the case of mass rapes, some two million women were deliberately-targeted victims in a gender-specific form of violence and torture (Grossmann, 1995: 193).

Designating women as 'victims' has been unpalatable for feminists holding that women could and should be subjects and not merely the

passive objects of men's policies. Victimhood denies agency and empowerment. Thus it has been argued, in particular by Claudia Koonz, that
'far from being helpless or even innocent, women made possible a murderous state in the name of concerns they defined as motherly. The fact
that women bore no responsibility for issuing orders from Berlin does
not obviate their complicity in carrying them out' (1987: 5). The second
sentence is certainly true of those who perpetrated evil deeds. But Koonz
goes further: it was not only women who were direct agents of evil deeds
who were villains, but also the wives of male malefactors, at every level.
They were, she says, guilty because they assisted the Nazi state in perpetrating its atrocities in ways which related precisely to the functions
assigned to them in patriarchal society – by providing a comfortable
home and family life for these men. Koonz argues that, because non-
Jewish German women accepted Nazi views about the polarity of the
sexes, and willingly retreated into their own domestic space, they were
agents who chose to maintain the home as a refuge of normality. Thus
they were complicit in Nazi crimes.

Some women became Nazi sympathizers because of the involvement
of their husband or another male relative. Some were sadistic *voyeuses*
who enjoyed the idea of their husband, father or brothers, as members of
the 'master race', dominating, baiting or murdering those who had been
dispossessed, degraded and dehumanized. There are sadists in any society, and these include women as well as men. There are also people who
lack moral fibre: in most societies, the heroine or hero is the exception
rather than the rule. 'Aryan' women who severed contact with Jewish
friends, and instructed their children to do the same, or who ceased to
shop at Jewish-owned stores, were at best selfish and cowardly. There
were also 'bystanders . . . [who] participated in [the] process of blocking
disturbing sensations'. Living near concentration camps, there were
'women whose nerves suffered because of the unavoidable sights and
sounds of persons being beaten' (Horowitz, 2000: 212). There were probably also women with limited horizons whose understanding of the
world outside their own home was negligible. Koonz almost implies this,
by basing her argument on women's acceptance of their domestic role;
but admitting it would undermine her argument. Therefore she says: 'far
from wanting to share their husbands' concerns, they *actively cultivated*

their own ignorance and facilitated his escape' from reality (my emphasis). Extrapolating from a few high-profile examples to arrive at generalizations of this character is perilous. Koonz might have remembered her own strictures about the dangers of 'group[ing] women – like members of a religious or ethnic minority – in a single category and view[ing] them as a single "problem"' (1976: 663). Further, her argument that 'in the Nazi world, man and woman operated in radically separated spheres' (1987: 420) is particularly shaky in wartime, when women were increasingly brought into work alongside men in both civilian and, eventually, military occupations, at the very time when the worst atrocities were being perpetrated.

There were women who collaborated in the worst crimes of the Nazis, as we have seen in this chapter. Women were, clearly, neither better nor worse than men. The difference was that men had more opportunity to commit crimes against humanity, given their greater role in the public sphere, including service in the *Wehrmacht*. It was when women were given the opportunity that their potential for evil could be judged. National Socialism gave them opportunities: firstly, it tried to politicize the private sphere, and then, especially during the war, it encouraged women into areas of the public sphere where evil deeds were routine – as warders, doctors, nurses, social workers and clerical workers in prisons, *Gestapo* offices, concentration camps, extermination camps. As a result, some women became perpetrators and some women were their victims. But what does not make sense is to label 'German women' in all their varieties collectively as either 'perpetrators' or 'victims'.

PART THREE

ASSESSMENT

7

Three issues: class, empowerment and international comparisons

The salience of class in Nazi Germany

Their obsession with race and 'value' led Nazi leaders to deny the significance of social class. The DAF claimed to represent 'all workers of hand and brain', and 'Aryans' who were 'hereditarily healthy', 'politically reliable' and socially responsible – by Nazi definition – all belonged to the 'master race'. This included working-class women. Whatever Tröger says about middle-class women being regarded as likely 'to produce ... "racially more valuable" offspring than women from the lower strata' (1984: 246), the majority of recipients of marriage loans were from the poorer sections of society, and the first family allowances were restricted to those in precarious financial circumstances (see Chapter 2). If middle-class women were under particular pressure to reproduce, it was probably because the trend towards small families was more strongly established in the middle classes, who were also generally better placed to afford the expense of a large family.

But while Nazi leaders denied the importance of class, there were clear class distinctions in Nazi Germany. Mason persuasively suggests that Nazi women's organizations 'were dominated by ... women with time and energy to spare, women who felt called upon to bring poor families up to bourgeois standards of self-reliance, thrift and cleanliness' (1976, I: 101). The patronizing emphasis on 'training courses' derived from the premise that there were millions of women and girls whose conduct of their life, family and home required improvement [Doc. 4]. Undoubtedly, the Nazi 'gold standard' was the middle-class home with its (normally) full-time wife and mother. Nonconformist lifestyles were to be discouraged and, if necessary, eliminated through the removal from the ethnic community of those who would not conform. In Itzehoe district, Schleswig-Holstein, 'men and women who were sterilized came . . . overwhelmingly from the urban working-class and from the rural lower classes' (Marnau, 1995: 321). These people were judged against middle-class standards of orderliness and thrift. In the BDM and women's Labour Service, those who met middle-class standards – in terms of manners and better educational qualifications – were regarded as the best leadership material and, probably even more than political enthusiasm, this was what counted.

Class becomes an issue particularly over women's employment in wartime. Yet it was not only in Germany that middle-class women feared being brought into factory work during the war; this was also evident in Britain. Hancock argues that 'the belief that only upper- and middle-class women evaded employment was probably false. The majority of women not in paid employment (58 percent in 1939) had working-class husbands. Yet the misconception persisted . . .' (1991: 77). Nevertheless, in Germany, middle-class women were most *conspicuously* successful in avoiding factory work. This was sometimes because they were married to men in influential political or professional positions who could and did pull rank. But it was probably also because middle-class women were more confident and articulate, and less fearful of official sanctions against recalcitrants. Yet, as Heineman shows, the burdens of employment and service in wartime fell disproportionately on young, unmarried women, of all classes.

The Nazi regime made no serious effort to alter Germany's prevailing class structure. It suited its policies to have substantial numbers of women working in industry and agriculture, particularly in the later 1930s and during the war. These were not areas where middle-class women were customarily active. The regime's officers spoke loudly and often about the need for equality of sacrifice in wartime, but did little to penalize abuses. For example, the SD in Württemberg reported in 1941 that a 'clientèle' of women with 'hats and painted fingernails . . . and large purses' had arranged with a store proprietor to acquire goods preferentially, while ordinary shoppers queued (Stephenson, 1985: 95). In 1944, Hitler himself opposed Goebbels' attempts to close down women's hairdressers, fashion houses and beauty parlours, fearful that this would antagonize German women. These were facilities predominantly used by middle-class women. The natural bias of Nazi leaders, who were mostly middle-class, was to favour the interests of the middle classes, as their policies demonstrated.

Was there anything 'emancipatory' about the Nazi women's organizations?

If women were subordinated to men in Nazi society, how could they have any agency or empowerment? Yet gender-segregated organizations were an article of Nazi faith. Thus NSF/DFW, BDM and Labour Service regional and local leaders, and NSF/DFW national leaders, were women. Did this afford them freedoms that women had generally not enjoyed before 1933? Koonz argues that 'the Nazi mobilization of wives, mothers, and daughters undercut masculine prerogatives and empowered some women by allying them with the state' (1993: 67). But this empowerment occurred within highly circumscribed areas, ones of little or no interest to men, particularly those governing the state. The women involved may have been 'working towards the *Führer*', but there is little evidence that the *Führer* either knew or cared about their activities (Kershaw, 1998: 527–73). Mason's view is more persuasive:

> Women were not entirely eliminated from public life . . . , rather their role was confined to the relatively broad sphere of what the party leadership considered to be specifically women's affairs. The element of surrogate emancipation involved in encouraging *some women* to run classes for *other women* in hygiene, baby-care, toy-making and domestic science is unmistakeable. (1976, I: 101, his emphasis)

Further, the NSF/DFW and, especially, the BDM and service schemes provided opportunities for professionally-qualified women, especially doctors who monitored the reproductive health of teenage girls. This mattered because women's opportunities in some areas of the professions were restricted, until wartime, at least.

Some have argued that Nazi youth organizations afforded young women the kind of escape from predictable routine and a predictable future that had not been open to more than a small minority of well-educated urban, middle-class young women before 1933. Certainly, some young women developed confidence of a kind that the Nazi regime is not normally credited with encouraging. Rempel regards BDM wartime activity in the occupied east as 'the Nazi version of female liberation, conditioned by wartime necessity, which produced its own kind of equality. . . . The BDM made it possible for some women to assume careers denied them for financial or other reasons' (1989: 152–53). Again, 'in the [BDM] girls could escape from the female role-model centred around family and children' that was typical of both traditional and Nazi ideals. 'They could pursue activities which were otherwise reserved for boys; and if they worked as functionaries for the [BDM] they might even approach the classic "masculine" type of the political organiser who was never at home' (Peukert, 1987: 28). Yet as Speitkamp rightly says, this was all within a system of regimentation and indoctrination, within a structure of 'established role-stereotypes' (1998: 227).

Certainly, there were strong attempts to subvert parental and church authority and to stamp Nazi authority on young females as well as males, through the BDM, Labour Service and, finally, war service. Even before 1939 it was clear that the young were to be instilled with a sense of service to the *Volksgemeinschaft*, service that was to be performed in a collective manner with other people of the same age and gender. Heineman argues that this broadened horizons and provided opportunities of a kind previously unavailable. And in Körle, both the BDM and the NSF 'allowed women to travel beyond the narrow confines of the village, brought them into contact with women from other regions and made them cross social class-boundaries . . . [and] helped to relax the principally endogamous marriage patterns which had prevailed in the village. In short, Nazism brought a certain "liberation" from the traditional confines of village life' (Wilke, 1987: 22).

Particularly while Germany was victorious, the war provided the ideal environment for utilizing the labour and idealism of young women in the service of the National Socialist 'idea'. They were removed from their familiar environment and deposited in a strange and perhaps inhospitable place where they would be moulded collectively through self-reliance, under Nazi leadership, and submission to the interests of their community. Perhaps their experience echoed that of Omer Bartov's soldiers on the eastern front, who were indoctrinated with race-hatred on a communal basis in an alien environment (1991). Yet if some women's horizons broadened, Wilke shows that, in Körle, the obverse was that in wartime other rural women were overburdened, with their private sphere invaded by evacuees and refugees.

It was uncontroversial – even expected – for young women to participate in the public sphere before marriage, as Heineman argues, but, as Frevert suggests, demands for involvement did not end with marriage: 'As millions of women were embraced by Nazi mass organisations and hundreds of thousands were appointed to positions of minor leadership, foreign observers never ceased to be amazed at the extent to which these supposedly "private" German women were being politically mobilized' (1989: 240). Two considerations must qualify the implication that this provided unprecedented opportunities for women. Firstly, as Frevert indicates, women were objects to be passively 'embraced' and 'politically mobilized'. Women as subjects in organizational life, the activist women in non-Nazi local and national associations before 1933, had been largely silenced. Similarly, Nazi women activists who had enjoyed some freedom before 1933 had to submit to party discipline; the alternative was exclusion from leadership positions.

Secondly, the Nazi women's organizations perhaps afforded space for women's agency, but that was only after free choice had been eliminated with the dissolution or *Gleichschaltung* of alternative groups. Scholtz-Klink boasted about 'all German women [being] under one leadership' as if this was a voluntary choice [Doc. 22]. In reality, every attempt was made to impose the will of a minority – including a tiny minority of women – on a majority who had, before 1933, overwhelmingly demonstrated that they preferred other options. That is the essential premise for any discussion of empowerment within Nazi women's organizations. If some Nazi women had considerable room for initiative within their own organization, it was because male leaders were completely uninterested in it. This has provoked suggestions that women had real opportunities for power within their own 'space', their separate women's sphere, as

Scholtz-Klink continued to claim long after 1945. Yet the only 'space' allowed them was a political backwater, with the women running their own little projects which had no influence, and often no bearing, on general party activity, and little influence on the mass of women who had chosen not to join the DFW. Whenever they emerged from this 'space', it was to work under the authority of male leaders of the NSDAP or organizations like the NSV.

Were women in Nazi Germany discriminated against to a greater extent than women elsewhere?

Ute Frevert rightly reminds us that 'not a single woman managed to rise to the decision-making centres of the party state. In this respect the Third Reich was no different from the parliamentary systems that preceded and followed it' (1989: 240). It also differed little from either dictatorships or parliamentary systems elsewhere. No woman in the USSR achieved Politburo membership until 1957, although gender equality featured in the Soviet constitution. Both Britain and the USA had in the inter-war years a solitary woman government minister. In Mussolini's Italy, no woman figured in the Fascist Party's leadership and the Fascist women's organization was politically powerless. In Republican France, women remained disenfranchised at national level until 1944, and the *Code Napoléon*'s patriarchal provisions gave men undisputed authority in family life until 1938. Women's political underrepresentation in Nazi Germany was not peculiar. It was, rather, typical of patriarchal society in both advanced industrial and largely agrarian societies.

Nor was it unusual to pay women less than men for the same work. Men's wages, it was commonly accepted in capitalist countries – and by their trade unions – contained an element of 'family allowance' because a man would probably have dependants. When jobs were scarce, as in the depression, this made (cheaper) women more attractive to hire. Governments did not normally intervene in the capitalist system to prevent this, but in Nazi Germany there were some cases where women were given equal pay with men in particularly hazardous areas of industry. Here, equal pay was a device for *discouraging* employers from employing women in jobs which threatened their reproductive health and redressing the employment balance in favour of men. Further, when Hitler's government sanctioned the breaching of equal pay for women in state employment, in 1933, it was not violating a universally acknowledged principle: in Britain, equal pay for women in the civil service and teaching was introduced only in the mid-1950s, and it took until 1970 for general equal pay legislation to be enacted. Equally, it was not unusual to exclude married women from certain areas of employment. Before 1944, other than exceptionally, British women teachers had to retire on marriage. In 1933, the Dollfuss government in Austria introduced legislation similar to the law of 30 June 1933 in Germany. Nazi leaders, like conservatives and churchmen in most places, both viewed women as a 'reserve army' to be afforded educational and employment opportunities when men did not suffice, and expected women to serve in the lower ranks of occupations, leaving plum jobs for men.

Regarding 'the politics of the body', contraception was strongly opposed and abortion illegal in any country where the Catholic Church was influential, well beyond 1945. Abortion was a criminal offence in Britain until 1967 and remains controversial in the USA. Again, interest in eugenics in the 1920s and 1930s was spread far wider than Germany. Proponents of 'social hygiene' measures were influential throughout the Anglo-Saxon and northern European world, with legislation to permit compulsory sterilization in Nordic countries, usually of 'feeble-minded' women who perhaps simply had poor eyesight, and had therefore failed at school. The numbers were small, but the policy persisted beyond 1945. In some states of the USA, sterilization was enforced mainly on blacks by whites. In Britain, unmarried mothers, or women regarded as incapable, were still being committed to psychiatric hospitals into the 1970s.

Yet there was nowhere else the massive scale of compulsory sterilization that was driven through to the very end of the Third Reich. In Itzehoe, for example, there were two sterilizations in early 1945. Murders of women – as 'euthanasia' – were still being perpetrated there in autumn 1944 (Marnau, 1995: 331). Officially-sanctioned murder, on racial or eugenic grounds, was what set Nazi Germany apart from other countries. Certainly, antisemitism was endemic in European society and rampant in some areas of eastern Europe particularly, with influential antisemites in the 1930s also in France. But only in Germany was persecution so comprehensive and consistent, and only in Germany were plans devised and executed to exterminate millions of people on racial or 'hereditary health' grounds. Nazi Germany utilized prejudices – against 'Gypsies' as well as Jews – which had currency elsewhere, and applied modern notions of perfectibility and cost-effectiveness to justify appalling policies which spoke euphemistically of 'cleansing the Fatherland' and 'special treatment' of racial 'enemies', the mentally or physically disabled and those who, because they did not conform, were 'asocial'. These policies affected men and women in ways which were often similar; this was true of perpetrators, victims and the majority who fitted neither of these categories. But the uniquely pernicious nature of the 'racial state' meant that in Nazi Germany women's crucial function as childbearers exposed them, peculiarly, at the very least to gross invasions of their privacy, and at worst to atrocious physical and mental cruelty.

PART FOUR

DOCUMENTS

1. HITLER AND WOMEN
2. ROSENBERG ON WOMEN'S EMANCIPATION
3. DARRÉ ON 'CLASSES OF WOMEN'
4. HOUSEHOLD SKILLS AND SOCIAL STABILITY
5. CARE OF 'VALUABLE' PREGNANT WOMEN
6. CANDIDATES FOR THE MOTHER'S CROSS
7. SOCIAL WORKERS TO IDENTIFY CANDIDATES FOR STERILIZATION
8. A DECISION TO STERILIZE
9. HIMMLER ON ABORTION AND *LEBENSBORN*
10. NO PROSECUTION OF LESBIANS
11. THE OVERBURDENED RURAL WOMAN
12. 'FORBIDDEN RELATIONS' WITH FOREIGNERS
13. WOMEN AND EMPLOYMENT IN A FUTURE WAR
14. WOMEN AND EMPLOYMENT IN WARTIME
15. TEACHERS AND 'POLITICAL RELIABILITY'
16. FARMING WOMEN'S BURDENS IN WARTIME
17. JEWISH SCHOOLGIRLS AND THE 'JEWISH QUESTION'
18. WOMEN STUDENTS IN WARTIME
19. THE AIMS OF THE BDM
20. AN AMERICAN VISITS A WOMEN'S LABOUR SERVICE CAMP
21. YOUNG WOMEN IN AUXILIARY WAR SERVICE
22. GERTRUD SCHOLTZ-KLINK ON THE NAZI WOMEN'S ORGANIZATIONS
23. THE DFW'S VARIED ACTIVITIES, 1935–44

24. NAZI WOMEN AND LOCAL WELFARE WORK
25. WOMEN'S MORALE AND THE STRESSES OF WAR ON MARRIAGE
26. CONSUMERS UNDER PRESSURE IN WARTIME
27. CIVILIANS AS BOMBING TARGETS
28. GERMAN WOMEN RAPED BY FOREIGN SOLDIERS
29. DENUNCIATIONS BY WOMEN IN WARTIME
30. THE DEPORTATION OF A JEWISH WOMAN
31. TRANSPORTS TO AUSCHWITZ, AUTUMN 1944

Document 1   Hitler and women

(a)   At the Nuremberg Party Rally in September 1936, Hitler reiterated his view that motherhood was woman's supreme function, and that a woman could make no greater contribution to the nation than the birth of several children. The reference here to the 'woman lawyer' came soon after his pronouncement that women should not appear as judges or counsel in courts of law.

If today a woman lawyer achieves great things and nearby there lives a mother with five, six, seven children, all of them healthy and well-brought up, then I would say: from the point of view of the eternal benefit to our people, the woman who has borne and brought up children and who has therefore given our nation life in the future, has achieved more and done more!

Bundesarchiv, NSD17/RAK, October 1936, 'Der Führer Adolf Hitler über die Aufgaben der deutschen Frau', p. 1.

*(b)   At the 1934 Nuremberg Party Rally, Hitler addressed 'for the first time in years', he said, the **NS-Frauenschaft**, on 8 September. He expounded his view that the sexes had separate functions, and, flattering his audience, emphasized the vital importance of both 'emotion' – in his view, woman's defining characteristic – and the 'smaller world' of the home.*

I can recall the difficult years of the movement's struggle. . . . I know that in those days there were countless women who remained unswervingly loyal to the movement and to me.

That was when the power of emotion demonstrated its greater strength and judgement. We know that the unfathomable intellect can be all too easily led astray, that seemingly intellectual arguments can lead men of low intellect to waver, and that it is precisely then that a woman's most profound inner instinct of self-preservation and preservation of the ethnic nation awakens. Woman has shown us that she understands what is right! At those times when this great movement seemed to many to falter and all were conspiring against us, the steadfastness and security of emotion prevailed as a force for stability when confronted with brooding intellect and apparent knowledge. . . . Throughout the ages, woman's feelings and, above all, her nature have consistently complemented man's intellect.

If it has often been the case in human life that men's and women's spheres of activity have become displaced from their natural order, this was not because woman aspired to dominate man. It was, on the contrary, because man was no longer entirely capable of fulfilling his own function. And that is the wonderful thing about nature and Providence: there can be no conflict in the relations between the two sexes as long as each fulfils the function assigned to it by nature. . . .

If it is said that man's world is the state, that man's world is his struggle, and his readiness to serve his community, so we might perhaps say that woman's world is a smaller one. For her world is her husband, her family, her children, and her home. But where would the larger world be if no one looked after the smaller world? How would the larger world survive if no one was prepared to make the concerns of the smaller world their life's work? No, the large world is constructed upon this small world! This large world cannot survive if the small world is unstable. Providence has entrusted to woman the care of this, her very own world, and only upon it can man's world be fashioned and constructed.

But these two worlds never stand in opposition to one another. They are mutually complementary, they belong together, just as husband and wife belong together.

We do not feel that it is right when a woman forces her way into man's world, onto what is essentially his territory. Rather, we feel it is natural when these two worlds remain separate from one another. To one belongs the power of feeling, the power of the soul! To the other belongs the power of vision, the power of firmness, of resolve, and willingness for action! On the one hand, this power calls on woman to volunteer her life in order to maintain and increase this vital cell, and on the other hand it requires from man the willingness to provide security for this life. . . .

Every child which a woman brings into the world is a battle which she wins for the existence over the extinction of her ethnic nation.

M. Domarus (ed.), *Hitler. Reden und Proklamationen 1932–1945*, volume I, 'Triumph' (1932–45), Verlagsdrückerei Schmidt, Neustadt a.d. Aisch, 1962, pp. 449–51.

Document 2   Rosenberg on women's emancipation

Alfred Rosenberg was one of Hitler's earliest associates and a leading exponent of the NSDAP's mystical 'blood and soil' tendency. Although Hitler retained him in the NSDAP's hierarchy for sentimental reasons, Rosenberg's influence on policy was minimal. This extract gives a flavour both of the antipathy felt by Nazi leaders to Enlightenment values in general and to liberalism and feminism in particular, and of the idea of 'polarity of the sexes' which appealed to some of them.

The invasion of the women's movement into the collapsing world of the nineteenth century proceeded on a broad front and was inevitably intensified by all the other destructive forces: world trade, democracy, Marxism, parliamentarism. . . .

Liberalism teaches: freedom, permissiveness, free trade, parliamentarism, women's emancipation, human equality, sexual equality etc., i.e. it is a sin against a law of nature, [which is] that creativity occurs only through the generation of tensions arising from polarity. . . . The German idea today, in the midst of the collapse of the feminized old world, demands: authority, a fine model of strength, the setting of limits, discipline, autarky (self-sufficiency), protection of the racial character, recognition of the eternal polarity of the sexes.

A. Rosenberg, *Der Mythos des 20. Jahrhunderts*, Hoheneichen-Verlag, Munich,
1935, pp. 497, 503.

Document 3   Darré on 'classes of women'

In 1930, Neuadel aus Blut und Boden, *a book by another Nazi 'blood and soil' theorist, R.W. Darré, was published. This extract shows that ideas which would be implemented in the Third Reich – including the creation of a racial hierarchy, the prevention of marriage among the 'worthless', and sterilization to prevent them from procreating – were already formulated and advocated before Hitler came to power.*

Class I: included in this are those girls for whom marriage appears to be desirable from every point of view. To ensure that only the really best are gathered together in this class, an upper limit should be determined for each age cohort with only a restricted percentage, perhaps 10 percent of the number of those who are fully suitable for marriage, accepted into it. . . . *Class II*: to this are assigned the remainder of all those girls who can marry without there being any objections from the point of view of their [potential] progeny. This class will generally be the most numerous, for which reason the creation of two sub-classes, IIa and IIb, may be considered. *Class III*: to this are allocated those girls against whose marriage there are no objections on moral or legal grounds, but whose hereditary value requires that reproduction be prevented. These girls will be allowed to marry once it can be guaranteed that their marriage will be childless (Sterilization!). *Class IV*: this comprises all those girls against whose marriage there are fundamentally serious objections. Thus not only is it not desirable for them to reproduce, but even their getting married must be opposed, because it would demean the term *German* marriage. To this category belong firstly all the mentally ill, as well as known prostitutes, whose genealogy in any case predicts their trade, and in addition habitual criminals etc.

Quoted in D. Münkel, *Nationalsozialistische Agrarpolitik und Bauernalltag,*
Campus Verlag, Frankfurt/New York, 1996, p. 428.

Document 4 Household skills and social stability

The Nazi leadership attributed many of contemporary society's ills – including an increase in family breakdown – to the massive increase in women's employment outside the home in the previous half-century. They believed that social order would be restored and the family safeguarded if young women had systematic training in housekeeping skills, and they used this to justify state intervention in the 'private sphere' of the family.

The entry of women into employment [outside the home] in most cases brought with it a neglect of training in housekeeping, since hardly had the girls left school than they rushed into a factory or prepared themselves for a career, and therefore hardly found time to learn household skills. By contrast, in better-off sections of society, training in housekeeping has generally been little regarded or neglected as a result of the . . . lack of respect for all domestic work. On the other hand, it was precisely the dual roles of working life and household duties, in which many married women and also many [single] girls found themselves, which necessitated a particularly good homecraft education so that both tasks could be performed more easily. . . .

The good of the whole state depends on whether women understand how to discharge their household duties, how to budget carefully and how to look after their children well and to bring them up. By contrast, ignorance on the part of women frequently spoils family life, and neglect of both the household and child-rearing are most often the causes of family break-up, of child mortality and of many criminal acts. Thus, the family stands or falls according to the ability and the character of the wife, and because the state is made up of families, as its cells, it must therefore have the greatest interest in the family's ability to thrive both internally and externally, and therefore it must take a hand in the training of girls for their future occupation as wives and mothers.

L. Marawske-Birkner, *Der weibliche Arbeitsdienst*, Leipzig, 1942, pp. 251–53.

Document 5   Care of 'valuable' pregnant women

Anxious to protect and nurture every unborn child of a 'valuable' woman, and to prevent abortion, the Nazi regime rationalized ante-natal care services and made them much more intrusive. Pregnant women who were not regarded as 'valuable' were excluded from these services and became candidates for compulsory sterilization.

It was left to National Socialism to bring order to this area. All organizations and institutions whose aim is to promote the welfare of expectant mothers, newly-delivered mothers and babies have been brought under the central leadership of the Reich Association for Mother and Child. . . .

The following facilities are available to pregnant women: advice on the possibility of economic assistance and the solution of personal and family problems; material support and the possible payment of a grant to cover the difference between earnings and maternity benefit. In a few cases, convalescence leave or welfare up to the fifth month after birth. Homes for single mothers serve the campaign against abortion, which is a priority with the offices for the welfare of pregnant women. . . .

Whereas earlier the principle on which the work of the advice centres was based was that every pregnant woman needed assistance, and therefore the state and the community were bound to render assistance to

her, today the guiding principle of the work is the following considera-
tion: will it benefit or damage the community as a whole in the present
and in the future? This is demonstrated in practical terms in the treatment of hereditarily diseased offspring, with the possibility of permitting
the termination of the pregnancy and making an application for sterilization and, on the other hand, in the preferential support of racially
healthy women.

E. Farrensteiner, 'Schwangerenfürsorge und Geburt', doctoral
dissertation, University of Rostock, 1939, p. 7.

Document 6   Candidates for the Mother's Cross

*The climax of gestures to elevate the status of the 'German mother', came
in 1938 with the announcement that mothers of at least four children would
receive the Honour Cross of the German Mother. The choice of decoration
was undoubtedly inspired by the highest military honour, the Iron Cross,
with childbirth a 'battle' (see Document 1b).*

... 2.   Among those who are unsuitable for this honour are mothers
who have a prison record or have been punished for reprehensible
behaviour, especially of the kind which contradicts the spirit of the
Honour Cross (for example, abortion). Also unworthy are mothers who –
although they have not been punished under the law – have seriously
damaged the image of the German mother (for example, through prostitution or non-punishable racial defilement).

3.   The award of the Honour Cross will be considered in all cases
where the offspring of the mother in question meet the requirements of
being able to function as capable racial comrades within the people's
community.

It follows that mothers from hereditarily ill and asocial families will
not be considered for the award of the Honour Cross. ... No mother
from an asocial large family [Grossfamilie] can apply for the Honour
Cross.

Award of the Honour Cross of the German Mother. Guidelines for the choice of
mothers who can be nominated. Order no. 37/39, 15.2.39 (*Verfügungen,
Anordnungen, Bekanntgaben*, 1939, volume I, p. 346).

Document 7   Social workers to identify candidates for sterilization

Social workers, who were mostly women, became key figures in the 'welfare' bureaucracy because they were in direct contact with the public. Thus they were deemed capable of judging the 'value' of individuals and families. Their opinions were often decisive in deciding who was 'hereditarily healthy', who was 'asocial', and who should be sterilized.

It is well-known that worthless people cause a lot of expense, and there was a time when an excessive amount of money was spent on this group. Today by contrast it frequently seems that nothing more can be done for such people. With these two extremes in mind, the question is what, and how much, should be done. Each of them must be put in a position where he can somehow support himself. The precondition of this is that his tasks, his environment and his relationship with society must be in accordance with his capabilities. . . .

It is very important that family social workers collaborate in . . . hereditary health measures. . . . During this summer, as an experiment, family social workers have already worked on some sterilization proposals. The reports of the social workers were absolutely excellent and proved to be of invaluable help to medical officers. . . .

This new field of work is the key to all our endeavours. Thus no social worker can be excluded from it. Family social workers, and also social workers from the Youth [Welfare] Office, from the Lung and Nursing sections, as well as senior social workers, should collaborate in this on a practical level. It is expected that each social worker will propose one case per month. That means that in a year of 10 months (allowing for holidays and sick leave), 10 cases annually should be processed by each social worker.

Minutes of the meeting of senior social workers in Hamburg on 10 November 1937, printed in A. Ebbinghaus (ed.), *Opfer und Täterinnen. Frauenbiographien im Nationalsozialismus*. Frankfurt/M: Fischer Taschenbuch Verlag, 1996, pp. 80–81.

Document 8   A decision to sterilize

Those who were forcibly sterilized in the Third Reich are counted in hundreds of thousands, but each one was a personal tragedy, and, for many of the victims, an incomprehensible one. The dramatizing of one case from a small south German town exemplifies how the decision to sterilize was conveyed to those affected.

Characters:	*the man; the woman; medical officer of health, Dr Lang.*
Scene:	*an office. Behind a desk, a man in a doctor's white coat; in front of the desk, a young couple in simple dress.*
The man:	But, doctor, you said that it would all right. That we would still be able to get married this year, my fiancée and I. [*He looks at the young woman beside him.*]
The medical officer [MO]:	I didn't tell you that. I said I would speak in support of you both, that's all.
The man:	That's what I meant, doctor. [*He takes his fiancée's hand. She smiles at him.*]
The MO:	Look, I wrote to the appropriate authorities, to the hereditary health court, and they wrote back with the decision that your fiancée – and I shall read this to you again – 'is, on the basis of the Law for the Protection of the Hereditary Health of the German People, to be refused a Certificate of Suitability to Marry'. I can't do anything more about it.
The man:	But Doctor Lang, she isn't deaf and dumb from birth. She's just very hard of hearing. A good hearing aid would perhaps make all the difference.
The MO:	There is nothing more you can do. And there's nothing more that I can do for you. You must do what the court has required of you.
The man:	And what is that?
The MO:	It tells you that in the decision that you have received. Your fiancée must not have children.
The man:	But why? [*He looks anxiously at his bride. She seems not to understand.*]

The MO:	The court has established that she suffers from a hereditary disease. So she must not have any children.
The man:	[*holding his fiancée's hand tightly*] But doctor, deaf and dumb people have healthy children, too, can't you see. . . .
The MO:	That's not the point. The court has decided that your fiancée must go to the hereditary health office at the beginning of July, and they will make the arrangements. And if she doesn't do that, then the police will take her there. It'll be done by force if necessary. Personally, I am sorry for you, but that's the way it is.
The man:	[*with resignation*] I don't understand it. I just don't understand it. Why does this have to happen to us?
The MO:	Now, don't lose heart altogether. After all, it doesn't say that you can't actually get married.

The man looks at the medical officer as if he has not really understood him.

The MO:	Don't get me wrong – if your fiancée is sterilized, then you can make another application. There'll be no danger then.

Now the man gazes at his fiancée, who seems not to have understood a word that has been said. He nods to her. She smiles and nods in return.

The man:	Is the operation dangerous?
The MO:	No more dangerous than an appendix. She'll soon get over it.
The man:	And then, doctor, we can never have children?
The MO:	[*slowly losing patience*] That's what I have been telling you all along.
The man:	And there's nothing we can do about it, doctor?
The MO:	Nothing. Absolutely nothing. Your fiancée must get it done. And now, if you please, I still have other patients to see.

U. Rothfuss, *Die Hitlerfahn' muss weg! Zwanzig dramatische Stationen in einer schwäbischen Kleinstadt*, Silberburg-Verlag, Tübingen, 1998, pp. 59–62.

Document 9   Himmler on abortion and 'Lebensborn'

Himmler's obsession with ideas of 'blood purity' and population policy was extreme. In 1940 he was concerned that, in spite of prohibitions and severe penalties, abortion rates remained high. With soldiers in wartime absent from home and stationed in unfamiliar places, where they formed new sexual relationships, illegitimate pregnancies increased. Himmler asked the army to support his 'Lebensborn' network of maternity homes to encourage pregnant women to carry their child to birth and to discourage resort to abortion.

Dear General Field Marshal Keitel

Today I have a request of considerable significance for the armed forces: Official statistics show that there are still some 600,000 abortions annually in Germany. I have been concerned for years about the fact that many abortions occur among those who can be counted as [racially] the best sections of German society. I do not believe that we can tolerate a situation where annually hundreds of thousands of valuable girls and women are lost as mothers of German stock because they have illicit abortions whose effect is often to render them sterile. We will have to contend for a long time yet with the witch-hunt experienced by the single pregnant woman; the aim of protecting German blood, however, has the highest priority.

It is interesting to think that, if we could prevent this scourge of abortion, and therefore give the German nation annually more than 600,000 children who would not otherwise be born, this population policy measure alone would result in 18 to 20 years in two hundred more regiments for the army. An extra 500,000 to 600,000 Germans each year would create a commensurate amount of extra wealth. The strength of our soldiers and workers would make a considerable contribution which would guarantee the maintenance and enhancement of Greater Germany.

It was with these considerations in mind that I founded 'Lebensborn' as a registered association in 1936. 'Lebensborn' leads the campaign against abortion in a positive way; in the Lebensborn homes, which are scattered all over the nation, any German mother of good blood can await in serenity the hour when she commits her life to her nation.

As a result of massive troop movements, the incidence of extra-marital pregnancies has, since the outbreak of war, reached a level which has not previously been recorded in Germany. I have been informed that the fathers of some 90% of all illegitimate children born in the Lebensborn homes are members of the armed forces.

Since the work of 'Lebensborn' requires means which are far beyond the resources of the Schutzstaffeln, the NSV and also [government] ministries have already directed substantial funds towards it.

I am asking you, esteemed General Field Marshal Keitel, to consider ways in which the armed forces might interest themselves in the work of 'Lebensborn' and to identify which funds available to the armed forces might be used to promote it.

Heil Hitler!

Institut für Zeitgeschichte Archiv (Munich), Fa202, letter from Himmler
to Field Marshal Keitel, undated (probably July 1940).

Document 10   No prosecution of lesbians

While section 175 of the Criminal Code classed gay men as criminals, lesbians were not mentioned. The possibility of extending its penalties to homosexual women was discussed over several years, which put lesbians on the defensive. But arguments against criminalizing lesbians consistently outweighed those in favour.

The results so far of the discussions of the official Commission on Reich Criminal Law do not envisage making unnatural acts between women punishable.

The main reasons for this are as follows.

Homosexual activity between women, apart from prostitutes, is not so widespread as it is among men and, given the more intense manners of social intercourse between women, it more readily escapes public notice. The greater resulting difficulty of establishing such behaviour would involve the danger of unfounded testimony and investigations. One major reason for punishing sex offences between men – namely, the distortion of public life by the development of personal ties of dependence – does not apply in the case of women because of their lesser position in state and public employment. Finally, women who indulge in unnatural sexual relations are not lost forever as procreative factors in the same way that homosexual men are, for experience shows that they later often resume normal relations.

Letter from the Reich Ministry of Justice, 18 June 1942, printed in G. Grau, *Hidden Holocaust? Gay and Lesbian Persecution in Germany 1933–45*, translated by Patrick Camiller, Cassell, London, 1995, pp. 83–84.

Document 11   The overburdened rural woman

Particularly with rapid industrialization from the later nineteenth century, the proportion of Germans working in agriculture declined. This posed a threat to Nazi population policy, because the rural population was, by the 1930s, unusual in continuing to have larger families. The NSDAP's newspaper, the Völkischer Beobachter, *details the unremittingly harsh life of the rural woman.*

The rural woman, whether she is a labourer or a farmer's wife, helps to carry the very heavy burden of agricultural work. Her day begins at 4 or 5 o'clock in the morning and does not end until 9 or 10 o'clock at night. Apart from all the housework, she looks after animals on the farm and also has to take them out into the fields, because the number of employed labourers has to be kept as small as possible. In the smaller concerns, the farmer's wife normally becomes involved in work in the fields; in larger ones she is less likely to do this but then there is that much more work for her in a large house and estate. The woman agricultural worker by contrast usually performs the same work as the man. She normally spends only a few hours each day in the house.

For all rural dwellers, the entire burden of work has increased considerably since the [1914–18] war, with the economic crisis forcing them to reduce the number of full-time employed labourers and to take on the extra work themselves. And this extra burden has in far the greatest measure fallen on the shoulders of the rural woman.

It is easy to see the consequences for the health of women and their offspring. A woman who has to perform hard physical work from her fifteenth year is old and exhausted by the time she is forty. Under these circumstances the number of children she has will be small, because she has neither the time to bring up many children nor the strength or the desire to do so. The children she has cannot be trained and supervised in the way that they should be; they are left to their own devices or locked up in the house until their mother comes home. This is the reason for the continuing high level of death in childhood in rural areas.

'Bevölkerungspolitik und Rassenpflege auf dem Lande', *Völkischer Beobachter*, 13/14 May 1934 (Racial Hygiene supplement).

Document 12   'Forbidden relations' with foreigners

(a)   In wartime, German women were repeatedly warned against having sexual relations with foreign workers, especially eastern Europeans. If they did, they were guilty of 'Rassenschande' ('racial defilement') and were harshly punished – but not as harshly as their foreign lover, who might be hanged.

Cases of (strictly forbidden) sexual relationships between Poles and Germans belonged to the particular sphere of competence of the *Gestapo*. The German girls and women involved were normally 'transferred' to a concentration camp; their arrest should, according to Himmler's guidelines of 8 March 1940, 'not, however, make it impossible for these people to be suitably abused by the population'. In fact, he regarded 'the effect of public humiliation as extraordinarily shocking', and had 'no objections if, for example, German women had their hair shaved off because of their dishonourable conduct or were led through their village with a placard explaining their offence'. Accordingly, this idea was subsequently adopted by many local NS party offices; thus towards the end of 1940 an 18 year-old girl 'with her head shaved bald and clothed in a sack' was dragged through her own district and forced to carry a placard with the following inscription: 'I am a depraved character because I went with a Pole. Therefore I am leaving this town in disgrace and going to prison.'

J. Woydt, *Ausländische Arbeitskräfte in Deutschland*, Distel Verlag, Heilbronn, 1987, pp. 116–17.

(b)   In small rural communities, where foreign workers were essential to the maintenance of a farm or business, even local officials of party and state might intercede for a woman and plead mitigating circumstances.

The Hanover Special Court considered the case of a farmer's widow from Harsfeld who was sentenced on 26.8.43 to one year and six months in prison because of 'association with a French prisoner-of-war'. Her father-in-law, as well as both the local *Reichsnährstand* (National Food Authority) leader and the mayor appealed for the early release of the woman concerned because the viability of the farm would otherwise be endangered. A similar case concerned a farmer's wife from Estorf. She was accused of the same 'offence' and in September 1943 she was sentenced to one year and three months in jail. She pleaded, in her own defence, that she did not want to lose the French prisoner-of-war as a worker. An application for suspension of her sentence was allowed by the local *Reichsnährstand* leader. . . .

D. Münkel, *Nationalsozialistische Agrarpolitik und Bauernalltag*,
Campus Verlag, Frankfurt/New York, 1996, pp. 412–13.

Document 13   Women and employment in a future war

With the reintroduction of rearmament and conscription in 1935, the government also considered the problems of a future war economy. A powerful and productive home front, they believed, would enable Germany to sustain a successful war effort. Here, a senior civil servant outlines the development of women's employment since 1933, and its potential in wartime.

In order to supply the war economy and other consumers with the necessary labour force, far-reaching preparations are necessary. The legal basis for the deployment of labour in wartime is the Law for German National Service, which was signed by the Führer on 21 May 1935. This details the obligation of all citizens who are not members of the armed forces and who are aged between 15 and 65 years of age. Exempt are only mothers with children under 15, if these live in the family home, and pregnant women. . . .

Of the 45 million men and women aged between 15 and 65 – if we subtract women with children under 15, pregnant women, the sick, pensioners, the severely disabled and those classed by the public welfare service as unfit for work – there are some 32 million available for both civil and military service. For two-thirds of the employed population, that is, for the 21 million or so men and women who work in blue-collar or white-collar jobs, the Labour Exchanges already hold the documentation which gives sufficient information about how they could be deployed in the event of war. . . .

The number of people eligible for National Service whose capabilities are so far undocumented is therefore not very large. Among them there is nevertheless one group whose deployment in the event of war will be essential. That is those women who are *not* currently employed. . . .

The development of women's employment in the period 1933 to 1936 was first of all determined by the principle that work-creation projects had to bring men back into employment. In accordance with the aims of NS population policy, the priority was that fathers of families should be put in a position to feed their family, and that single men should be put in a position where they could start a family. And so the proportion of women in the German industrial workforce has steadily declined. According to the results of reports by factories to the National Statistical Office's Industrial Survey, the proportion of women working in industry has dropped from 30.1 percent in the first half of 1933 to 24.5 percent in the first half of 1936. This is consistent with the development of women's employment in the economy as a whole. According to figures from the sickness insurance funds, the number of women as a proportion of all employees has fallen gradually from 36.1 percent in the first half of 1933 to 31.3 percent. However, it does seem that the decline in women's employment in the industrial workforce levelled out around the middle of the year 1936.

The experience of the [1914–18] war shows that placing non-employed women who have never before worked in industrial concerns, or in agriculture etc., in work for the war economy has only rather limited benefits. The reasons for this are too many to detail here. Suffice it to say that, to prepare for the replacement of male workers by women, it is imperative to determine now which kinds of work in war-related and essential industries are to be considered, taking account of [women's] physical capabilities. . . . For a start, mining and the heavy iron industry can be excluded from this survey, because the possibilities for employing women in them are too small. On the other hand, surveys in the textile and clothing industries are superfluous because the possibilities for employing women there are already well-known. Surveys in the precision engineering, electro-technical and iron and steel processing industries are in progress. On this basis, guidelines for the employment of women in industrial concerns in the event of war can be compiled.

The limits which there currently are to the employment of women, through prescription of the number of hours worked and the ban on employment in certain sectors, will on the whole be revoked in the event of war, as far as that can be justified to the population as a whole. . . .

Institut für Zeitgeschichte, MA 468, Varia (II), 55, frames 5719–23,
2 February 1937, Labour Deployment in Wartime. Speaker:
Oberregierungsrat Nolte.

Document 14   Women and employment in wartime

Attempts to persuade economically inactive women into employment in wartime met resistance from them, especially – but not only – if they were middle-class. This ultimately led to the introduction of labour conscription for women, in January 1943.

On the subject of the limited success [of attempts to attract more women into war work], Dresden, for example, reports that out of 1,250 women invited to a recruitment meeting only 600 turned up, of whom only 120 said they were prepared to take up employment. The majority of these, however, then chose to withdraw their consent for a variety of reasons. A similar picture was reported from Brunswick. . . . From Leipzig, according to a report of 13.5.1941, it was stated among other things that the first, and so far the only, woman had presented herself at the employment office there on 8.5.1941. In Halle, of 120 women invited to a recruitment meeting only 40 turned up, of whom only 20 had given a positive response. Further, a report from Weimar states that so far there is no news of women volunteering to take up work. Similarly, from Dortmund it is unanimously reported from the entire area that there has so far been no noticeable success in getting German women to volunteer for work. The report mentions, for example, that women who are as yet not employed are showing no more enthusiasm for work than formerly. Out of 223 mostly childless women who were invited, only 17 have been persuaded into part-time employment. From Aachen it is reported that, on the subject of women's employment, a policy of 'wait and see' persists. In Halle, of 87 wives of conscripted workers in the Eulenburg celluloid factory who were asked to take on work, a total of only 5 women agreed to take on full-time work and 5 part-time work 'after much humming and hawing and lengthy persuasion by the manager'. Of the remaining 77, only a few produced justifiable reasons for not working. . . .

In some reports it is mentioned that the population expects women from the higher levels of society to show a good example. Available information, they say, shows that [those who have taken on work] are almost exclusively women in humble circumstances, while often women from more favoured circumstances produce a multitude of reasons which prevent them from working.

H. Boberach (ed.), Meldungen aus dem Reich, Deutscher
Taschenbuch Verlag, Munich, 1968, pp. 146–48.

Document 15   Teachers and 'political reliability'

NSDAP local branch and district officials reported to their superiors on the political attitudes of people in their area, particularly those in politically sensitive occupations like school-teaching. Four such reports, from Trier in 1935–36, show the kinds of assessment that were made, without the subjects' knowledge. The 'Opferring' was created, after NSDAP membership was closed at 2.5 million on 1.5.33, for those who wanted to demonstrate loyalty to the NSDAP by paying it a subscription. Individuals, families and small places are rendered anonymous in the original to comply with German law.

(a)   [Teacher] 'A' became a member of both the Opferring and the NS-Frauenschaft on 1 July 1934. She does not take our newspapers and is closely associated with the clergy and the Paramenten Association [a Catholic group]. As I was told in confidence, 'A' is anything but a National Socialist. Her entire current demeanour towards us can only be considered a façade in order to maintain her position. . . .

(b)   [Teacher] 'A' is not a member of the NSDAP but she does belong to the Bund Deutscher Mädel. Her father, teacher 'B', belongs to the Opferring, and two sons are in the SA. The family 'B' participates very actively in fund-raising etc. From the political point of view, the family

'B', and in particular the daughter 'A', can be considered politically reliable. . . .

(c)   Teacher 'A' has been a member of the NSLB since 1.7.33, of the NSV since October 1933 and of the RLB [National Air-raid Protection Association] since October 1933. Teacher 'B' has belonged to the NSLB since 1.7.33, the NSV since October 1933, the RLB since September 1933. Nothing is known to the detriment of either. They are in no way active in the [National Socialist] movement, not even in the NSLB. In political terms, they are neither better nor worse than other women teachers in Trier. The tight National Socialist supervision of schools that has been imposed will ensure that, if there is any question of a permanent appointment, in the case of both of them instruction and education are carried out in the correct spirit. . . .

(d)   In the border area of 'R' it has still not been possible to establish a BDM [group], in spite of the greatest efforts; on the contrary, in this place 100% of the girls at the elementary school are organised in the [Marian] Maidens' Congregation. The blame for this can be squarely laid at the door of teacher 'A' who is employed there.

> F.J. Heyen, *Nationalsozialismus im Alltag. Quellen zur Geschichte des*
> *Nationalsozialismus vornehmlich im Raum Mainz-Koblenz-Trier*,
> Boppard, 1967, pp. 256–57.

Document 16   Farming women's burdens in wartime

With men conscripted, women were left to run small family businesses with very little assistance. This was particularly onerous on the land, where men had normally performed the heaviest work; in wartime, then, women had to assume more tasks, including physically taxing ones. Government exhortations to still greater efforts were not received well by them.

The village of Kanndorf . . . [in the Jura, has] a cultivable area of 83 hectares. To manage this land, there are only two adult male full-time workers aged between twenty and sixty; the only other men are two sixteen year-old youths, two delivery boys and a child. . . . [One holding] with a cultivable area of 10.60 hectares and some farm animals – a horse, six cows and three pigs – is worked by the farmer's wife and her three daughters. Her other children, four sons, are in the armed forces. A sixty-four year-old farmer's wife runs a cultivable area of 8.40 hectares with five cows, three calves and six pigs, with only her twenty-one year-old daughter and a fourteen year-old *Pflichtjahr* girl to help her. Her five sons are in the armed forces.

Under these circumstances, it is not difficult to guess at the thoughts running through such a woman's head when she is bombarded on radio, in the press, in appeals and at meetings, with slogans about making the utmost effort, village community, mobilization of every last reserve of work and effort, a rise in the production of oil-producing crops, increased rape-seed production.... Such a farmer's wife would wonder, if Reich Minister Dr Goebbels' recent leading article in *Das Reich* were shoved in front of her nose, about all the layabouts who there must surely be when 'people are just waiting at home to be summoned and deployed'. These farmers' wives and their women assistants belong rather to those groups of worn out and exhausted people who, if this goes on much longer, one day will simply give out, like a workhorse at the end of its tether. . . .

> H. Focke and U. Reimer, *Alltag unterm Hakenkreuz.*
> *Wie die Nazis das Leben der Deutschen veränderten*,
> volume 1, Rowohlt, Reinbek bei Hamburg,
> 1979, pp. 175–76.

Document 17 Jewish schoolgirls and the 'Jewish question'

(a) In April 1934, the father of a Jewish senior school pupil wrote to the Hamburg education authority to complain about his daughter's being subjected to Hitler's views on the 'Jewish question' in class.

My daughter Friedel attends the Helene-Lange senior school. Apart from her, there is another Jewish pupil who was, however, absent from the class on the days in question.

On 12 April in the German hour, the teacher, Frau Ahlborn, read out the passage on the Jewish question from the second chapter of Hitler's *Mein Kampf*. . . .

The reading was interrupted half-way through the chapter by the end of the class and the conclusion was deferred until the next day. Frau

Ahlborn made no comment on the reading. The reading contained asser-
tions which no self-respecting Jewish schoolgirl can accept. . . .

My daughter returned home in an agitated state. I spoke with Frau
Ahlborn about the matter on the same day, and with head teacher
Grüber on the following day. Frau Ahlborn told me that she had been
instructed by the head teacher to have this chapter read. She was aware
of the difficult position of Jewish pupils. It was, however, her duty to
promote the girls' National Socialist education by discussing the Jewish
question. What kind of discussion she would have at the end of the
reading she had not fully considered.

Head teacher Grüber told me that he had ordered the reading. He felt
that this kind of treatment of the Jewish question was necessary in order
to protect his classes from the danger of being psychologically influenced
by their Jewish classmates.

I have agreed with the head teacher and Frau Ahlborn that Friedel will
not take part in classes which deal with the Jewish question.

I would now like the *Land* education authorities to answer the following question: are [they] trying to make it impossible for Jewish schoolgirls to remain in the state schools by having instruction in the Jewish
question which damages their self-respect?

*(b) The teacher also gave her side of the story, which manifests both
clear antisemitism and anti-intellectualism which accorded with Nazi educational policy, especially for girls.*

Any instruction about fundamental principles is rendered extremely difficult by the presence of even just one Jewish girl in class, particularly in
the senior years. Even when the Jewish girls are restrained about what
they say, when they take part in a class they almost always ask the kinds
of question which – often unintentionally – disrupt the atmosphere.
Particularly today, we can be effective with children and young girls only
if we have a strong community spirit, because otherwise there are many
things that they cannot experience. We do not want to train them to
debate; rather, we want to have an effect on their feelings and on their
will. We want to let them experience things like a work of art or the
principles of race and their tasks as girls and women in the German

ethnic community. But how can we do that when every new experience is nipped in the bud by an intellectual question of an alien kind! . . . When one comes to the race question or the Jewish question, as one often does in the German class, the Jewish girls immediately put their hands up and one has the choice of ignoring them or listening to their interjections and refuting them. If one does the former, the others get the impression that one is afraid of interjections, and if one does the latter, the effect of the interjection is seldom without effect on some of the pupils.

H. Focke and U. Reimer, *Alltag unterm Hakenkreuz. Wie die Nazis*
das Leben der Deutschen veränderten, volume 1, Rowohlt,
Reinbek bei Hamburg, 1979, pp. 99–101.

Document 18   Women students in wartime

In wartime, young men were conscripted from civilian sectors, including universities, into the armed forces. While the number of women students had declined since 1931, by the later 1930s the government was anxious to encourage women to study, and during the war women attended universities and colleges in unprecedented numbers, to mixed reactions.

1.   Compared with the winter semester of 1941/42, student numbers in many universities show a decline, which is mostly attributable to the return to their units of a large number of men on leave from the armed forces following the end of that semester. . . . By contrast, it is reported from the universities of Berlin, Freiburg, Halle, Marburg and Würzburg that the numbers attending lectures have risen sharply, which was most unexpected in view of the recall of soldiers on leave who were at university. The University of Freiburg has even reached its highest numbers for years, with 4,244 matriculated students compared with 3,659 in the preceding semester; similarly, at the University of Würzburg the total numbers matriculated stand at 1,637 compared with 1,445 in the winter semester, which is the highest figure since the summer semester of 1937.

2.   This unexpected increase in student numbers is attributable above all to a renewed massive influx of female students into the various faculties, a trend which has been highlighted in previous reports. . . . In Berlin, for example, the number of students has increased by 20 percent.

In its Faculty of Foreign Studies, female students account for as much as 85 percent of the total, while in the Arts Faculty the figure is 77 percent and in the Mathematics/Natural Sciences Faculty it is 58 percent. This means that for the first time in the history of the University of Berlin, women are in a clear majority in three faculties. At the University of Freiburg, where female students are in a majority (1,555 women compared with 1,480 men), there are 145 men in their first semester compared with 362 women. In the other universities, too, the proportion of male to female students is shifting increasingly in favour of the latter. . . .

The women students prefer now, as in the past, to study medicine or arts. The intake of women students, which was already observed in the previous semester, continues undiminished, so that in the Arts Faculties of Freiburg, Göttingen, Halle and Marburg female students are already in a majority. In the Arts Faculty at Freiburg, the number of women students is actually five times that of the men. In Giessen, women students in Arts subjects are twice as numerous as the men. In the natural sciences faculties, too, available reports indicate a recent strong influx of women (Berlin, Göttingen, Giessen, Würzburg). In the Mathematics/Natural Sciences Faculty at Berlin, e.g., the proportion of women has risen from 35 percent in the winter semester of 1941/42 to 58 percent in the current semester (113 new matriculations, as opposed to 72 in winter semester 1941/42). In Würzburg, e.g., in some lecture halls there were only about two male students out of an audience of forty or fifty. . . .

In view of the acute shortage of recruits for the graduate professions, prevailing opinion is that, if the massive gaps left by men can to some extent be filled by women, then the significant growth in the number of women studying is entirely appropriate. That goes, for example, for the teaching profession, for occupations in which knowledge of foreign languages and cultures is required, for medicine etc. Also, in view of the heightened demand that there will be in the expanded Reich after the end of the war, the possibilities for an increased deployment of women are at least a solution. – Nevertheless, it is therefore imperative that these female students pursue their studies with real seriousness and the necessary diligence, and that, above all, they aim for a proper conclusion to their studies. Regrettably, as almost all the reports show, this can be said of only some of the current intake of female students. With the best will in the world, one cannot avoid the impression that a considerable number of women students have embarked on their studies in order to avoid working for the war effort. Among these, medical studies are particularly favoured because female students in a Medical Faculty are largely exempted from labour conscription. The idea of an 'escape from the factory into the lecture hall' derives from the deficient zeal with which many female students approach their studies. Lecturers often complain about the 'immature and foolish' attitude of the women students, and express the fear that the universities are becoming more and more like 'a continuation of senior school' or 'a marriage bureau' (Göttingen, Kiel, among others). A large number of female students [it is said] would never finish their studies, and many of them had never had any intention of doing so.

> 'The position in German universities in the summer semester of 1942',
> Institut für Zeitgeschichte, MA 441/6, 'Meldungen aus dem Reich',
> frames 2–757139–41.

Document 19   The aims of the BDM

Baldur von Schirach, the Hitler Youth's leader, outlined in 1934 the purpose and aims of the BDM. His priority was to promote uniformity, discipline, industriousness and service, compared with the alleged purposelessness and decadence to which young people had been consigned since 1918.

The human material with which we are working is, as far as the older age cohorts are concerned, not yet the product of our education but the result of educational experiments of an era which was essentially divided. Unemployed and desperate parents, Marxist teachers, smutty films, trashy writers gave these youngsters their 'education'. . . . The BDM should demonstrate to girls the realities of their struggle for existence; it should train them to be neither genteel young ladies nor hooligans. Whoever is organized in the BDM will learn that the new state assigns to girls, too, their tasks and requires self-discipline and the fulfilment of duties. As boys aim to be strong, so girls aim to be beautiful . . . , something to which the harmonious development of the body is intrinsic. The ever-increasing sporting activities of the BDM serve this aim, as does ideological training. Every social evening, every camp takes place against this background. The generation that wants to mould the German future needs heroic women. Delicate 'ladies' and those who neglect their bodies and let themselves degenerate into depravity do not belong to this future. The BDM will create proud and noble women who, conscious of their supreme value, want to belong only to the ranks of their equals.

They (the girls) can dance and be happy, but they should understand that they will have no private life; rather, they will remain a part of their community and its exalted aims. Girls will willingly approach their future destiny as mothers of the new generation.

Baldur von Schirach, quoted in R. Wiggershaus, *Frauen unterm Nationalsozialismus*, Peter Hammer Verlag, Wuppertal, 1984, pp. 40–41.

Document 20   An American visits a women's Labour Service camp

Hitler's regime was concerned, especially at first, to impress foreigners. Visitors were escorted to official projects and shown carefully-prepared versions of them. This American woman doctor viewed Labour Service camps for girls in 1934.

We visited some of the voluntary labor camps for girls where high-school graduates who have passed their college entrance examination join with peasant girls in a life of hard physical work and total lack of the ordinary comforts of life. I think of a camp near Stettin, a bleak, unheated house, large dormitories with springless cots, straw sacks for mattresses, rough army blankets. The girls had to go from the second story [sic] to the basement to wash and the basins and showers had warm water only twice a week. They worked in vegetable gardens, they milked the cows, fed the pigs and geese and fowl, they even cleaned the stalls and pig-pens, and of course they washed the clothes and scrubbed the floors and did the cooking. Many of them were gently bred, but you could not pick them out, for all were in rough clothes, all rosy and energetic and full of vigor. When their six months' training is over they were to go to the country, to the new settlements, where they would relieve the settlers' wives, taking charge of the house and the barnyard while the wife was working in the field.

I thought of William James' vision of each youth and maiden giving a year of service to the country [the USA] and though I could not possibly imagine American girls doing work such as these German girls are capable of, still it would be a beautiful thing to see the same spirit over here. . . .

A. Hamilton, M.D., 'Woman's Place in Germany', *Survey Graphic*,
volume 23 (January 1934), p. 29.

Document 21   Young women in auxiliary war service

The Women's Labour Service was increasingly utilized in wartime for tasks with the armed forces. They could find themselves in mortal danger.

[In autumn 1944, Lisa] and other *Arbeitsmaiden* [members of the women's Labour Service] . . . were conscripted as anti-aircraft auxiliaries. . . . 'We each had ten hours on duty and ten hours free. First we were stationed in a barracks. After it was destroyed by bombing, we lived in a huge tent. We girls each had a kitbag with a tarpaulin, rather like a sailor's kitbag. . . . In January 1945 fate overtook us. There was a massive British air-raid by low-flying craft. One fired at our gun so that everything was mown down by machine-gun bursts. The NCO took a direct hit. We flew through the air and landed some distance away. My steel helmet fell off my head, the strap broken. I felt blood on my face, coming from my left temple. My thigh was full of splinters from a grenade. But the NCO . . . the NCO had his stomach ripped open, and his intestines were hanging out. I stood in front of him, unable to move. "Lisa, take my pistol and shoot me dead!" I couldn't do it. I have a hard exterior but a soft centre. I was dreadfully sorry for him. Such a nice guy, about 36 years old, and he had to be tortured like that. "Lisa, take my pistol and shoot me dead!" That's all he said, and his voice got weaker and weaker. We were all around him, crying. . . . I had a first-aid dressing with the cut [in my head] simply pressed together.'

'Die Flakhelferin im Café. Über Lisa G.', in G. Szepansky, *'Blitzmädel'*,
'Heldenmutter', *'Kriegerwitwe'. Frauenleben im Zweiten Weltkrieg*,
Fischer Taschenbuch Verlag, Frankfurt/M, 1986, pp. 47–48.

Document 22 Gertrud Scholtz-Klink on the Nazi women's organizations

The leader of the Nazi women's organizations first addressed a Party Rally in 1934. The co-ordination process, by which all existing women's organizations were either dissolved or brought under her leadership in the Deutsches Frauenwerk, was by this time far advanced. For her, a 'working woman' was one who was active in a women's organization.

. . . One of the hardest tasks was to give women due credit in the construction work of this state, by recognizing all the countless sacrifices which women had made during the struggle for the German future – without, however, falling into the error of the old women's movement by portraying woman as something exceptional in the nation.

We therefore have the obligation to let women, as the female citizens of the state responsible for maintaining the state as a living organism, have the kind of organization which is appropriate to woman's nature and at the same time is in accord with the demands of the National Socialist world view.

The external structure for this has already been created. Today we have in Germany something that amazes foreigners and also many of our own men: all German women under one leadership! . . .

As women in our nation, we see our immediate task as being to transmit the National Socialist world view to women in such a way that it is intelligible and clear. To this end, the Deutsches Frauenwerk has been created, in which all working German women are gathered together regardless of which position they are working in.

. . . I would like to thank all the associations, the leaders and their members who have sincerely and with the greatest good will opened the door to their heart; all these sincere and willing people will acknowledge with me that we are at the beginning of our organizational development and that together we still have some way to go to closer amalgamation. For we know very clearly that our goal, as creators of new concepts, must never be 'yesterday' and 'today', but the 'tomorrow' of our nation. . . .

I have already said to you that we are well aware that pretty speeches are of no value to us if we do not succeed by our deeds in making it clear to our people, in our case to our women, what National Socialism means.

Therefore we have set about translating National Socialist prescriptions into practical work and on this basis we have created our sections in the NS-Frauenschaft.

First and foremost, for all German women, is the section 'Training of mothers and mothers' service'.

Being a mother unites women from all classes and all walks of life.

Gertrud Scholtz-Klink, 'Rede an die deutsche Frau', Reichsparteitag, Nürnberg, 8 September 1934, printed in G. Scholtz-Klink, *Die Frau im Dritten Reich*, Grabert Verlag, Tübingen, 1978, pp. 496–511.

Document 23   The DFW's varied activities, 1935–44

The wide range of the DFW's activities resulted from its virtual monopoly of women's organizational life. Mostly, however, it merely sponsored events which were mounted by its constituent organizations. But under the Four Year Plan of 1936, and especially in wartime, its sections, particularly National Economy/Domestic Economy, instructed women about making use of available commodities. The following extracts record the DFW's activities in Stuttgart.

9 December 1935
The DFW, along with the Employment Office, organizes a discussion evening for women domestic servants under forty-five years of age, who are forbidden by law to continue to work for Jewish families after 31 December 1935. Households in Stuttgart were called on to provide new jobs for these women.

2 November 1936
Frau Anne Klenk of the DFW's section for National Economy and Domestic Economy speaks in the Hindenburg Building. She deals with questions about the new Four Year Plan, settlement policy, the so-called Stew Sunday (*Eintopfsonntag*) and the recently inaugurated 'campaign against waste' ('*Kampf dem Verderb*').

17 September 1937
The South Tyrolean poet, Maria Rubatscher, reads from her own work at an event sponsored by the NSF and the DFW, in the German Overseas Institute.

1 March 1940

In collaboration with women composers, the Association of Communities of German Women Artists and Friends of Artists, within the DFW, gives a concert in the Music College featuring works by the Stuttgart composer Hilde Kocher-Klein and the Munich composer, Philippine Schick.

28 February 1941

During 1940, the Mothers' Service of the DFW in Stuttgart held 286 courses in infant care, child-rearing, care of the sick, cookery and housekeeping, needlework and household crafts, at which 5,494 women and girls were instructed.

30/31 May 1942

During this month, teachers and administrators of the Swabian Women's Union (since 1938, the DFW, Gau Württemberg-Hohenzollern, Swabian Women's Union, registered organization, Stuttgart) ought to fill in personnel questionnaires for the NSDAP; this can, however, be avoided.

21 October 1942

The DFW opens a fashion and housekeeping advice centre in Crown Prince Street.

18 November 1942

In the lecture hall of the TWS, the DFW demonstrates how gas can be conserved in households for the benefit of the armaments industry in Greater Stuttgart.

9 February 1943

In collaboration with the Guild of Women Dressmakers of Stuttgart, the DFW's section National Economy/Domestic Economy organizes in the Hindenburg Building a teaching demonstration of how to alter second-hand clothes.

29 September 1943

The DFW repeats its much-visited and free cookery demonstration of up-to-date recipes at no. 3 Crown Prince Street, and organizes for the first time cookery courses for grass widowers [men whose wives were evacuated].

21 November 1943

The DFW organizes twice weekly bakery demonstrations featuring pastries and biscuits for Christmas, in Crown Prince Street.

9 December 1944

37th bombing raid [on Stuttgart]. . . . 24 dead, 55 injured.

The Gau NSF leader and Gau leader of the DFW, Anny Haindl, calls on women and girls in Württemberg to volunteer for the Women's Auxiliary Army Corps: 'The struggle is being waged fiercely on the borders of our Fatherland. It's a matter of life or death. The German woman is well aware of that. Therefore she is determined not to surrender the essence of her world, her family and her home, to the enemy without a fight. On the contrary, she is resolved to defend with all her might and with deep fanaticism, even with weapons in her hand, if it comes to that. As a Women's Auxiliary, she has that opportunity. She will stand shoulder-to-shoulder with her man as his best comrade, and, above all, she will replace him where she can. The times in which we live are hard, especially for us women, but we shall be even harder. Our destiny is in our own hands.'

K. Leipner (ed.), *Chronik der Stadt Stuttgart, 1933–1945*, Klett-Cotta, Stuttgart, 1982, pp. 252, 330, 424, 657, 735, 833, 858, 863, 880, 926, 935, 1011.

Document 24   Nazi women and local welfare work

The war gave Nazi women's organizations a new focus, with fresh areas to recruit from, like Alsace which was seized from France and incorporated into Gau Baden in 1940. However, this reservoir of recruits was rather small, contrary to their boasts, and consisted chiefly of those who could be pressured into assisting the tiny number of genuine enthusiasts.

At the start of the war, the *NS-Frauenschaft*'s section for Neighbourhood Aid expanded massively. Because of the increasing shortage of domestic servants and the increase in women's employment, and through the diminishing availability of paid staff for shops and farming concerns, and not least because of terror bombing, the need for friendly local support has put the ideas of 'neighbourhood' and '*Volksgemeinschaft*' to the test.

In purely organizational terms, the extent of this welfare work could never have been mastered unless the recognition that the *Volksgemeinschaft* can only exist if it becomes a reality in the smallest household had not been exemplified in the years of preparatory work by the *NS-Frauenschaft*'s 'Neighbourhood Aid'. With the growing volume of tasks, the number of Neighbourhood Aid Assistants also increased. While at the beginning of the war there were in Gau Baden-Alsace 160,000 women involved, this number has risen to 217,000 at the present time. They all work almost without exception as unpaid volunteers, making themselves available to help for days or hours. It is, of course, compulsory for all Block and Cell *NS-Frauenschaft* leaders to work in Neighbourhood Aid, while the employed members of the [*NS-Frauenschaft*'s] Youth Groups make themselves available in their free time, for example by giving help to the wife of a small farmer at harvest time.

Priority is given to supporting mothers with several children, and also to assisting the farmer's wife at particularly busy times, as well as to assisting the employed housewife who has to cope with a huge amount of work. As the war has continued, it has become obvious that there are ever more areas where help is required. Things that fall into the category of neighbourly aid are collecting ration cards for the woman running a business on her own, darning socks for soldiers, giving a hand in the kitchen of a large concern, taking care of sewing and mending for the employed woman and the farmer's wife, giving information at railway stations. And if, in a night of terror, thousands of women in a town that has been hit [by bombs] commit themselves to rescuing and retrieving, and, armed with cleaning equipment, set to work in damaged homes, and to cleaning up splinters and debris in food shops, to looking after children and people who have been injured, and above all to standing ready in each local branch to offer help of whatever kind is needed, as if it were the most natural thing in the world – what is all this but neighbourly aid in its finest sense? As for the individual organisations involved, they work in particularly close comradeship with the NSV.

In spite of all the many millions of working hours put in, it is clear that, given the many dimensions of Neighbourhood Aid, we can never describe everything that is done, because an untold amount of neighbourly support is naturally given in private. And that is how it should be; after all, the basic premise of this neighbourly assistance by the *NS-Frauenschaft* is that everyone should be educated to be ready to provide it as a matter of course. And the German *Volksgemeinschaft*, which is admired but poorly understood throughout the world, does not need to be publicized and verified with figures – it speaks for itself!

'The NS-Frauenschaft, Gau Baden-Elsass. Comradeship from woman to woman (Strassburg, 6 June 1944)',*Völkischer Beobachter*, Wednesday, 7 June 1944.

Document 25 Women's morale and the stresses of war on marriage

The home front in wartime consisted disproportionately of women. As well as incessantly worrying about conscripted male relatives, they had to sustain their household under increasingly difficult circumstances. Especially in towns, this meant fear of and disruption by enemy bombing, as well as coping with shortages and rationing. The differing, and traumatic, experience of soldiers meant that, when they were home on leave, communication was sometimes difficult and some relationships came under severe strain.

According to recent reports, the mood among women following the arduous campaigns [against the Red Army] and consistent retreat in the east is calm but very dejected. They are waiting anxiously to see what will happen in Russia. Many women view retreat by our troops as a sign of a general weakening of our ability to resist. . . .

Women are taking less interest in the detailed events of the war. Young women in particular are apathetic. Frequently a positive war-weariness is evident. They go to any lengths to avoid mention of anything connected with developments in the war, by, e.g., refusing to listen to radio broadcasts or watch films about them and leaving the current events sections of the newspaper unread. In general, only those women who have close relatives at the front, as well as women of the educated classes, show much interest in current events. . . .

Many women are also anxious about the effect that the long duration of the war is beginning to have on the strength of, and mutual feelings in, their marriage. People's lives have been altered and influenced by having been separated now for years, apart from short intervals, by the way in which total war has altered living conditions, and, further, by the substantial demands now being made of each individual. The front-line soldier who is home on leave often no longer shows any comprehension of the realities of running a household under wartime conditions and remains indifferent to the many daily worries of the home front. The result is that increasingly married couples are drifting apart. Wives anxiously point out that the time together in the fleeting period of leave, to which they had eagerly looked forward, has been sullied by frequent arguments. This is the case even in marriages which were formerly idyllically harmonious.

H. Boberach (ed.), *Meldungen aus dem Reich*, Deutscher Taschenbuch Verlag, Munich, 1968. 'Current events and their impact on opinion and attitudes among women', 18 November 1943, pp. 360–61.

Document 26   Consumers under pressure in wartime

Food-producing areas at least had enough to eat. In the towns, there were complaints about shortages of food, coal and other materials virtually from the start of the war. Even so, Germans did not suffer dire shortage (as in 1916–18) until the last stages of the war.

(a)   18 March 1940

From the entire country there are reports saying that there is great ill-feeling among the population on account of difficulties in buying non-rationed goods. This applies especially to foodstuffs and tobacco, vegetables, fruit in general and citrus fruit in particular, things that are quite as important for the daily diet as the foodstuffs which are controlled by rationing.

It is mentioned in this connection that especially working women, who can normally do their shopping only in the evening, make complaints about not being able to obtain goods other than those which are rationed. And a larger number of housewives, who do not have the time to stand for hours in a queue for some items, are affected, too.

H. Focke and U. Reimer, *Alltag unterm Hakenkreuz. Wie die Nazis das Leben der Deutschen veränderten*, volume 1, Rowohlt, Reinbek bei Hamburg, 1979, p. 182.

(b) It is reported from all parts of the Gau [Württemberg-Hohenzollern] that there is increasing anxiety among women about shopping for food. . . . Women often stand for hours to obtain supplies of fruit, vegetables and, especially, potatoes. Since each woman is allowed only 2–3 pounds of potatoes at a time, women with larger families can often be seen queuing at several different shops in order to obtain a greater supply. The picture of women queuing is very evocative of the [First] World War, when almost every kind of foodstuff was obtainable only in this way, and the comments of the women queuing underline that, with most of them actually uttering the words 'just like in the World War'. . . .

A further example of growing anxiety about food shortages is a scene which took place at the last weekly market in Bismarck Square in Stuttgart. The first women came as early as 5 o'clock in the morning to queue up. They were mostly industrial workers who were hoping to get their supplies before they went to work, because they would not be able to get anything after the day's work. Around 6 o'clock more of them came, including a woman with several children [eine kinderreiche Frau]. She wanted to go to the head of the queue because she had a pass entitling her to preferential treatment. In a matter of seconds the women were involved in a huge brawl, and it took several policemen to separate them.

Staatsarchiv Ludwigsburg, K110, Bü48, Sicherheitsdienst
RFSS – SD-Leitabschnitt Stuttgart, 'Betr.: Allgemeine Stimmung
und Lage', 1 September 1941, pp. 36–37.

Document 27 Civilians as bombing targets

(a) *Allied bombing of German cities intensified in 1943. In 'Operation Gomorrha' in July–August, Hamburg endured ten continuous days of fire-bombing. Ilse Grassmann, mother of four, recorded her experiences before and during the raids.*

[Late June 1943] . . . A terror attack on Hamburg is being prepared. It's not just Hamburgers who are finding leaflets, but it's also those who in all secrecy listen to enemy broadcasts. You can sense panic everywhere. It's so good that at least our two older sons are no longer in Hamburg. No one can now leave Hamburg without permission. The individual regions of Germany are divided into discrete districts. You can leave your home area only with the permission of the NSDAP local branch leader. Without this permission, you will not receive a ration card anywhere else. These ration cards tie us to a place and to a specified shop. You can get food only where you are registered. A new application for new ration cards can be made only with the authorization of both [NSDAP] local branches; thus the circle is closed. This war is taking on characteristics that are disturbing.

27 July. . . . The bombs fall continuously. The house shakes, through the concrete floor of the cellar you sense that the earth is moving. There are hairline cracks, the supports start to shift, and people perch on their seats as if they were already dead. . . . Another massive impact, now the light goes out. Delivered pitilessly into the darkness and gloom, we are now waiting for the end. Finally we are able to light a candle. . . . The air-raid warden comes and tells us: 'some of the houses in our street are already burning, and we obviously have to leave the cellar. Leave any luggage here, the children are more important. If the emergency exit has fallen in, we'll have to try to break through into the next house'.

Quoted in J. Szodrzynski, 'Das Ende der "Volksgemeinschaft"? Die Hamburger Bevölkerung in der "Trummergesellschaft" ab 1943', in F. Bajohr and J. Szodrzynski (eds), *Hamburg in der NS-Zeit. Ergebnisse neuerer Forschung*, Ergebnisse Verlag, Hamburg, 1995, pp. 295–96.

(b)   The last days of the war were terrifying for German civilians. In the towns, they were mercilessly bombarded by enemy air power and, increasingly, by the enemy on the ground too.

Inge made her way eastwards with her two small children. She was evacuated to East Prussia by the NSV because of the frequent air attacks on Berlin. . . . But Inge was not there long before, in midsummer 1944, the rumble of the approaching front became audible. In the first few days, she thought it was a storm. As she said so, the others laughed. 'It sounds like a storm!' The old farmer said bitterly: 'A fine storm! The storm of war!' Absolutely terrified, she fled from the theatre of war back to Berlin. Nowhere was safe. Now the sirens wailed at ever shorter intervals. With her two little ones, Eva by the hand and Dieter on her arm, she hurried to the air-raid shelter in Landsberger Avenue, near her home. . . .

The final battle for Berlin had begun. Inge's father was conscripted into the *Volkssturm* (Home Guard). . . . The air-raid warden still talked about planned exercises, about holding out and wonder weapons, when bridges in Berlin had already been blown up by the SS, and Soviet soldiers with multiple rocket launchers were bombarding the centre of the city from [the suburbs]. A neighbour knocked at the door: 'Come to the cellar! The Russians will soon be here'. Inge woke the children from their afternoon sleep. With her three year-old daughter on her right and her two year-old son on her left, she sat in the cellar and waited for the war to end. She had so often longed for it, but now she felt no joy at the thought of it. Her feelings were numb, consumed by the strains of the struggle for survival. She had heard nothing of Karlheinz [her husband] for a long time. Day after day she waited for the postwoman, with mixed feelings. It could after all be . . . news of his death.

'Kriegerwitwe. Über Inge D.', in G. Szepansky, '*Blitzmädel*', '*Heldenmutter*', '*Kriegerwitwe*'. *Frauenleben im Zweiten Weltkrieg*, Fischer Taschenbuch Verlag, Frankfurt/M, 1986, pp. 54–55.

Document 28   German women raped by foreign soldiers

When German towns and villages were taken by the Allies, in early 1945, the invading soldiers sometimes took revenge by raping German women. This reached epidemic proportions among Soviet troops in the east, but it also occurred in western Germany. Here, French soldiers are the perpetrators in a south German village.

20 April 1945. The worst thing of all happened to the women and girls. No female person between the ages of 12 and 80 was safe from rape. According to the local doctor . . . 152 women required medical attention because they had been raped. Fifty of them were infected [with a sexually transmitted disease], two pregnancies were confirmed. The 68-year-old wife of a farmer . . . was forced to lie on the bed – of all places, at the feet of her husband who was at death's door – and was raped by 10 [French soldiers]. Her husband died the next day. There wasn't an officer to be seen. . . . Clearly the officers closed their eyes, because it was only

German women. It is probable that a number of women who were raped kept quiet out of shame, so that the number of these tragic cases is actually higher than is recorded above.

Hauptstaatsarchiv Stuttgart, J170, Bü13, Landkreis Leonberg,
Gemeinde Merklingen a.W., 'Geschichtliche Darstellung der
letzten Kriegstage', 11 October 1948.

Document 29   Denunciations by women in wartime

Ordinary Germans who were not Nazis sometimes settled private scores by denouncing an acquaintance or even a spouse to the police, claiming that s/he had made treasonable or merely critical comments about the regime. Particularly in wartime, this could be literally deadly.

(a)   Satrup (Schleswig-Holstein) – November 1943
At first the relationship with the married couple J., who were renting rooms from Frau Schulz, seemed good. Then in 1943 a dispute developed about the rent. Tensions mounted visibly, until, after a quarrel on 15.11.43, [Schulz] denounced Hermann J. to Head of Department H. for various utterances and actions that were hostile to the state [including calling the *Führer* a house painter]. . . .

   Head of Department H., who knew Hermann J. as a good, hardworking man with a 'big mouth', conveyed the report to the *Landrat* and the police authorities. Gestapo official P. from Flensburg found an instruction on his desk to question Frau Schulz. Without knowing the facts of the case or the accused, he questioned [Frau Schulz], who repeated all the political comments made by her tenant and also named as witnesses [two] other women [who] confirmed some of the comments. J. himself was interrogated on 7 and 8.2.1944 and was arrested on 11.2. A month later he was taken to Berlin. In the proceedings on 6.6.1944 before . . . the People's Court, Frau Schulz repeated her statement again, and it was confirmed by others. Hermann J. was sentenced to death and executed on 17.7.1944.

(b)   Berlin – 1944
(1)   . . . In 1940, Frau Maag reported her divorced husband, Arthur M., to his superiors at the Police Department – Section Command Charlottenburg for 'aiding and abetting Jews'. She accused him and a colleague

of frequenting the house of the Jewish manufacturer Karl Joel over a period of 18 months and receiving gifts. In the proceedings on 16.5.1941, Maag was sentenced to six months in prison for serious passive bribery.

(2) ... The former Minister of the Interior in Hesse and Social Democratic trade union leader, Leuschner, lived with his family on the same landing as [Frau Maag]. Following personal disagreements, Frau Maag was not on good terms with Frau Leuschner. In 1942, Frau L. was summoned to the Gestapo for having allegedly made comments hostile to the state to Frau Maag. When Frau L. contested this, she was released with no adverse consequences. On information from Frau Maag, the Gestapo searched the Leuschners' apartment and confiscated a large amount of fruit for a hospital. ...

As early as 9.5.1942, Gau [NSDAP] officer Becker was brought in as [Frau Maag's] lodger to spy on Herr Leuschner. After his apartment had been searched in connection with the attempt on Hitler's life on 20.7.1944, Leuschner visited it only occasionally and, when he did, he entered by the back door. His wife was arrested because she would not reveal his whereabouts. Frau Maag watched what Leuschner did and informed the Gestapo. She also told the officers that Leuschner often stayed with his former cleaner, whom she knew by the name of 'Mariechen'. On the basis of this information, the Gestapo traced Frau Marie S. and was able to arrest Leuschner there on 16.8.1944. Leuschner was later sentenced to death and hanged.

R. Wolters, *Verrat für die Volksgemeinschaft. Denunziantinnen im Dritten Reich*, Centaurus-Verlagsgesellschaft, Pfaffenweiler, 1996, pp. 64–67.

Document 30   The deportation of a Jewish woman

At first, the Jewish wives of 'Aryans' were protected from deportation to incarceration and probable death. But the death of the 'Aryan' husband left the Jewish widow exposed. Being well-integrated into a neighbourhood was not enough to protect her from being deported, as this dramatized account illustrates.

Characters:	*Rosa Creuzberger; 1st SA Man; 2nd SA Man; Girl; Onlookers*
Scene:	*At the entrance to a house. In the background, a notice on the house, 'The Lime Tree Inn'. Two armed SA men stand at the*

door and look inside the house. In the background, a small crowd. An elderly woman comes out, wearing an apron.

1st SA Man:	Rosa Creuzberger, born Hoffmann, date of birth 26.9.1889?
Creuzberger:	Yes, that's me.
1st SA Man:	Jewess?
Creuzberger:	Why do you need to know?
1st SA Man:	You have to come with us.
Creuzberger:	Where to?
2nd SA Man:	We don't know. You must come with us.
Creuzberger:	Can I get changed?
1st SA Man:	It's all right if you fetch a coat. But come straight back. We haven't much time.

Rosa Creuzberger disappears into the house.

2nd SA Man:	[*sings insinuatingly*] Between Calw and Althengstett the road goes left, there sit three Jews, ugh, yuck, what a pong! Between . . .
1st SA Man:	Be quiet. You really shouldn't do that.
2nd SA Man:	[*seems absolutely amazed*] Why?
1st SA Man:	Don't be so daft. Here she comes. We don't need to go on about it, she's to come with us.

Rosa Creuzberger comes out of the house, in a coat with a Jewish star on the lapel.

Creuzberger:	So where am I being taken?
1st SA Man:	All Jews are being taken away. You mean you didn't know that?
Creuzberger:	But my husband was an . . . an 'Aryan' [*she emphasizes this word*].
2nd SA Man:	Your husband is dead. And Jewish widows of Aryans are also being taken away.
1st SA Man:	These are our instructions [*he shows her a piece of paper*], and an order is an order. Are you ready?
Creuzberger:	And where are you taking me?
1st SA Man:	First of all, to the Langen, up in the tower. And then we'll see.
Creuzberger:	But my husband . . .
2nd SA Man:	Your husband doesn't count any more. You are a Jew, and that's all there is to it.

Creuzberger:	But you two have always come to our inn. You've always enjoyed my cooking.
1st SA Man:	That's got nothing to do with it. And now we're not going to talk about it any more. Come along.

[*Seizes her by the arm. The second one takes the other side.*]

Creuzberger:	[*to the crowd*] Can't you help me! Can't you help me!
A Man:	[*from the crowd, timidly*] This won't do. She's been the landlady of the Lime Tree for years. What do you want with her? She hasn't done anything!

The SA men stop. Look at the crowd. Stare at one after the other.

1st SA Man:	Who's got something to say? Let him come forward. A Jew-lover? Did I really hear that correctly?

The people in the crowd look away. No one comes forward, some go off.

Creuzberger:	[*to a girl who sticks her head out of the entrance to the house and looks at her*] I'll be back soon. Keep my house in order! I'll be back soon.

[*The SA men first smirk and then laugh. Then they go off with the woman.*]
Short pause.
A man from the crowd comes forward and turns to the audience:

The Man:	In September 1943, only three months after the death of her 'Aryan' husband in an accident, Frau Rosa Creuzberger, was deported to Auschwitz and, like many hundreds of thousands of her fellow-victims, put to death in the gas chambers. Until then she had been for many years the landlady of the Lime Tree Inn.

U. Rothfuss, *Die Hitlerfahn' muss weg! Zwanzig dramatische Stationen in einer schwäbischen Kleinstadt*, Silberburg-Verlag, Tübingen, 1998, pp. 70–73.

Document 31   Transports to Auschwitz, autumn 1944

Resi Weglein was deported, with her husband, on 20 August 1942 from her home in Ulm to the Theresienstadt 'ghetto', where she worked in extraordinarily difficult and distressing conditions as a nurse for the rest of the war. She describes the final transports of Jews from Theresienstadt to Auschwitz.

To give the impression that it was quite harmless, the first transport [on the Jewish new year] was disguised as a labour transport. 3,000 men were ordered to report within twelve hours to the departure area. . . . In September 1944 there were between 20,000 and 30,000 of us in the camp. The women could not understand that the men were seized from them, and it was even less comprehensible that the best men from [a construction unit], who had been promised that they would never be transported, were selected to leave the camp. The women swarmed into the Magdeburg barracks and volunteered to go with the men to be able to work with them at the new destination. This offer was unnecessary, as will become apparent. To be accommodating, 50 women were chosen to accompany the men's transport. One can imagine the sorrow and desperation of the women who were left behind. Three days after the first transport, it was the turn of the next 3,000 people. Almost all the holders of the highest war decorations [from 1914–18] were among them, and 500 women had to travel with them. The ghetto looked liked an anthill that had been destroyed. Everyone had a relative or close friend in the transport. . . .

Yes, it was a very clever system that kept devising new forms of suffering. The transports cast an awful shadow over the whole of October 1944, and we did not have a moment's peace by day or by night.

After the second transport of men, a children's transport was assembled. Boys and girls aged 12 to 16 were torn from their parents. . . .

The fourth transport included all the women whose husbands had already gone, except for those working in the mica insulation works. They volunteered to go, but to no avail, because all of those working in war industry were exempted from the transports. . . .

For the sixth transport, people from all occupations had to appear in front of the SS. . . . We nurses stood in alphabetical order for hours in the [hospital] yard. The men in command took plenty of time to choose. They were sitting in heated rooms, and knowing that we were outside in the cold meant nothing to them. Because my name was at the end of the alphabet, unfortunately my turn came very late. Like my husband, I was examined by [SS leader] Möhs. He did not ask me much, and naturally I did not know how the die had been cast. I breathed a sigh of relief that the camp commandant supported me.

R. Weglein, *Als Krankenschwester im KZ Theresienstadt. Erinnerungen einer Ulmer Jüdin*, Silberburg-Verlag, Stuttgart, 1988, pp. 67–69.

Glossary

Altreich (lit., old Reich) Germany within its borders of 1937.

autarky Self-sufficiency, intensified from 1936 in the Four Year Plan.

Autobahn (pl. *Autobahnen* – motorway) The major German roads built from 1933.

BDF (*Bund Deutscher Frauenvereine*) Federation of German Women's Organizations – a liberal, middle-class combine founded in 1894, dissolved in May 1933.

BDM (*Bund Deutscher Mädel*) League of German Girls – the section of the NSDAP's youth organization, the Hitler Youth, for girls of 14 to 18 years of age.

Beauty of Labour Project promoted by the DAF to improve the working environment in factories.

BKL (*Bund Königin Luise*) Queen Luise League – a conservative and nationalist women's organization, founded in 1923, dissolved in 1934.

Block The smallest unit of the NSDAP's territorial organization, from 1936 consisting of 40 to 60 households.

Cell Unit of the NSDAP's territorial organization, from 1936 consisting of four to six blocks.

Concordat Treaty between the Vatican and the German government, signed on 20 July 1933, by which the Catholic Church agreed to the dissolution of its political organizations in return for the immunity of non-political groups. The Nazi regime began to violate this provision almost immediately.

DAF (*Deutsche Arbeitsfront*) German Labour Front – the largest mass organization in Nazi Germany, which replaced the trade unions after their dissolution on 2 May 1933 and expropriated their assets. Membership for blue- and white-collar workers was in theory voluntary; in practice, non-members faced discrimination. Its leader was Robert Ley.

DFO (*Deutscher Frauenorden*) German Women's Order – Elsbeth Zander's organization, affiliated to the NSDAP in 1928 and dissolved in 1931 when the NSF was founded.

DFW (*Deutsches Frauenwerk*) German Women's Enterprise – the umbrella organization into which 'co-ordinated' women's groups were forced; founded in 1933 and under the NSF's leadership.

Doppelverdiener (lit., double earner) An employed married woman whose husband was also employed. Mostly applied to those in the public service.

Evangelical Church The Protestant Church in Germany.

Four Year Plan Economic strategy launched in September 1936 to prepare Germany for a future war by channelling resources, directing production and promoting autarky.

Führer (leader)   The title assumed by Adolf Hitler as leader of the NSDAP. After 1933, used to describe him as leader of Germany.

Führerprinzip (leadership principle)   Line management by which all authority came from the top down, with unquestioning obedience required from those below.

Gau   The largest territorial unit of the NSDAP, of which there were thirty-two in 1933 and forty from autumn 1938, after the annexation of Austria and the Sudetenland.

Gestapo (Secret State Police)   The much-feared political police force with limited numbers but extensive extra-legal powers.

Gleichschaltung ('co-ordination')   Term used for the dissolution of non-Nazi institutions and organizations in 1933–34 and the imposition of a Nazi monopoly in political life and over social group activity.

Greater Germany   Territory ruled by the Nazi regime after the annexation of Austria in March 1938, later including the Sudetenland, Bohemia and Moravia, Memel [Map 2].

Greater German Reich   German territory after conquests in eastern and western Europe, including Alsace, Lorraine, Luxembourg, as well as Danzig-West Prussia and the Wartheland in Poland [Map 3].

JFB (*Jüdischer Frauenbund*)   Jewish Women's Association – founded in 1904, forcibly dissolved in 1938.

Kreis (district)   Second largest unit of the NSDAP's territorial organization, into which the *Gaue* were divided.

Kristallnacht ('night of broken glass')   9/10 November 1938, the massive officially-orchestrated pogrom against Jewish property and persons.

KPD (*Kommunistische Partei Deutschlands*)   German Communist Party – founded in 1918, declared illegal in February 1933.

Land (pl., *Länder*)   Federal state of Germany, e.g., Baden, Bavaria, Prussia.

Luftwaffe   The German military air force, whose commander was Göring.

Mischling   The term used by Nazis for those with one or two Jewish grandparents.

NSDAP (*Nationalsozialistische Deutsche Arbeiterpartei*)   National Socialist German Workers' Party – the Nazi Party, 1920–45.

NSF (*Nationalsozialistische Frauenschaft*)   Nazi Women's Group – the elite organization of women within the NSDAP, founded in 1931.

NSLB (*Nationalsozialistischer Lehrerbund*)   Nazi Teachers' Association – to which 90 percent of German teachers belonged by 1936.

NSV (*Nationalsozialistische Volkswohlfahrt*)   Nazi People's Welfare – a large organization within the NSDAP, providing welfare and supervised assistance selectively to 'valuable' Germans.

Ortsgruppe (local branch)   Unit of the NSDAP's territorial organization into which *Kreise* were divided, consisting of a village, a small town, or an area within a city.

Reichsbahn   The German state railway network.

RdK (*Reichsbund der Kinderreichen*)   National Association of Large Families – a propaganda organization inherited by the Nazis, used to promote the desirability of 'valuable' large families.

RNS (*Reichsnährstand*)   National Food Estate – the Nazi organization for farmers and agricultural policy, founded in September 1933.

Reichstag   Lower house of the German legislature.

SA (*Sturm Abteilungen*)   Storm Troopers – the strong-arm paramilitary organization of the NSDAP whose leadership was purged in June 1934.

SD (*Sicherheitsdienst*)   Security Service – part of the *Reichssicherheitshauptamt* (Reich Main Security Office) which was a branch of the SS responsible for surveillance of the population and monitoring of the popular mood.

SPD (*Sozialdemokratische Partei Deutschlands*)   German Social Democratic Party – founded in 1875, dissolved in June 1933.

SS (*Schutzstaffeln*)   Protection Squads – the black-uniformed paramilitary organization of the NSDAP which was led by Himmler and fanatically loyal to both him and Hitler.

Volksgemeinschaft (people's ethnic community)   Applied to the 'Aryan', 'valuable' population of Germany collectively, explicitly excluding all others.

Wehrmacht (the armed forces)   Collective term for the German army, navy and air force.

Who's who?

Bormann, Martin (1900–45)   Hess's secretary, who succeeded him as head of the NSDAP's central office in 1941 and became Hitler's close confidant from 1941 to 1945.

Brüning, Heinrich (1885–1970)   Leader of the Catholic Centre Party and Reich Chancellor, 1930–32. His failure to construct a parliamentary majority led to rule by Presidential decree and the demise of parliamentary democracy.

Goebbels, Joseph (1897–1945)   NSDAP *Gauleiter* of Berlin and Reich Minister of Propaganda and Popular Enlightenment in Hitler's government. He incited the violence of *Kristallnacht*, became General Plenipotentiary for Total War in July 1944.

Göring, Hermann (1893–1946)   Appointed Prussian Interior Minister on 30 January 1933, Commander-in-Chief of the *Luftwaffe* in 1935, and Plenipotentiary for the Four Year Plan in 1936, he directed the 'Aryanization' of Jewish businesses.

Hess, Rudolf (1894–1987)   Hitler's private secretary who, from 1933, was NSDAP Deputy of the *Führer* and a government minister, until his flight to Scotland in 1941. After the war, he was imprisoned in Spandau for the remainder of his life.

Hilgenfeldt, Erich (1897–1945)   From May 1933, leader of the NSV. From February 1934, Leader of the Office of the *Frauenschaft* in the Supreme Leadership of the Party's Organization, giving him nominal overlordship of the NSF/DFW which ensured their co-operation in NSV projects.

Himmler, Heinrich (1900–45)   Chief of the German Police from 1936, he was *Reichsführer-SS* (supreme leader of the *Schutzstaffeln*). His positions as head of the SS and the *Gestapo* and, from 1943 to 1945, as Reich Minister of the Interior gave him enormous power. He implemented Nazi racist policies in occupied Poland, and, above all, in the concentration and extermination camps over which he presided.

Hitler, Adolf (1889–1945)   *Führer* of the NSDAP and, from 30 January 1933, Reich Chancellor. He presided over and encouraged racist and murderous policies, both in Germany and in occupied countries during the war.

Ley, Robert (1890–1945)   NSDAP *Gauleiter* who, from 1933 to 1945, was leader of the DAF. From 1932, he was leader of the NSDAP's organization.

Rüdiger, Jutta (b. 1910)   ANSt activist at Würzburg university, she graduated in psychology. Leader of the BDM, 1937–45.

Scholtz-Klink, Gertrud (b. 1902)   DFO leader in Gau Baden and, from 1934, leader of both the NSF and the DFW, and *Reichsfrauenführerin* (National Women's

Leader). She married three times and was mother of eleven children, several of whom did not survive childhood. She was used as a show-piece of German womanhood both at home and abroad, but she had no authority outside the women's organizations.

Speer, Albert (1905–81) Architect who from 1933 designed major Nazi rallies and events, as well as major buildings in Berlin. He was Minister for Armaments and War Production, 1942–45, mobilizing Germany's resources and exploiting forced foreign labourers.

Strasser, Gregor (1892–1934) NSDAP Organization Leader, 1928–32. Resigned, December 1932; was murdered in the Night of the Long Knives, 30 June 1934.

Wagner, Robert (1895–1946) NSDAP *Gauleiter* of Baden, 1925–45, and head of the government of Baden, 1933–45. He was head of the civil administration of occupied Alsace, 1940–45.

Zander, Elsbeth (b. 1888) Leader of the *Deutscher Frauenorden*, a racist and patriotic women's organization which was affiliated to the NSDAP in 1928. On the creation of the *NS-Frauenschaft* on 1 October 1931, the DFO was dissolved and Zander became NSF leader, until her resignation in 1933.

References

Sources cited

1   Bundesarchiv Koblenz (BAK), NS25/75, fol. 1, Hauptamt für Kommunalpolitik, Rundschreiben Nr 6, 14 February 1933.
2   Staatsarchiv Ludwigsburg (StAL), K110, Bü44, SD 'Lagebericht', 1 February 1939, p. 14.
3   Ibid.
4   BAK, NSD30/1836, *Informationsdienst für die soziale Arbeit der NSV*, 'Landjahr und Landdienst', February 1939, S. 87.
5   StAL, K110, Bü46, SD 'Lagebericht', 1 July 1939, p. 25.
6   Ibid., p. 46.
7   Hauptstaatsarchiv Stuttgart (HStAS), J170: Bü1 (Aalen), Gemeinde Zipplingen.
8   StAL, K110, Bü48, SD 'Lagebericht', 1 September 1941, p. 45.
9   Ibid., p. 44.
10 HStAS, J170, Bü8, Kreis Heilbronn, Gemeinde Hausen a.d.Z., n.d.

Official publications cited

Deutsche Hochschulstatistik, 1934/35.
Statistisches Jahrbuch: 1914, 1934, 1935, 1938, 1941/42.

Books and essays cited

Abrams, L. and Harvey, E. (eds) (1996) *Gender Relations in German History. Power, Agency and Experience from the Sixteenth to the Twentieth Century*. London: UCL Press.

Abrams, L. and Harvey, E. (1996a) 'Introduction', in Abrams/Harvey (eds), *Gender Relations*, pp. 1–37.

Arbogast, C. (1998) *Herrschaftsinstanzen der württembergischen NSDAP*. Munich: Oldenbourg.

Bajohr, S. (1979) *Die Hälfte der Fabrik. Geschichte der Frauenarbeit in Deutschland 1914–1945*. Marburg: Verlag Arbeiterbewegung und Gesellschaftswissenschaft.

Bartov, O. (1991) *Hitler's Army: Soldiers, Nazis and War in the Third Reich*. New York and Oxford: Oxford University Press.

Bauer, T. (1996) *Nationalsozialistische Agrarpolitik und bäuerliches Verhalten im Zweiten Weltkrieg. Eine Regionalstudie zur ländlichen Gesellschaft in Bayern.* Frankfurt/M: Peter Lang.

Beck, E.R. (1986) *Under The Bombs. The German Home Front 1942–1945.* Lexington, KY: The University of Kentucky Press.

Bennett, R. (1998) *Under the Shadow of the Swastika. The Moral Dilemmas of Resistance and Collaboration in Hitler's Europe.* London: Macmillan.

Benz, W. (2000) *The Holocaust. A Short History.* London: Profile Books.

Bergen, D. (1996) *Twisted Cross. The German Christian Movement in the Third Reich.* Chapel Hill, NC: University of North Carolina Press.

Bessel, R. (1993) *Germany after the First World War.* Oxford: Clarendon Press.

Boak, H. (1989) ' "Our Last Hope": women's votes for Hitler – a reappraisal', *German Studies Review*, volume XII, no. 2, pp. 289–310.

Bock, G. (1984) 'Racism and sexism in Nazi Germany: motherhood, compulsory sterilization, and the state', in Bridenthal et al. (eds), *When Biology Became Destiny*, pp. 271–96.

Bock, G. (1986) *Zwangssterilisation im Nationalsozialismus. Studien zur Rassenpolitik und Frauenpolitik.* Opladen: Westdeutscher Verlag.

Bock, G. (1994) 'Antinatalism, maternity and paternity in National Socialist racism', in D.F. Crew (ed.), *Nazism and German Society, 1933–1945.* London and New York: Routledge, pp. 110–40.

Böltken, A. (1995) *Führerinnen im 'Führerstaat'. Gertrud Scholtz-Klink, Trude Mohr, Jutta Rüdiger und Inge Viermetz.* Pfaffenweiler: Centaurus-Verlagsgesellschaft.

Botwinick, R.S. (1992) *Winzig, Germany, 1933–1946. The History of a Town under the Third Reich.* Westport, CT, and London: Praeger.

Bridenthal, R., Grossmann, A. and Kaplan, M. (eds) (1984) *When Biology Became Destiny. Women in Weimar and Nazi Germany.* New York: Monthly Review Press.

Bronnen, B. (ed.) (1998) *Geschichte vom Überleben. Frauentagebücher aus der NS-Zeit.* Munich: C.H. Beck Verlag.

Burleigh, M. (1994) *Death and Deliverance. 'Euthanasia' in Germany 1900–1945.* Cambridge: Cambridge University Press.

Burleigh, M. (2000) *The Third Reich. A New History.* London: Macmillan.

Burleigh, M. and Wippermann, W. (1991) *The Racial State. Germany 1933–1945.* Cambridge: Cambridge University Press.

Büttner, U. (1993) *'Gomorrha': Hamburg im Bombenkrieg. Die Wirkung der Luftangriffe auf Bevölkerung und Wirtschaft.* Hamburg: Lütcke and Wulff.

Corni, G. and Gies, H. (1997) *Brot, Butter, Kanonen. Die Ernährungswirtschaft in Deutschland unter der Diktatur Hitlers.* Berlin: Akademie Verlag.

Czarnowski, G. (1991) *Das Kontrollierte Paar. Ehe- und Sexualpolitik im Nationalsozialismus.* Weinheim.

Czarnowski, G. (1996) ' "The value of marriage for the *Volksgemeinschaft*": policies towards women and marriage under National Socialism', in R. Bessel (ed.), *Fascist Italy and Nazi Germany. Comparisons and Contrasts.* Cambridge: Cambridge University Press, pp. 94–112.

Dammer, S. (1981) 'Kinder, Küche, Kriegsarbeit – Die Schulung der Frauen durch die NS-Frauenschaft', in Frauengruppe Faschismusforschung, *Mutterkreuz und Arbeitsbuch*, pp. 215–45.

Daniel, U. (1997) *The War from Within. German Working-class Women in the First World War*. Oxford and New York: Berg.

Farquharson, J.E. (1976) *The Plough and the Swastika. The NSDAP and Agriculture in Germany, 1928–45*. London and Beverly Hills, CA: Sage.

Focke, H. and Reimer, U. (1979) *Alltag unterm Hakenkreuz. Wie die Nazis das Leben der Deutschen veränderten*, Band 1. Hamburg: Rowohlt Taschenbuch Verlag.

Frauengruppe Faschismusforschung (ed.) (1981) *Mutterkreuz und Arbeitsbuch. Zur Geschichte der Frauen in der Weimarer Republik und im Nationalsozialismus*. Frankfurt/M: Fischer Taschenbuch Verlag.

Frevert, U. (1989) *Women in German History. From Bourgeois Emancipation to Sexual Liberation*. Oxford/Hamburg/New York: Berg.

Fröhlich, E. (1981) 'Die Partei auf lokaler Ebene. Zwischen gesellschaftlicher Assimilation und Veränderungsdynamik', in G. Hirschfeld and L. Kettenacker (eds), *Der 'Führerstaat': Mythos und Realität. Studien zur Struktur und Politik des Dritten Reiches*. Stuttgart: Klett-Cotta, pp. 255–69.

Gellately, R. (1990) *The Gestapo and German Society. Enforcing Racial Policy 1933–1945*. Oxford and New York: The Clarendon Press.

Gellately, R. (1990a) 'Surveillance and disobedience: aspects of the political policing of Nazi Germany', in Nicosia/Stokes (eds), *Germans against Nazism*, pp. 15–31.

Gersdorff, U. von (1969) *Frauen im Kriegsdienst 1914–1945*. Stuttgart: Deutsche Verlags-Anstalt.

Giles, G.J. (1985) *Students and National Socialism in Germany*. Princeton, NJ: Princeton University Press.

Goldhagen, D.J. (1996) *Hitler's Willing Executioners. Ordinary Germans and the Holocaust*. London: Little, Brown and Company.

Grill, J.H. (1983) *The Nazi Movement in Baden, 1920–1945*. Chapel Hill, NC: University of North Carolina Press.

Grossmann, A. (1995) *Reforming Sex. The German Movement for Birth Control and Abortion Reform, 1920–1950*. New York and Oxford: Oxford University Press.

Hahn, C. (1981) 'Der öffentliche Dienst und die Frauen – Beamtinnen in der Weimarer Republik', in Frauengruppe Faschismusforschung, *Mutterkreuz und Arbeitsbuch*, pp. 49–78.

Hancock, E. (1991) *National Socialist Leadership and Total War 1941–45*. New York: St Martin's Press.

Harvey, E. (1997) 'Culture and society in Weimar Germany: the impact of modernism and mass culture', in Fulbrook, M. (ed.), *German History since 1800*. London: Arnold, pp. 279–97.

Harvey, E. (1998) '"Die deutsche Frau im Osten": "Rasse", Geschlecht und öffentlicher Raum im besetzten Polen 1940–1944', *Archiv für Sozialgeschichte*, volume 38, pp. 191–214.

Heineman, E. (1999) *What Difference Does a Husband Make? Women and Marital Status in Nazi and Postwar Germany*. Berkeley, Los Angeles, CA, and London: University of California Press.

Herbert, U. (1997) *Hitler's Foreign Workers*. Cambridge: Cambridge University Press.

Hitler, A. (1936) *Mein Kampf* (172nd–173rd edn). Munich: Frz. Eher Verlag.

Homze, E. (1967) *Foreign Labor in Nazi Germany*. Princeton, NJ: Princeton University Press.

Horowitz, G.J. (2000) 'Places far away, places very near: Mauthausen, the camps of the Shoah, and the bystanders', in O. Bartov (ed.), *The Holocaust. Origins, Implementation, Aftermath*. London and New York: Routledge, pp. 206–18.

Jarausch, K.H. (1990) *The Unfree Professions. German Lawyers, Teachers and Engineers, 1900–1950*. New York and Oxford: Oxford University Press.

Jureit, U. (1999) *Erinnerungsmuster. Zur Methodik lebensgeschichtlicher Interviews mit Überlebenden der Konzentrations- und Vernichtungslager*. Hamburg: Ergebnisse Verlag.

Kaiser, J.-C. (1982) 'Das Frauenwerk der evangelischen Kirche. Zum Problem des Verbandsprotestantismus im Dritten Reich', in H. Dollinger, H. Gründer and A. Hanschmidt (eds), *Weltpolitik, Europagedanke, Regionalismus. Festschrift für Heinz Gollwitzer zum 65. Geburtstag am 30. Januar 1982*. Münster: Aschendorff, pp. 483–508.

Kaminsky, U. (1999) 'Verfolgung im Arbeitermilieu Hamburgs aus erfahrungsgeschichtliche Sicht – Sozialdemokraten und Kommunisten zwischen Widerstand und Anpassung', and '"Vergessene Opfer" – Zwangssterilisierte, "Asoziale", Deserteure, Fremdarbeiter', in S. Baumbach, U. Kaminsky, A. Kenkmann and B. Meyer, *Rückblenden. Lebensgeschichtliche Interviews mit Verfolgten des NS-Regimes in Hamburg*. Hamburg: Ergebnisse Verlag, pp. 206–317 and 318–57.

Kaplan, M.A. (1979) *The Jewish Feminist Movement in Germany. The Campaigns of the Jüdischer Frauenbund, 1904–1938*. Westport, CT, and London: Greenwood Press.

Kaplan, M.A. (1984) 'Sisterhood under siege: feminism and anti-semitism in Germany, 1904–1938', in Bridenthal et al. (eds), *When Biology Became Destiny*, pp. 174–96.

Kaplan, M.A. (1998) *Between Dignity and Despair. Jewish Life in Nazi Germany*. New York and Oxford: Oxford University Press.

Kater, M. (1983) 'Frauen in der NS-Bewegung', *Vierteljahrshefte für Zeitgeschichte*, volume 31, no. 2, pp. 202–41.

Kater, M. (1989), *Doctors under Hitler*. Chapel Hill, NC, and London: University of North Carolina Press.

Kershaw, I. (1998) *Hitler 1889–1936: Hubris*. London: Allen Lane, The Penguin Press.

Kirkpatrick, C. (1939) *Woman in Nazi Germany*. London: Jarrolds.

Klinksiek, D. (1982) *Die Frau im NS-Staat*. Stuttgart: Deutsche Verlags-Anstalt.

Koonz, C. (1976) 'Conflicting allegiances: political ideology and women legislators in Weimar Germany', *Signs*, volume I, no. 3, pp. 663–83.

Koonz, C. (1987) *Mothers in the Fatherland. Women, the Family and Nazi Politics*. New York: St Martin's Press.

Koonz, C. (1993) 'Eugenics, gender, and ethics in Nazi Germany: the debate about involuntary sterilization 1933–1936', in T. Childers and J. Caplan (eds), *Reevaluating the Third Reich*. New York and London: Holmes and Meier, pp. 66–85.

Kundrus, B. (1995) *Kriegerfrauen. Familienpolitik und Geschlechterverhältnisse im Ersten und Zweiten Weltkrieg*. Hamburg: Hans Christians Verlag.

Kundrus, B. (1996) 'Frauen und Nationalsozialismus. Überlegungen zum Stand der Forschung', *Archiv für Sozialgeschichte*, volume 36, pp. 481–99.

Lacey, K. (1996) 'Driving the message home: Nazi propaganda in the private sphere', in Abrams/Harvey (eds), *Gender Relations*, pp. 189–210.

Lewy, G. (2000) *The Nazi Persecution of the Gypsies*. Oxford: Oxford University Press.

Lück, M. (1979) *Die Frau im Männerstaat*. Frankfurt/M: Peter Lang Verlag.

Lode, M. (1938) 'Women under Hitler's yoke', *The Communist International*, volume XIV, no. 10, pp. 42–6.

Lohalm, U. (2001) '. . . *anständig und aufopferungsbereit*'. *Öffentlicher Dienst und Nationalsozialismus in Hamburg 1933 bis 1945*. Hamburg: Ergebnisse Verlag.

McLaren, A. (1990) *A History of Contraception. From Antiquity to the Present Day*. Oxford and Cambridge, MA: Blackwell.

Marnau, B. (1995) '". . . empfinde ich das Urteil als hart und unrichtig": Zwangssterilisation im Kreis Steinburg/Holstein', in M. Salewski and G. Schulze-Wegener (eds), *Kriegsjahr 1944. Im Grossen und im Kleinen*. Stuttgart: Franz Steiner Verlag.

Maschmann, M. (1965) *Account Rendered: A Dossier on My Former Self*. Trans. by Geoffrey Strahan. London: Abelard Schumann.

Mason, T. (1976) 'Women in Germany, 1925–1940. Family, welfare and work', *History Workshop Journal*, nos I, 74–113, and II, 5–32. Reprinted as Chapter 5 in Jane Caplan (ed.) (1995) *Nazism, Fascism and the Working Class. Essays by Tim Mason*, Cambridge and New York: Cambridge University Press, pp. 131–211.

Michalka, W. (1985) *Das Dritte Reich*, Band 2. Munich: Deutscher Taschenbuch Verlag.

Michel, A. (1999) '"Alte Kämpferinnen". Dora Horn-Zippelius und Gertrud Gilg, Propaganda- und Gauschulungsleiterinnen der NS-Frauenschaft in Baden', in M. Kissener and J. Scholtyseck (eds), *Die Führer der Provinz. NS-Biographien aus Baden und Württemberg*. Konstanz: UVK Universitätsverlag Konstanz, pp. 225–65.

Milton, S. (1984) 'Women and the Holocaust: the case of German and German-Jewish women', in Bridenthal et al. (eds), *When Biology Became Destiny*, pp. 297–333.

Mommsen, H. (1991) 'The political legacy of the German resistance: a historiographical critique', in D.C. Large (ed.), *Contending with Hitler. Varieties of German Resistance in the Third Reich*. New York: Cambridge University Press, p. 161.

Mühlfeld, C. and Schönweiss, F. (1989) *Nationalsozialistische Familienpolitik. Familiensoziologische Analyse der nationalsozialistische Familienpolitik*. Stuttgart: Ferdinand Enke Verlag.

Münkel, D. (1996) *Nationalsozialistische Agrarpolitik und Bauernalltag*. Frankfurt/ New York: Campus Verlag.

Neiberger, A. (1998) 'An uncommon bond of friendship: family and survival in Auschwitz', in R. Rohrlich (ed.), *Resisting the Holocaust*. Oxford and New York: Berg, pp. 133–49.

Nicosia, F.R. and Stokes, L.D. (eds) (1990) *Germans against Nazism. Nonconformity, Opposition and Resistance in the Third Reich. Essays in Honour of Peter Hoffmann*. Oxford and Providence, RI: Berg.

Noakes, J. (1987) 'Social outcasts in the Third Reich', in R. Bessel (ed.), *Life in the Third Reich*. Oxford: Oxford University Press, pp. 83–96.

Noakes, J. (ed.) (1998) 'Women' and 'Sex and population policy', Chapters 45 and 46 in *Nazism, 1919–1945. A Documentary Reader*. Exeter: University of Exeter Press, volume 4, 'The German Home Front in World War II', pp. 302–95.

Noakes, J. and Pridham, G. (eds) (1983) *Nazism, 1919–1945. A Documentary Reader*. Exeter: University of Exeter Press, volume 1, 'The rise to power'.

Noakes, J. and Pridham, G. (eds) (1986) *Nazism, 1919–1945. A Documentary Reader*. Exeter: University of Exeter Press, volume 2, 'State, economy and society'.

Nolan, M. (1997) 'Work, gender and everyday life in twentieth century Germany', in I. Kershaw and M. Lewin (eds), *Stalinism and Nazism. Dictatorships in Comparison*. Cambridge: Cambridge University Press, pp. 311–42.

Overy, R. (1988) '"Blitzkriegwirtschaft"? Finanzpolitik, Lebensstandard und Arbeitseinsatz in Deutschland 1939–1942', *Vierteljahrshefte für Zeitgeschichte*, no. 3, pp. 379–435.

Owings, A. (1994) *Frauen. German Women Recall the Third Reich*. New Brunswick, NJ: Rutgers University Press.

Paucker, A. (1999) *Deutsche Juden im Widerstand 1933–1945. Tatsachen und Probleme*. Berlin: Eppler and Buntdruck.

Pauwels, J.R. (1984) *Women, Nazis, and Universities. Female University Students in the Third Reich, 1933–1945*. Westport, CT: Greenwood Press.

Peukert, D.J.K. (1987) *Inside Nazi Germany. Conformity, Opposition and Racism in Everyday Life*. London: Batsford.

Pine, L. (1995) 'Hashude: the imprisonment of "asocial" families in the Third Reich', *German History*, volume 13, no. 2, pp. 182–97.

Pine, L. (1997) *The Nazi Family, 1933–1945*. Oxford: Berg.

Proctor, R.N. (1988) *Racial Hygiene. Medicine under the Nazis*. Cambridge, MA, and London: Harvard University Press.

Quack, S. (1991) 'Everyday life and emigration: the role of women', in H. Lehmann and J.J. Sheehan (eds), *An Interrupted Past. German-speaking Historians in the United States after 1933*. New York and Cambridge: Cambridge University Press, pp. 102–8.

Reagin, N.R. (1995) *A German Women's Movement. Class and Gender in Hanover, 1880–1933*. Chapel Hill, NC, and London: University of North Carolina Press.

Reagin, N.R. (2001) '*Marktordnung* and autarkic housekeeping: housewives and private consumption under the Four-Year Plan, 1936–39', *German History*, volume 19, no. 2, pp. 162–84.

Reese, D. (1981) 'Bund Deutscher Mädel – Zur Geschichte der weiblichen deutschen Jugend im Dritten Reich', in Frauengruppe Faschismusforschung, *Mutterkreuz und Arbeitsbuch*, pp. 163–87.

Reese, D. (1989) *Straff, aber nicht stramm – herb, aber nicht derb. Zur Vergesellschaftung von Mädchen durch den Bund Deutscher Mädel im sozialkulturellen Vergleich zweier Milieus.* Weinheim and Basel: Beltz Verlag.

Rempel, G. (1989) *Hitler's Children. The Hitler Youth and the SS.* Chapel Hill, NC: University of North Carolina Press.

Rinderle, W. and Norling, B. (1993) *The Nazi Impact on a German Village.* Lexington, KY: The University Press of Kentucky.

Rosenhaft, E. (1992) 'Women in modern Germany', in G. Martel (ed.), *Modern Germany Reconsidered, 1870–1945.* London and New York: Routledge, pp. 140–58.

Rupp, L. (1978) *Mobilizing Women for War. German and American Propaganda, 1939–1945.* Princeton, NJ: Princeton University Press.

Said, E. (1981) 'Zur Situation der Lehrerinnen in der Zeit des Nationalsozialismus', in Frauengruppe Faschismusforschung, *Mutterkreuz und Arbeitsbuch*, pp. 105–30.

Saldern, A. von (1994) 'Victims or perpetrators? Controversies about the role of women in the Nazi state', in D.F. Crew (ed.), *Nazism and German Society, 1933–1945.* London and New York: Routledge, pp. 141–65.

Schefer, G. (1981) 'Wo Unterdrückung ist, da ist auch Widerstand – Frauen gegen Faschismus und Krieg', in Frauengruppe Faschismusforschung, *Mutterkreuz und Arbeitsbuch*, pp. 273–91.

Schmitt-Linsenhoff, V. et al. (eds) (1981) *Informationsblätter zu der Ausstellung 'Frauenalltag und Frauenbewegung in Frankfurt 1890–1980'. Historisches Museum Frankfurt.* Frankfurt/M: Fuldaer Verlagsanstalt.

Schnabel, T. (1986) *Württemberg zwischen Weimar und Bonn 1928–1945/46.* Stuttgart: Kohlhammer.

Schoenbaum, D. (1967) 'The Third Reich and women', chapter VI in *Hitler's Social Revolution. Class and Status in Nazi Germany, 1933–1939.* London: Weidenfeld and Nicolson, pp. 187–201.

Schoppmann, C. (1995) 'The position of lesbian women in the Nazi period', in G. Grau (ed.), *Hidden Holocaust. Gay and Lesbian Persecution in Germany 1933–45.* Trans. by Patrick Camiller. London and New York: Cassell, pp. 8–15.

Scholtz-Klink, G. (1978) *Die Frau im Dritten Reich.* Tübingen: Grabert Verlag.

Schupetta, I. (1981) 'Jedes das Ihre – Frauenerwerbstätigkeit und Einsatz von Fremdarbeitern/-arbeiterinnen im Zweiten Weltkrieg', in Frauengruppe Faschismusforschung, *Mutterkreuz und Arbeitsbuch*, pp. 292–317.

Shorter, E. (1982) *A History of Women's Bodies.* New York: Basic Books.

Sorge, M.K. (1986) *The Other Price of Hitler's War. German Military and Civilian Losses Resulting from World War II.* Westport, CT: Greenwood Press.

Speitkamp, W. (1998) *Jugend in der Neuzeit. Deutschland vom 16. bis zum 20. Jahrhundert.* Göttingen: Vandenhoeck and Ruprecht.

Staff, I. (ed.) (1964) *Justiz im Dritten Reich. Eine Dokumentation.* Frankfurt/M: Fischer Bücherei.

Stephenson, J. (1975) *Women in Nazi Society*. London and Totowa, NJ: Croom Helm and Barnes and Noble.

Stephenson, J. (1975a) 'Girls' higher education in the 1930s', *Journal of Contemporary History*, volume 10, no. 1, pp. 41–69.

Stephenson, J. (1979) '"Reichsbund der Kinderreichen": the League of Large Families in the population policy of Nazi Germany', *European Studies Review*, volume 9, no. 3, pp. 351–75.

Stephenson, J. (1981) *The Nazi Organisation of Women*. London and Totowa, NJ: Croom Helm and Barnes and Noble.

Stephenson, J. (1982) 'Women's labor service in Nazi Germany', *Central European History*, volume XV, no. 3, pp. 241–65.

Stephenson, J. (1983) 'Propaganda, autarky and the German housewife', in D. Welch (ed.), *Nazi Propaganda. The Power and the Limitations*. London and Totowa, NJ: Croom Helm and Barnes and Noble, pp. 117–42.

Stephenson, J. (1985) 'War and society in Württemberg, 1939–1945: beating the system', *German Studies Review*, volume VIII, no. 1, pp. 89–105.

Stephenson, J. (1987) '"Emancipation" and its problems: war and society in Württemberg, 1939–1945', *European History Quarterly*, volume 17, no. 3, pp. 345–65.

Stephenson, J. (1990) '"Resistance" to "no surrender": popular disobedience in Württemberg in 1945', in Nicosia/Stokes (eds), *Germans against Nazism*, pp. 351–67.

Szepansky, G. (1986) *'Blitzmädel', 'Heldenmutter', 'Kriegerwitwe'. Frauenleben im Zweiten Weltkrieg*. Frankfurt/M: Fischer Taschenbuchverlag.

Thalmann, R. (1984) *Frausein im Dritten Reich*. Munich: Hanser.

Tröger, A. (1981) 'Die Frau im wesensgemässen Einsatz', in Frauengruppe Faschismusforschung, *Mutterkreuz und Arbeitsbuch*, pp. 246–72.

Tröger, A. (1984) 'The creation of a female assembly-line proletariat', in Bridenthal et al. (eds), *When Biology Became Destiny*, pp. 237–70.

Usborne, C. (1992) *The Politics of the Body in Weimar Germany*. Ann Arbor, MI: University of Michigan Press.

Weyrather, I. (1981) 'Numerus Clausus für Frauen – Studentinnen im Nationalsozialismus', in Frauengruppe Faschismusforschung, *Mutterkreuz und Arbeitsbuch*, pp. 131–62.

Wickert, Christl (1994) 'Frauenwiderstand und Dissens im Kriegsalltag', in Peter Steinbach and Johannes Tuchel (eds), *Widerstand gegen den Nationalsozialismus*. Berlin: Akademie Verlag, pp. 411–25.

Wiggershaus, R. (1984) *Frauen unterm Nationalsozialismus*. Wuppertal: Peter Hammer Verlag.

Wilke, G. (1987) 'Village life in Nazi Germany', in R. Bessel (ed.), *Life in the Third Reich*. Oxford: Oxford University Press, pp. 17–24.

Wilke, G. and Wagner, K. (1981) 'Family and household: social structures in a German village between the two world wars', in R.J. Evans and W.R. Lee (eds), *The German Family*. London and Totowa, NJ: Croom Helm and Barnes and Noble, pp. 120–47.

Willmot, L. (1985) 'The debate on the introduction of an Auxiliary Military Service Law for women in the Third Reich and its consequences, August 1944–April 1945', *German History*, volume 2, pp. 10–20.

Winkler, D. (1977) *Frauenarbeit im 'Dritten Reich'*. Hamburg: Hoffmann and Campe.

Wippermann, W. (1998) *Umstrittene Vergangenheit. Fakten und Kontroversen zum Nationalsozialismus*. Berlin: Elefanten Press.

Wittmann, I. (1981) '"Echte Weiblichkeit ist ein Dienen" – Die Hausgehilfin in der Weimarer Republik und im Nationalsozialismus', in Frauengruppe Faschismusforschung, *Mutterkreuz und Arbeitsbuch*, pp. 15–48.

Wolters, R. (1996) *Verrat für die Volksgemeinschaft. Denunziantinnen im Dritten Reich*. Pfaffenweiler: Centaurus-Verlagsgesellschaft.

Woycke, J. (1988) *Birth Control in Germany, 1871–1933*. London and New York: Routledge.

Zentner, C. (ed.) (1975) 'Die Reichsfrauenführerin im Kreuzverhör', in *Dokumentation: Das Dritte Reich. Ein Volk, ein Reich, ein Führer*. Hamburg: John Jahr Verlag, pp. 218–20, 262–4.

Zimmermann, M. (1998) 'Die nationalsozialistische "Lösung der Zigeunerfrage",' in U. Herbert (ed.), *Nationalsozialistische Vernichtungspolitik 1939–1945. Neue Forschungen und Kontroversen*. Frankfurt/Main: Fischer Taschenbuch Verlag, pp. 235–62.

Guide to further reading

NB   Books and essays which appear in the list of References or have already been cited in the Guide are noted here by author's surname and date of publication.

Printed primary sources on women in Nazi Germany, especially for the years 1933–39, are scattered. There are useful small sections in Ebbinghaus, A. (ed.) (1996) *Opfer und Täterinnen. Frauenbiographien des Nationalsozialismus*. Frankfurt/M: Fischer Taschenbuch Verlag; Focke/Reimer (1979); Noakes/Pridham (1986) and Klinksiek (1982). The Second World War is better served. The major volume of documents is Gersdorff (1969), which concentrates on women's wartime employment, especially work with the *Wehrmacht*. There are also two substantial sections in Noakes (1998), as well as key documents on women's employment and morale in Boberach, H. (ed.) (1968) *Meldungen aus dem Reich*. Munich: Deutscher Taschenbuch Verlag, and documents on denunciations in Wolters (1996). Scholtz-Klink (1978) is a collection of publications of the *Reichsfrauenführung*, compiled by its former leader. Books and essays with evocative interviews with survivors and/or memoirs include Bronnen (1998); Jureit (1999); Haste, C. (2001) *Nazi Women: Hitler's Seduction of a Nation*. London: Channel 4 Books; Kaminsky (1999); Owings (1994); Szepansky, G. (1983) *Frauen leisten Widerstand*. Frankfurt/M: Fischer Taschenbuch Verlag; Szepansky (1986). A particularly valuable contemporary account is given by an American sociologist who undertook field-work in Germany in 1936–37: Kirkpatrick (1939).

Books and essays which address several of the themes discussed here include Bridenthal et al. (1984); Burleigh, M. (ed.) (1996) *Confronting the Nazi Past. New Debates on Modern German History*. London: Collins and Brown; Burleigh/Wippermann (1991); Focke/Reimer (1979); Frauengruppe Faschismusforschung (1981); Frevert (1989); Heineman (1999); Klinksiek (1982); Koonz (1987); Kuhn, A. (ed.) (1994) *Frauenleben im NS-Alltag*. Pfaffenweiler: Centaurus; Kundrus (1996); Lück (1979); Mason (1976); Noakes (1998); Noakes/Pridham (1986); Nolan (1997); Pine (1997); Rosenhaft (1992); Rupp (1978); Schoenbaum (1967); Stephenson (1975); Stephenson, J. (1992) 'Modernization, emancipation, mobilization: Nazi society reconsidered', in L.E. Jones and J. Retallack (eds), *Elections, Mass Politics and Social Change in Modern Germany*. New York and Cambridge: Cambridge University Press, pp. 223–43; Thalmann (1984); Westenrieder, N. (1984) *'Deutsche Frauen und Mädchen!' Vom Alltagsleben 1933–1945*. Düsseldorf: Droste; Wippermann (1998).

On marriage, motherhood, reproduction and sexual politics – especially compulsory sterilization – the works of Gisela Bock are particularly valuable: (1984),

(1986), (1994), and also Bock, G. (1994a) 'Nazi gender policies and women's history', in Thébaud, F. (ed.), *A History of Women in the West. V. Toward a Cultural Identity in the Twentieth Century*. Cambridge, MA, and London: The Belknap Press, pp. 149–76. There is a perceptive contemporary account in Glass, D.V. (1940) 'German policy and the birth rate', in *Population Policies and Movements*. Oxford: Clarendon Press, pp. 269–313. See also Bridenthal et al. (1984); Czarnowski (1991), (1996); Czarnowski, G. (1999) 'Women's crimes, state crimes: abortion in Nazi Germany', in M.L. Arnot and C. Usborne (eds), *Gender and Crime in Modern Europe*. London: UCL Press, pp. 238–56; Grossmann (1995); Heineman (1999); Klinksiek (1982); Koonz (1987); Mason (1976); Mühlfeld/Schönweiss (1989); Pine (1995), (1997); Schoppmann (1995); Schoppmann, C., 'National Socialist policies towards female homosexuality', in Abrams/Harvey (1996), pp. 177–87; Schoppmann, C. (1991) *Nationalsozialistische Sexualpolitik und weibliche Homosexualität*. Pfaffenweiler: Centaurus; Stephenson (1975), (1979); Wippermann (1998). On prostitution, see Paul, C. (1994) *Zwangsprostitution. Staatlich errichtete Bordelle im Nationalsozialismus*. Berlin: Verlag Edition Hentrich. On Himmler's *Lebensborn*, see Noakes (1998); Schmitz-Köster, D. (1997) *'Deutsche Mutter, bist Du bereit . . .'. Alltag im Lebensborn*. Berlin: Aufbau-Verlag; Seidler, F.W. (1992) 'Lebensborn e.V. der SS. Vom Gerüchte zur Legende', in U. Backes, E. Jesse and R. Zitelmann (eds), *Die Schatten der Vergangenheit*. Frankfurt/M and Berlin: Ullstein, pp. 291–318. For eugenics and 'euthanasia', the work of Michael Burleigh is essential reading: (1994), (1996), (2000), and Burleigh/Wippermann (1991); see also Ebbinghaus (1996); Heineman (1999); Koonz (1993); Noakes (1987); Pine (1995), (1997).

Women's employment generally is discussed in Mason (1976); Nolan (1997); Overy (1988); Rupp (1978); Stephenson (1975); Wippermann (1998). On women in industry, see especially Bajohr (1979); Tröger (1981), (1984); Winkler (1977); and Sachse, C. (1987) *Industrial Housewives. Women's Social Work in the Factories of Nazi Germany*. Trans. by H. Kiesling and D. Rosenberg. New York and London: Haworth Press. Gersdorff (1969) deals with wartime employment questions. On the professions generally, see Jarausch (1990); Stephenson (1975); Stephenson, J. (1990) 'Women and the Professions in Germany, 1900–1945', in G. Cocks and K.H. Jarausch (eds), *German Professions, 1800–1945*. New York and Oxford: Oxford University Press, pp. 270–88. On individual professions, see Bajohr, S. and Bajohr, K.R. (1980) 'Die Diskriminierung der Juristin in Deutschland bis 1945', *Kritische Justiz*, volume 13, no. 1, pp. 39–50, on lawyers; Kater (1989) on doctors; Said (1981) on teachers. On the important role of social workers in racist policies, see Ebbinghaus (1996); Heineman (1999); Kundrus (1995), (1996). And on nurses' role in 'euthanasia', see Burleigh (2000); McFarland-Icke, B.R. (1999) *Nurses in Nazi Germany. Moral Choice in History*. Princeton, NJ: Princeton University Press. On domestic service, see Mason (1976) and Wittmann (1981); and on women in agriculture, see Bauer (1996); Farquharson (1976); Münkel (1996); Stephenson (1987); Wilke (1987); Wilke/Wagner (1981).

Girls' education is discussed generally in Klinksiek (1982); Stephenson (1975). On schooling, see Lück (1979); Speitkamp (1998). On universities, see Pauwels

(1984); Stephenson (1975a); Weyrather (1981). The BDM is covered by Reese (1981), (1989), with relevant sections in Böltken (1995) and Rempel (1989). See also the essays in Reese, D. (ed.) (2001) *Die BDM-Generation*. Potsdam: Verlag Berlin-Brandenburg. Maschmann (1965) gives a fairly remorseful insider's view. Peukert (1987) discusses dissident youth. On the women's Labour Service, see Bajohr, S. 'Weiblicher Arbeitsdienst im "Dritten Reich" zwischen Ideologie und Ökonomie', *Vierteljahrshefte für Zeitegeschichte*, volume 28, no. 3, pp. 331–57; Gersdorff (1969); Harvey (1998); Maschmann (1965); Stephenson (1982).

The Nazi women's organizations are considered in Böltken (1995); Dammer (1981); Kater (1983); Klinksiek (1982); Koonz (1987); Noakes (1998); Stephenson (1981), (1983). Scholtz-Klink (1978) gives a defensive insider's view. Koonz (1987) and Zentner (1975) feature postwar interviews with Scholtz-Klink. Church youth and women's organizations are discussed in Bergen (1996); Kaiser (1982); Wiggershaus (1984). The Jewish women's organization is covered by Kaplan (1979), (1984), (1998). Broadcasting directed at women features in Lacey (1996) and Lacey, K. (1996a) *Feminine Frequencies. Gender, German Radio, and the Public Sphere, 1923–1945*. Ann Arbor, MI: The University of Michigan Press. On women as consumers, see Lacey (1996); Reagin (2001); Stephenson (1983).

For women in wartime, Noakes (1998) is invaluable. Also useful are Beck (1986); Gersdorff (1969); Kitchen, M. (1995) *Nazi Germany at War*. London: Longman; Kundrus (1995); Noakes, J. (1992) 'Germany', in J. Noakes (ed.), *The Civilian in War*. Exeter: Exeter University Press, pp. 35–61; Stephenson (1981), (1987); Szepansky (1986); Winkler (1977). Women and resistance figure in Kaminsky (1999); Löwenthal, R., and Mühlen, P. von zur (eds) (1984) *Widerstand und Verweigerung in Deutschland 1933 bis 1945*. Bonn: Dietz Taschenbuch; Paucker (1999); Schefer (1981); Szepansky (1983); Wickert (1994). On women and denunciation, see Gellately (1990); Gellately, R. (2001) *Backing Hitler. Consent and Coercion in Nazi Germany*. New York and Oxford: Oxford University Press; Schubert, H. (1990) *Judasfrauen. Zehn Fallgeschichten weiblicher Denunzianten im 'Dritten Reich'*. Frankfurt/M: Luchterhand Literaturverlag; Wolters (1996). On the notorious wife of a concentration camp commandant, see Przyrembel, A. (2001) 'Transfixed by an image – Ilse Koch, the "Kommandeuse of Buchenwald"', *German History*, volume 19, no. 3, pp. 369–99.

Jewish women's experience and the Holocaust are analysed in Jureit (1999); Kaplan (1998); Koonz (1987); Milton (1984); Neiberger (1998); Pine (1997). See also, on this and on the 'death marches', Goldhagen (1996). On '*Mischlinge*', see Noakes, J. (1989) 'The development of Nazi policy towards the German-Jewish "Mischlinge" 1933–1945', *Leo Baeck Yearbook*, volume XXXIV, pp. 291–354; Koehn, I. (1978) *Mischling, Second Degree: My Childhood in Nazi Germany*. London: H. Hamilton. The fate of Sinti and Roma 'Gypsies' is recounted in Lewy (2000); Zimmermann (1998). On coerced foreign women workers, see Herbert (1997); Homze (1967); Kuhn, A. (ed.) (1994) *Frauenleben im NS-Alltag*. Pfaffenweiler: Centaurus; Schupetta (1981). On women in concentration camps and their warders, see Ebbinghaus (1996); Koonz (1987); Milton (1984); Morrison, J. (2000) *Ravensbrück*. London and New York: Markus Wiener; Neiberger (1998).

The essentials of the 'victims and perpetrators' dispute are conveyed in Bock (1986), (1994); Böltken (1995); Ebbinghaus (1996); Gravenhorst, L., and Tatschmurat, C. (eds) (1990) *Töchterfragen: NS-Frauengeschichte*. Freiburg: Kore; Heineman (1999); Grossmann, A. (1991) 'Feminist debates about women and National Socialism', *Gender and History*, volume 3, no. 3, pp. 350–58; Koonz (1987); Kundrus (1996); Saldern (1994); Wolters (1996).

Index

Aachen xvii, 156
abortion xiii, 7, 29, 33, 35, 37–40, 123,
    126, 137, 139, 145, 146, 150
  Abortion, Central Office to Combat
    Homosexuality and 39
  abortionists xvii, 38–9
agency 4, 115, 127, 133, 135
agriculture xv, 14, 17, 59, 66, 67–8,
    79–81, 124, 132, 152, 155 *see also*
    employment; foreign workers
air force 112, 182, 183, 185
air-raid 89, 96, 97, 119, 165, 174
  alarms/sirens 74, 97, 174
  protection 93, 96, 106
    RLB (National Air-raid Protection
    Association) 158
  shelter 97, 103, 175
  warden 174, 175
Allies xvii, 96, 97, 107, 108, 173, 175
  'camp followers' of 107
  occupation by 100, 106
  'unconditional surrender' demand by
    xvii, 96
Alsace 14, 105, 169, 182, 186
  see also NSDAP: *Gau* Baden-Alsace
Altreich 92, 104, 105, 181
America(n) (USA) xiii, xvii, 6, 26, 44, 50,
    63, 77, 107, 108, 136, 137
anti-natalism 33
antisemitic/ism 15, 23, 137, 160 *see also*
    Jews
armaments *see* industry: armaments
armed forces (*Wehrmacht*) xvi, xvii, 4,
    17, 46, 54, 55, 56, 61, 63, 74, 81,
    95, 102, 118, 122, 128, 150, 151,
    154, 159, 161, 165, 183
  anti-aircraft work in 78, 81, 165
  signals duties in 78
  Women's Auxiliary Army Corps of 169

'women's battalion' xvii, 95
  see also conscription; rearmament
'Aryan(s)' 12, 13, 16, 18, 23, 25, 26, 27,
    28, 32, 33, 40, 41, 48, 49, 60, 61,
    72, 75, 79, 88, 90, 98, 99, 100,
    114, 115, 116, 117, 118, 122, 125,
    126, 127, 131, 177, 178, 179, 183
'Aryanization' 185
'asocial(s)' 13, 14, 16, 20, 31, 33, 35, 36,
    40, 41, 43, 44, 45, 48, 58, 66, 81,
    89, 112, 116, 119, 120, 138, 146,
    147
'assisting family members' *see*
    employment
atrocities 6, 13, 104, 107, 127, 128
  death-marches 96, 121
  pogrom xvi, 116, 182
    Kristallnacht ('night of broken glass')
    xvi, 87, 182, 185
Austria(n) xv, 91, 119, 137, 182
autarky 78, 89, 97, 143, 181
  'campaign against waste' 78, 97,
    167

Baden 12, 30, 84, 86, 90, 91, 100, 105,
    182, 186
  Karlsruhe 91
  Lahr 30
  Oberschopfheim 95
  see also NSDAP: *Gau* Baden
Baltic States 14, 104
Bartov, Omer 135
Bauer, Theresia 124
Bavaria 12, 29, 79, 106, 123, 182
  Bad Windesheim 106
BDM (*Bund Deutscher Mädel*) *see* Nazi
    youth organizations
Bednarski, Ruth 71
Belgium 122

Benjamin, Hilde 12
Berlin xvii, 12, 19, 28, 32, 34, 38, 41, 47,
    56, 64, 81, 89, 95, 101, 102, 103,
    107, 111, 117, 118, 127, 174, 175,
    176, 186 *see also* NSDAP: *Gau*
    Berlin
birth control 34, 37–40
  advice centres 37, 38
birth rate 26, 29, 32, 33, 37, 38, 40, 45,
    48
Black(s) 12, 137
  African-Americans 12
  Germans 33, 116
    'Rhineland Bastards' 116
black market 58, 97, 98, 99
  bartering 98, 99
  hoarding 98, 99
  illicit slaughtering 98
'blood and soil' 17, 143
Boak, Helen 15
Bock, Gisela 25, 30, 33, 35, 37, 45, 50,
    125, 126
Bohemia 118, 182
Böltken, Andrea 126
bombing xvii, 46, 48, 57, 58, 74, 78, 93,
    95, 96, 97, 100, 101, 102, 103,
    105, 106, 121, 140, 165, 169, 171,
    173, 174
  area xvii, 101
bordello(s) 39, 44, 45, 124, 126
Bormann, Martin xvii, 43, 95, 185
Bremen 36
Britain/British xvi, 26, 63, 96, 132, 136,
    137, 165
  RAF 96
Brüning, Heinrich 51, 185
Brunswick 156
Bülbring, Edith 63
Bund Deutscher Frauenvereine (BDF) *see*
    women's organizations
Bund Königin Luise (BKL) *see* women's
    organizations
Burleigh, Michael 25, 114

Cammens, Minna 110
camp(s), penal 110, 111, 112, 113, 114,
    115, 116, 117, 118, 119, 120, 127,
    128, 180, 195
  camps for 'Gypsies' 36

concentration 13, 35, 36, 44, 45, 47,
    48, 58, 61, 77, 96, 111, 112, 113,
    114, 115, 116, 118, 119, 120, 121,
    124, 126, 127, 128, 153, 185
  Buchenwald 113
  commandant(s) 113, 121, 180
  'family' 120
  Helmbrechts 121
  Majdanek 113
  Theresienstadt 118, 119, 121,
    179
  women's 119
    Lichtenberg 119
    Moringen 119
    Ravensbrück 111, 112, 119, 120
  extermination 13, 33, 96, 110, 117,
    118, 121, 128, 185
  Auschwitz 20, 110, 118, 119, 120,
    121, 140, 179
  gas chambers in 113, 121, 179
  warders 112, 113, 121, 126, 128
Canadians 107
census 9, 11, 53
Central Office to Combat Homosexuality
    and Abortion 39
Certificate of Suitability for Marriage 28,
    34, 35, 36, 148
childcare 9, 39, 60, 65, 73, 80, 89, 93,
    104, 105, 168
Christian church(es) 3, 6, 8, 15, 39, 41,
    42, 43, 82, 88, 134, 137, 181
  Catholic (Roman) 11, 37, 43, 75, 87,
    123, 137, 157, 158, 181
  convent 99
  nuns 65
  Evangelical (Protestant) 6, 11, 15, 37,
    82, 87, 181
  Confessing Church 87
  German Christians 87
  other Christians 11
  Jehovah's Witnesses 111, 118
  women's organizations *see* women's
    organizations
  youth organizations *see* youth
    organizations
civil service 50, 137
civilian(s) 46, 54, 55, 58, 94, 95, 98, 106,
    109, 116, 122, 128, 140, 161, 173,
    174

defeatism among 95, 96, 106
morale of 94
class 11, 14, 15, 38, 45, 82, 83, 98, 131,
132, 134, 167
lower class 115, 132
middle class 6, 8, 10, 12, 14, 15, 33,
50, 56, 61, 62, 65, 77, 78, 81, 82,
91, 115, 119, 131, 132, 133, 134,
156, 181
upper class 65, 115, 132
working class 8, 10, 12, 14, 23, 60, 61,
62, 71, 77, 78, 82, 91, 131, 132
Cold War 23
Cologne 97
Concordat (1933) xiv, 76, 85, 87, 181
conscription,
labour xvii, 55, 56, 58, 60, 66, 67, 68,
116, 156, 163
military xv, 36, 40, 54, 55, 56, 62, 65,
67, 68, 69, 72, 94, 95, 122, 154,
157, 158, 161, 171, 175
service schemes 81, 165
conservatism 75
conservative(s) 8, 12, 16, 26, 29, 42, 51,
52, 63, 70, 83, 137
consumerism 6, 62
consumer(s) 18, 97, 98, 140, 154, 172
shortages 74, 100 *see also* food;
wartime: shortages
'Stew Sunday' 167
'war gardens' 100
see also industry: consumer goods
contraception/ives xvi, 6, 7, 37–40, 137
court(s) 29, 141, 148–9
Hereditary Health 35, 148
People's 176
Special 154
Czarnowski, Gabriele 28

DAF (German Labour Front) 60, 61, 90,
131, 181, 185
'Beauty of Labour' section of 60, 181
social workers of 60
women's section of 60, 90, 92
Danzig-West Prussia 182
Darmstadt 31
Darré, R.W. 18, 139, 143
Das Reich 159
denunciation/tor 112, 114, 115, 140, 176

depression xiii, 8, 9, 15, 19, 26, 38, 50, 51,
52, 53, 54, 59, 63, 66, 83, 84, 136
Diehl, Guida 82
discrimination xiv, 5, 26, 33, 35, 41, 51,
52, 71, 98, 116, 121, 136, 181
against Jews xiv, 13, 33, 71, 116, 121
against women xiv, 5, 35, 41, 51, 52,
125, 136
underrepresentation of women 5, 136
division of labour 3, 17, 19, 82
divorce xv, 8, 28, 29, 48, 118, 176
'postmortem divorce' xvii, 49
Dollfuss, E. 137
Dortmund 156
double burden 10, 60
'double earner' (*Doppelverdiener*) 51, 63, 181
Dresden 97, 156
Duisburg 108
Düsseldorf 110

East Prussia *see* Prussia
eastern Europe(an) 39, 47, 94, 99, 104,
105, 122, 123, 124, 137, 153, 182
education 8, 64, 70–5, 80, 91, 132, 137,
145, 158, 160, 163
classics 72, 73
foreign languages 72–4
poor academic standards 75
science 72, 73
Education Ministry, Prussian 73
Education Ministry, Reich 79
election(s) xiii, xiv, 15, 17, 50, 84
elite, Nazi 74, 77, 78, 91, 92, 106, 182
emancipation 9, 18, 133, 139, 143
employment xv, 6, 7, 8, 10, 11, 12, 28,
29, 43, 46, 50–5, 59, 60, 62, 64,
70, 72, 91, 95, 97, 99, 103, 122,
125, 132, 136, 137, 139, 144, 151,
154–7, 169, 170, 172, 181 *see also*
agriculture; industry
absenteeism 97
'assisting family members' 9, 12, 29,
53, 56, 67
clerical work/er(s) 12, 50, 53, 61–3, 81,
113, 114, 115, 120, 125, 128
domestic servant(s)/service 12, 53, 56,
61, 65, 66, 67, 167, 169
Hausgehilfin (maid) 67
exchanges, labour 155

factory work 9, 12, 50, 55, 59, 60, 61,
  62, 66, 68, 105, 125, 132, 144, 163
  assembly lines 59
  Eulenburg factory 157
farm(ing) 3, 9, 12, 18, 27, 54, 61, 62,
  66, 67, 101
  figures 57, 58
  half-day shifts 54
  home workers 59
  married women 6, 51, 52, 54, 56, 60,
    63
  office work see clerical work
  part-time 51, 156, 157
  poor productivity 97
  reserve army 53, 137
  service industries 53–4
  shorthand typist 12, 61
  small business 9, 12, 27, 54, 66, 67,
    158, 170
  trade 3, 52, 61
  unemployed/ment 28, 41, 50, 51, 52,
    54, 58, 59, 66, 72, 77, 80, 163
  benefit 30
  work see employment
employment office 56, 57, 156, 167
enemy/ies, Germany's 16, 49, 94, 95, 96,
  100, 106, 109, 113, 122, 169, 171,
  173, 174 see also 'racial enemy/ies'
English 107, 111
Enlightenment 143
Estorf 154
ethnic Germans 14, 78, 104
eugenics 25, 26, 34, 126, 137
  social hygiene 15, 26, 137
'euthanasia' 65, 112, 114, 117, 119, 137,
  186
  'life unworthy of life' 33, 117
evacuated/ion 46, 57, 58, 74, 78, 97,
  101, 102, 106, 119, 168
evacuees 68, 100, 102, 105, 107, 135
  migrants, voluntary 100, 101

family/ies 3, 6, 7, 8, 9, 10, 11, 12, 13, 14,
  17, 18, 19, 23, 27, 30, 31, 32, 33,
  36, 38, 39, 40, 41, 43, 49, 51, 52,
  55, 56, 57, 67, 69, 83, 93, 100,
  102, 106, 112, 115, 116, 117, 127,
  131, 132, 134, 136, 144, 145, 147,
  152, 154, 155, 157, 167, 169, 182

allowance(s) xv, 30, 33, 48, 131, 136
  Honour Book of the xv, 32
  large xv, 31, 32, 36
    Grossfamilie(n) 32, 146
  Jewish xv
  rural 39
  two-child 30, 32
  urban 39
  see also RdK – Reichsbund der
    Kinderreichen
farm(s) 67, 68, 69, 79, 101, 102, 107,
  124, 153, 154, 169
farmer(s) 54, 66, 81, 99, 174, 182
  wives of 29, 47, 56, 67–9, 82, 101, 123,
    139, 152, 154, 158, 159, 170, 175
  see also employment: farm(ing)
Farquharson, John 82
fascism 23, 125
'feebleminded(ness)' 34, 35
feminism/ist(s) 9, 13, 18, 25, 63, 85, 125,
  126, 143
  antifeminism/ist 15, 25, 72
  'Nazi feminists' 84
  radical 82, 85
  'women's rightists' 41
fertility 7, 25, 32, 35, 37, 40, 70
  infertility 29, 35, 45
'Final Solution' 120
Flensburg 176
food xvi, 30, 69, 97, 99, 100, 102, 110,
  123, 170, 174
  'nutritional hierarchy' 124
  shortages 97–100, 105, 108, 172–3
    in camps, penal 120
  Jews and 100, 116, 118
forced/coerced workers 14, 35, 46, 47,
  55, 124, 186 see also foreign
  workers
'foreign children's care units' 123
foreign worker(s) 14, 42, 46, 47, 48, 55,
  58, 60, 68, 69, 98, 99, 100, 121–4,
  153, 186
  civilian 122
  deportation of 121, 123
  in agriculture 124
  in industry 124
  male workers 46–8
  migrant 122
  Pole(s) 14, 47, 55, 123–4, 153

women workers 47, 58, 121–4
  Belgian 122
  French 122
  Polish 123, 124
  'Ostarbeiter' ('eastern workers')/Soviet
    122, 123
  Russian 123
Förster, Hedwig 73
Four Year Plan xv, 79, 94, 97, 167, 181,
  185
France xvi, 95, 111, 122, 136, 138, 169
  Code Napoléon 136
  French 100, 107, 111, 122, 154, 175
Frevert, Ute 135, 136
Fuchs, Berta 110
Führer 16, 42, 101, 133, 141, 154, 176,
  182, 185
Führerprinzip 16, 182

Galen, Clemens von (Bishop of Münster)
  119
gas 96, 168
  attacks 96
  chambers *see* camp(s): extermination
  masks 96
Gersdorff, Ursula von 74, 82
Gestapo see police
ghetto 118, 119, 179, 180
  ghettoized 5
Gleichschaltung 83, 85, 86, 88, 135, 166,
  181, 182
Goebbels, Joseph 41, 56, 57, 133, 159,
  185
  Magda 90
  'total war' speech 56
Goldhagen, Daniel 113, 121
Göring, Hermann xv, 79, 182, 185
government 9, 26, 30, 31, 32, 34, 36, 42,
  43, 47, 51, 55, 56, 57, 59, 60, 66,
  74, 75, 78, 92, 96, 97, 101, 103,
  112, 122, 136, 137, 151, 154, 161,
  185, 186
Greater German Reich 14, 43, 182
Greater Germany 31, 54, 55, 150,
  182
Greece 98
Grill, Johnpeter H. 86
Grossmann, Atina 34
Gürtner, Franz 42

'Gypsies' 116, 118, 119, 138
  'Gypsy camp', Auschwitz 121
  Roma and Sinti 12, 33, 71, 116, 118

Haenel, Franziska 113, 114
Haindl, Anny 169
Halle 156, 157
Hamburg xvii, 12, 40, 45, 58, 86, 97,
  101, 113, 147, 159, 173
  education authorities 159–60
  jail 40, 113
  'Operation Gomorrha' xvii, 173
Hancock, Eleanor 57, 132
Hanover 82, 154
Hashude 36
Heineman, Elizabeth 27, 41, 43, 57, 82,
  132, 134, 135
Herbert, Ulrich 122, 124
'hereditary disease' 12, 13, 14, 20, 26,
  28, 33, 34, 36, 112, 146, 149
'hereditary health' 13,14, 16, 29, 65, 89,
  131, 138, 147
  Hereditary Health Courts/office 35,
    148, 149
Hess, Rudolf xvi, 31, 42, 43, 185
Hesse 69, 177
  Körle 69, 134, 135
Heymann, Aenne 110
Hilgenfeldt, Erich 88, 185
Himmler, Heinrich 18, 39, 40, 42, 43,
  44, 56, 139, 150, 153, 183, 185
  Himmler Ordinance xvi, 38
Hitler xiv, xv, xvii, 15, 16, 17, 18, 26, 42,
  43, 48, 51, 55, 56, 64, 70, 75, 83,
  85, 86, 88, 94, 95, 96, 97, 98, 106,
  109, 112, 121, 125, 133, 137, 139,
  141, 142, 143, 151, 159, 164, 177,
  181, 185
  Mein Kampf 159
Hitler Youth *see* Nazi youth
  organizations
Holocaust 13, 23
home front 17, 49, 57, 94, 95, 96, 154,
  171, 172
homecraft xvi, 60, 73, 76, 78, 104, 145
homosexual 41, 44, 151
  Homosexuality and Abortion, Central
    Office to Combat 39
  gay 13, 14, 43, 44, 151

lesbian(s) 13, 14, 40, 41, 43, 44, 139, 151
  sex offences 151
hospital(s) 61, 65, 74, 177, 180
hostages 110, 119
  'collective responsibility' 110
Hungarian 122

ideology, ideological 16, 33, 52, 60, 70, 71, 73, 78, 89, 93
  courses/training in 75, 88, 89, 103, 104, 163
illegitimacy xvi, 24, 41–3, 151
industry 4, 7, 10, 50, 52, 53, 54, 58, 59, 60, 61, 66, 67, 98, 99, 101, 120, 123, 132, 136, 155, 173
  armaments 58, 59, 120, 168
    munitions 81
  clerical work in 62
  consumer goods 10, 58, 59, 61
    clothing 155
    foodstuffs 58
    paper-making 58
    textiles 58, 155
  factory social workers 60
  producer goods 58, 59, 60
    building industry 59
    metal trades 59
  war(-related) 54, 58, 60, 61
industrialization 17, 152
infanticide 40
  child-murderers 40, 119
inflation 8
informers 114
intellectual 7, 70, 73, 75, 141, 161
  anti-intellectualism 73, 160
Iron Cross 31, 146
Italy 136
  Fascist Party 136
    women's organization 136

Jarausch, Konrad 63
Jewish xiv, xv, 26, 33, 66, 104, 119, 120, 121, 127, 139, 140, 159, 160, 167, 177, 182, 185
  morale 117, 120
Jew(s) xiv, xv, xvi, 11, 12, 13, 14, 33, 63, 71, 72, 87, 94, 96, 98, 99, 100,

104, 109, 110, 111, 112, 113, 115, 116, 117, 118, 138, 176, 178, 179
  deportation of xvi, 88, 117, 118, 140, 177, 179
  emigration 117
  'Jewish question' 139, 159, 161
  Jewish star 178
  JFB – *Jüdischer Frauenbund see* women's organizations
  Judaism 83
  Rosenstrasse protest 118
  'submarines' 118
  see also antisemitism
Judæo-Christian 3, 83
Jungmädel see Nazi youth organizations

Kaiser, Jochen-Christoph 83
Kanndorf 158
Kaplan, Marion 71, 99
Kater, Michael 64, 85
Keitel, Field Marshal 150, 151
'kinderreich' 31–2, 173, 182 *see also* RdK – *Reichsbund der Kinderreichen*
Kirchner, Johanna 111
Kirkpatrick, Clifford 28, 38, 45
Klenk, Anne 167
Koch, Ilse 113
Koonz, Claudia 11, 127, 128, 133
KPD *see* political parties
Kristallnacht see atrocities: pogrom
Krupp 61, 123

labour(ers) 29, 53, 55, 59, 61, 62, 66, 67, 68, 79, 80, 89, 117, 134, 154
  protection 60
  shortage(s) 53–5, 62, 66, 67, 162, 169
  slave 58, 106
  see also agriculture; employment; foreign workers; industry
labour-saving 66, 67, 89
Labour Service *see* Nazi service schemes
law, codes of
  Civil 8, 10, 19
  Criminal xiii, 37, 38, 41, 44, 151
    Criminal Law, Commission on Reich 151
laws:
  Law of 30 May 1932 xiii, 51, 52
  Law of 30 June 1933 xiv, 52, 137

Law Against the Establishment of Parties 34
Law for German National Service 154
Law for the Prevention of Hereditarily Diseased Offspring xiv, 34
Law for the Protection of Mothers in Gainful Employment 60
Law for the Protection of the Hereditary Health of the German People 148
Law for the Protection of the People and the State xiv, 38, 45
Law for the Restoration of the Professional Civil Service xiv, 63
Law on the Hitler Youth xv, 76
Law to Reduce Unemployment xiv, 28, 52
Marriage Health Law xv, 28, 35, 36
'Lebensborn' 39, 42, 114, 123, 139, 150, 151
    Germanization 114, 123
Leipzig 156
Lenz, Fritz 45
Leuschner, Wilhelm 177
Ley, Robert 90, 181, 185
liberal(s) 18, 26, 41, 82, 181
    anti-liberal 52
liberalism 15, 18, 143
life expectancy, women's 7
local authorities 36, 61, 62
    health/social service departments 45, 48
Lorraine 14, 105, 182
Lotze, Irmgard 81
Lübeck xvii, 97
Luxembourg 14, 182

Marburg 95
marital status 11, 103
    married women xiii, 8, 9, 12, 16, 18, 38, 40, 42, 48, 53, 54, 56, 57, 64, 137, 144, 181
    single mother(s) 13, 14, 40–3, 137, 145, 150
        prejudice against 42
    single women xv, 8, 9, 12, 17, 18, 35, 36, 39, 41–3, 45, 48, 51, 53, 57, 58, 63, 93, 103, 132, 144
    widow(s) xvii, 8, 11, 43, 48, 154, 177–8

marriage xv, 5, 10, 24, 26–9, 32, 35, 36, 43, 45, 46, 48, 49, 52, 62, 64, 65, 66, 67, 118, 134, 135, 137, 140, 143, 144, 163, 171, 172
    bigamy 43
    loan(s) xiv, xv, 28, 30, 32, 34, 35, 41, 42, 45, 52, 131
    'mixed' 118
    'postmortem marriage' xvi, 43
Marriage Health Law see laws
Marxism/Marxist 15, 23, 38, 50, 87, 125, 143, 163
Maschmann, Melita 77, 104
Mason, Tim 29, 51, 52, 59, 62, 131, 133
McLaren, Angus 32
Mecklenburg 119
medical advances 7
Memel 182
middle class see class
miscarriage(s) 40, 123
miscegenation 26, 28
'mischling' 26, 63, 118, 182
Möhs, SS leader 180
Molotov–Ribbentrop pact xvi, 14
Mommsen, Hans 109
morale, civilian/women's 94, 140, 171
        see also Jewish: morale
Moravia 182
mortality 145
    infant 7, 27, 39, 40
    maternal 7
mother(s) 5, 8, 9, 16, 19, 25, 29, 30, 31, 36, 39, 41, 42, 48, 78, 81, 85, 93, 97, 98, 101, 117, 123, 126, 132, 133, 145, 146, 150, 153, 154, 164, 167, 170, 186
    Honour Cards 31
    Honour Cross xvi, 31, 40, 139, 146
    Mother's Day 31, 33
motherhood 27, 30, 33, 50, 70, 126, 141
    'compulsory motherhood' 30, 125
    maternity allowance 60, 145
motorways (Autobahnen) 59, 181
Munich xiii, 84, 101, 110
Münkel, Daniela 67
Mussolini, Benito 136

National Statistical Office 155
Nazi 'Brown Nurses' 65

Nazi ideology *see* ideology
Nazi leaders/ship 5, 6, 12, 13, 14, 15, 16,
    17, 18, 19, 25, 26, 47, 88, 109,
    116, 125, 131, 133, 135, 137, 144
Nazi service schemes 58, 61, 65, 66, 68,
    79–82, 106, 112, 133
  Frauendienst (Women's Service) 79
  Girls' Land Service 79
  Household Year 79
  Labour Service xvi, 19, 58, 62, 66, 68,
      79–82, 85, 90, 91, 104, 132, 133,
      134, 139, 164, 165
    Auxiliary War Service xvi, xvii, 62,
        81, 139, 165
    camp(s) 80, 139, 164
    leaders 80–1
  Land Service (*Landdienst*) 79, 81
  Land Year (*Landjahr*) 79, 81
  Pflichtjahr (Compulsory Year of
      Service) xv, 66, 68, 79, 81, 93, 159
  see also conscription
Nazi women's organizations 4, 14, 15,
    18, 19, 29, 30, 65, 75, 77, 83, 86,
    93, 131, 133, 135, 139, 166, 169
  DFO – *Deutscher Frauenorden* xiii, 83,
      181, 185, 186
  DFW – *Deutsches Frauenwerk* xiv, xv,
      85, 86, 87, 88, 89, 90, 91, 92, 96,
      98, 102, 103, 105, 106, 136, 139,
      166, 167, 168, 169, 181, 185
    Auxiliary Service section of 89, 96
    Border/Foreign section of 89
    Culture/Education/Training section
        of 89
    Finance section of 89
    Frauenhilfsdienst (Women's Auxiliary
        Service) section of 93
    Law and Arbitration section of 89
    local branch 104, 170
    Mothers' Service section of xv, 87,
        89, 92, 105, 167, 168
    National economy/Domestic
        economy section of 86, 89, 92, 98,
        105, 167, 168
      homecraft courses of 60
    Neighbourhood Aid section of 102,
        104, 169, 170
    Organization/Personnel section of
        89
    Press and Propaganda section of 89
    women's media 92 *see also*
        women's magazines
  NSF – *NS-Frauenschaft* xiii, xiv, 28, 43,
      60, 64, 76, 79, 84, 85, 88, 89, 91,
      92, 103, 104, 105, 106, 112, 123,
      134, 141, 157, 167, 169, 170, 171,
      181, 182, 185, 186
    block 84, 92, 103, 104, 170
    cell 84, 92, 103, 104, 170
    children's groups 76
    district NSF leader 84, 90, 105, 123
      Strasbourg 105
    Gau NSF leader 84, 169
    leaders 133, 170, 186
    local branch NSF leader(s) 84
    youth groups 170
  NSF/DFW 91, 93, 97, 103, 104, 105,
      106, 133
    leaders 90, 133, 185 *see also* Scholtz-
        Klink, Gertrud
Nazi youth organizations
  Bund Deutscher Mädel (BDM) xiv, xvi,
      32, 75, 76, 77, 78, 91
    BDM – 'Faith and Beauty' 76, 78
    leaders 77–8
  Hitler Youth (HJ) xvi, 31, 75, 76, 77,
      90
  Jungmädel (JM) 75, 76
Netherlands 98
  Dutch 12
  Holland 122
'new woman' 6
non-'Aryan(s)' xiv, 18, 20, 28, 44, 46, 53,
    63, 71, 112, 115, 116, 117, 126
Nordic countries 137
  Scandinavians 12
NSDAP xiii, xiv, xvi, 4, 15, 16, 17, 18,
    19, 29, 31, 32, 42, 43, 47, 50, 61,
    71, 74, 83, 84, 85, 90, 105, 106,
    136, 143, 152, 153, 157, 168, 174,
    177, 181, 182, 183, 185, 186
  block 181
  cell 181
  Gau (region) 84, 104, 105, 182
    Baden 169, 185, 186
    Baden-Alsace 170
    Berlin 185
    Württemberg-Hohenzollern 173

Gauleiter 84, 185, 186
Kreis (district) 157, 182
  leaders 85, 93, 105, 136
    Strasbourg district 105
  local branch 157, 174, 182
    leader 29, 174
  Nazi Doctors' Association 186
  programme xiii, 18
NSLB – *NS-Lehrerbund* 64, 85, 158, 182
NSV (National Socialist People's Welfare
  organization) 19, 30, 57, 65, 88,
  89, 97, 101, 104, 105, 136, 151,
  158, 170, 174, 182, 185
  Mother and Child section of 30, 145
Nuremberg Laws xv, 28, 66
Nuremberg Party Rally 88, 141, 166

occupied countries 47, 49, 57, 65, 78, 96,
  98, 105, 107, 122, 134, 185
Opferring 157
opposition 13, 109–12, 119
  anti-fascist girls' group 111
  Baum Group 111
  communist 109, 111, 112, 113,
  119
  'inner emigration' of 13
  Knöchel organization 110
  political xiv, 13, 53
  religious 13
  resistance 109, 110, 111
  Rote Kapelle 111
  Saefkow group 111
  socialist 109, 111, 112, 114
  White Rose group 109, 110
Overy, Richard 57, 58, 60

pacifist(s) 13, 63, 114
patriarch(al) 5, 10, 11, 17, 20, 47, 72,
  112, 127, 136
patriarchy 3, 4, 125, 126
Paucker, Arnold 111
perpetrate/or(s) 4, 109, 112, 115, 124–8,
  137, 138, 175
persecution/ed 23, 26, 33, 40, 44, 87, 90,
  96, 104, 114, 115, 117, 118, 121,
  138
Pflichtjahr see Nazi service schemes
Pine, Lisa 27, 32
pogrom *see* atrocities

Poland/Poles xvi, 14, 55, 98, 104, 121,
  123, 124, 153, 182, 185
  Soviet eastern 104
'polarity of the sexes' 17, 127, 143
police 41, 45, 112, 124, 149, 173, 176,
  182, 185
  Gestapo 13, 39, 40, 76, 86, 99, 109,
  110, 113, 114, 115, 118, 119, 128,
  153, 176, 177, 182, 185
'political education' 78, 103 *see also*
  ideology: courses/training in
political parties 10, 13
  Bavarian People's Party 15
  Centre Party 15, 185
  Communist Party (KPD) 12, 13, 15, 37,
  42, 76, 82, 83, 85, 110, 119, 182
  conservative 15
  peasant 15
  Social Democratic Party (SPD) 12, 13,
  15, 26, 37, 63, 76, 78, 82, 85, 94,
  110, 114, 183
political reliability 139, 157
  'politically reliable' 88, 91, 131, 158
  'politically unreliable' 13, 44, 63
Pomerania 12
Pope Pius XI 37
population 9, 11, 24, 30, 34, 39, 47, 51,
  94, 95, 102, 115, 117, 153, 154,
  156, 157, 172, 183
  demographic decline 26
  expert(s) 38, 45
  fecundity 23, 27
  growth 9, 27, 44, 52
  Jewish 117
  policy 16, 26, 32, 150, 152, 155
  see also birth rate
postal service 62
postwar 103, 104
POWs 46, 47, 55, 95, 98, 122, 154
prejudice
  against 'Gypsies' 138
  against single mothers 42
  anti-liberal 52
  conservative 63
  political 63
  misogynist/sexist 68, 74, 110
  see also race/racial
prison 61, 111, 113, 115, 118, 119, 128,
  146, 153, 154, 177

Plötzensee 111
Spandau 185
warder(s) 113, 114
prisoner(s) 58, 96, 107, 111, 113, 114,
        119, 120, 121
    political 119
prisoner(s)-of-war *see* POWs
pro-natalism/ist 23, 32, 33
professional(s) 12, 64, 72, 82, 85, 96,
        112, 114, 115, 116, 132
    organizations 64
profession(s) 8, 50, 52, 53, 63, 65, 71,
        73, 74, 77, 133, 162
    bureaucrats 65
    civil servants 64
    doctor(s) xiv, 14, 26, 28, 34, 35, 38,
        39, 40, 44, 63, 64, 65, 112, 114,
        123, 128, 133, 148, 149, 164,
        175
        paediatrician 114
    economist 120
    graduates 65
        history 114
    law 63
        judiciary 29, 64, 141
        lawyer(s) xv, 12, 14, 64, 65,
        141
    medical officer(s) 147–9
    medicine 63, 73
    midwives 30, 39
    nurse(s)/ing 9, 14, 65, 81, 112, 114,
        121, 128, 179, 180
        psychiatric 114
    pharmacologists 63
    social work/ers 13, 14, 27, 30, 40,
        65, 73, 102, 112, 114, 128, 139,
        147
    teacher(s)/ing 15, 44, 63, 64, 65, 73,
        75, 76, 77, 83, 87, 101, 102, 112,
        137, 139, 157, 158, 159, 160, 162,
        163, 168, 182
        confessional 83
        General German Women Teachers'
        Union 85
        Union of Catholic German Women
        Teachers 87
        Union of German Evangelical
        Women Teachers 87
    university staff 63, 65

propaganda 23, 29, 31, 32, 47, 55, 64,
        69, 73, 76, 84, 88, 95, 97, 103,
        106, 111, 182, 185
    anti-war 111
prostitute(s) 13, 14, 40, 41, 43, 44, 45,
        119, 124, 144, 151
prostitution 35, 41, 48, 118, 124, 126,
        146 *see also* bordello(s)
Prussia 26, 71, 73, 102, 182, 185
    East xvii, 12, 102, 174
public health offices 27
public transport 60, 62, 81, 97
    railway (*Reichsbahn*) 61, 182
    railway stations 170

race/racial(ly) 12, 23, 25, 26, 27, 65, 87,
        90, 122, 125, 131, 137, 138
    'biology' 70
    body 25, 33
    character/identity 18, 143
    'crimes' 118
    'defilement'/'pollution' 47, 146, 153
        'polluting German blood' 48
    elite 43
    'enemy/ies' 33, 35, 48, 63, 71, 96, 98,
        126, 138
    hierarchy 143
    'hygiene' 26, 34
    'inferior' 12, 47
    'nordic' 12
    policy/ies 23, 27, 104, 125
    prejudice 23, 33, 63, 70, 138
    see also 'Aryan(s)', persecution/ed
    state 25, 138
    theories of racial development 12
        'valuable' 12, 13, 16, 19, 20, 25,
        26, 27–33, 37, 38, 39, 41, 42, 43,
        46, 48, 55, 65, 72, 75, 78, 88, 89,
        91, 92, 94, 96, 98, 114, 125, 131,
        145, 150, 182, 183
    'value' 12, 16, 19, 31, 33–4, 40, 69, 90,
        123, 131, 144, 147
    'worthless' 12–13, 16, 20, 26, 30, 33,
        36, 37, 40, 65, 90, 114, 116, 117,
        123, 125, 143, 147
race-hatred 135
'race question' 161
racism/ist 25, 34, 75, 89, 117, 124, 126,
        185, 186

radio 68, 92, 102, 105, 159, 171, 173
rape 107, 124, 126, 140, 175, 176
rationing xvi, 62, 98, 99, 101, 171,
    172
  clothing stamps 100
  non-rationed goods 172
  ration card(s) 99, 100, 102, 103, 112,
    170, 174
rations 120, 122
  food 120
RdK (*Reichsbund der Kinderreichen*) xv, 48,
    92, 182
Reagin, Nancy 82, 89
rearmament 54, 59, 66, 94, 97, 154
Red Army 96, 103, 106, 107, 121, 126,
    171
  Soviet soldiers 175
Red Cross 57, 89, 105
Reese, Dagmar 75, 76
refugees 100, 102, 106, 135
Reichsbund Deutsche Familie
  letter centres 48
Reichsfrauenführerin 85, 185
Reichsfrauenführung (RFF) 89, 91, 92, 103,
    104
  Press and Propaganda section of 92
Reichsnährstand 68, 79, 90, 154, 183
Reichstag xiii, xiv, 17, 51, 183
religion 11, 88
  see also Christian churches
religious 11, 13, 82, 85, 86, 87, 89, 128
Rempel, Gerhard 134
reproduction/ive 5, 7, 23, 25, 27, 28, 30,
    33, 40, 52, 55, 60, 123, 125, 126,
    131, 133, 136, 144
resources 57
Reysz, Rosel 105
Rhineland 12, 112
RLB *see* air-raid: protection
Romania 14, 104
Rosenberg, Alfred 17, 139, 143
Rosenhaft, Eve 5, 114
Rüdiger, Jutta 77, 185
Ruhr 101, 112
rural 6, 12, 47, 50, 67, 92, 101
  women 15, 18, 39, 40, 101, 135, 139,
    152
Russia(n) 107, 123, 171, 175
Rüthers, Hella 113, 119

SA (Storm Troopers) 17, 83, 84, 157, 177,
    178, 179, 183
Saarburg 87
Saldern, Adelheid von 92, 126
'Salon Kitty' 41
Schäffer, Margarete 112
Schirach, Baldur von 163
Schleswig-Holstein 132
  Itzehoe 132, 137
  Satrup 176
Schoenbaum, David 125
  'secondary racism' 125
Scholl, Sophie 110
Scholtz-Klink, Gertrud xiv, 84, 85, 86,
    88, 89, 90, 91, 93, 103, 104,
    106, 111, 135, 136, 139, 166,
    185 *see also* Nazi women's
    organizations: NSF/DFW: leaders;
    Reichsfrauenführerin
school(s) xiv, 33, 62, 70–5, 81, 101, 116,
    139, 144, 158, 160, 163
  Adolf-Hitler-Schools 74
  coeducation 73
  confessional 72, 75, 87
  elementary 66, 70, 71, 73, 158
  Jewish 71
  middle 71, 76
  Napoleas 74
  private 76
  senior xv, 63, 71, 72, 73, 74, 76, 159, 163
Schoppmann, Claudia 44
Schupetta, Ingrid 58, 122
SD – *Sicherheitsdienst* 36, 40, 56, 69, 78,
    132, 183
separate spheres 4, 128
  private sphere 4, 19, 20, 23, 27, 37, 93,
    115, 125, 128, 135, 144
  public sphere 4, 7, 16, 19, 23, 27, 93,
    128, 135
service 18, 68, 70, 79, 80, 81, 83, 88, 93,
    132, 134, 163
  National Service 155
  service projects 18 *see also* Nazi service
    schemes
sexism 25 *see also* prejudice: misogynist/
    sexist
sexual: abuse, 107, 124 *see also* rape
  conduct 41, 43, 44
  favours 69, 108, 123

intercourse 26, 47, 81
  adultery xvii, 48
  morality 35, 43
    double standard in 35, 41, 47
  promiscuity/ous 35, 41, 102, 115
  relationships 47, 115, 124, 150, 152, 153
sexuality 41, 43, 44
sexually transmitted diseases 38, 44, 45, 46, 47, 175
  gonorrhea 44
  syphilis 44
shortage(s) 63, 78, 80, 81, 100
  coal/fuel 74, 100
  housing 108
  see also food; labour; wartime
Shorter, Edward 44
Siemens 61, 120
Silesia 12, 66, 102
  Upper 102
Slav(s) 12, 116
  Sorbian 116
social engineering 20, 80, 101
Soviet Union (USSR) xvi, 6, 23, 55, 96, 106, 107, 121, 122, 123, 136
  constitution 136
  domestic policy 15
  Five Year Plan 15
  October Revolution 6, 15
  Politburo 136
Spanish Civil War 96
SPD see political parties
Speer, Albert 56, 57, 186
Speitkamp, Winfried 134
Sprengel, Rita 120
SS – Schutzstaffeln 39, 42, 43, 74, 78, 100, 106, 113, 114, 118, 119, 120, 121, 151, 175, 180, 183, 185
  Das Schwarze Korps 43
  female auxiliary corps 78
  leadership 120
  wives of 113
sterilization xiv, 25, 26, 34, 35, 36, 41, 45, 65, 114, 116, 117, 123, 125, 126, 132, 137, 139, 143, 145, 146, 147, 149, 186
Stettin 164
Strasser, Gregor 84, 186
student(s) 14, 53, 71, 72, 74, 75, 79, 80, 139, 161, 162, 163 see also university

Stuttgart 99, 101, 103, 167, 168, 169, 173
Sudetenland xvi, 91, 182
Szepansky, Gerda 46, 75, 95, 102

tax 30, 42, 62, 66
Thalmann, Rita 113, 126
The Racial State 25
torture 112, 113, 114, 126
'total war' 54, 56, 94, 172, 185
  Goebbels' speech on 56
trade unions 110, 119, 136, 177, 181
traditional 6, 8, 9, 10, 19, 29, 37, 39, 40, 50, 52, 55, 59, 61, 65, 67, 75, 82, 110, 112, 115, 134
Trier 157, 158
Tröger, Annemarie 61, 131

Ukrainian 66
Ulm 179
university(ies) xvi, 7, 71, 72–5, 78, 80, 161, 163
  Abitur (university entrance) 75
  ANSt (Nazi women students' group) 75, 79, 96, 185
  arts subjects 74, 162
  Berlin 161, 162
  economics 74
  Freiburg 161, 162
  Giessen 162
  Göttingen 162
  Halle 161, 162
  law 74
  Marburg 161, 162
  medicine 72, 74, 162, 163
  natural sciences 162
  pharmacy 74
  sciences 72, 74
  Technical 74
  Würzburg 161, 162, 185
'Untermensch' ('subhuman'), 47, 60, 123
urban 3, 6, 8, 11, 17, 61, 68, 76, 101

Vatican xiv, 76, 181
Versailles treaty xiii, 17, 71, 94, 95
victims 4, 109, 114, 115, 117, 118, 124–6, 128, 138, 148
Viermetz, Inge 114
Vogt, Marthe 63

Völkischer Beobachter 152
Volksgemeinschaft (people's ethnic
 community) 19, 20, 79, 101, 132,
 134, 146, 161, 169, 170, 171, 183,
Volkssturm (home guard) 106, 175

wages/pay 59, 62, 66, 68, 105, 120, 122,
 136
 equal pay 136, 137
 unpaid 105
Wagner, Robert 84, 186
Walb, Lore 81
war xvi, 4, 8, 14, 29, 39, 42, 43, 44, 45,
 46, 47, 48, 49, 50, 54, 55, 56, 57,
 58, 59, 60, 62, 65, 66, 67, 68, 69,
 72, 73, 74, 75, 77, 78, 80, 82, 91,
 93, 94, 95, 96, 98, 99, 100, 105,
 106, 111, 112, 115, 117, 120, 121,
 122, 125, 126, 128, 132, 134, 139,
 140, 151, 154, 155, 156, 161, 162,
 169, 170, 171, 172, 174, 175, 179,
 185
 economy 23, 154, 155
 First World War (1914–18) 7, 17, 54,
  57, 94, 95, 152, 155, 172, 173,
  180
  stab-in-the-back 94, 98
 home front 17, 94, 96
 industry/ies 61, 180
 Second World War 13, 14, 38, 46, 48
  wives' allowance 56, 68
 total war 54, 94
war-effort 54, 67, 82, 95, 120, 121, 154,
 163
war-weariness 171
Wartheland 104, 182
wartime 8, 38, 46, 54, 55, 58, 61, 62, 66,
 68, 69, 74, 75, 79, 81, 94, 103,
 105, 128, 132, 133, 134, 135, 139,
 140, 154, 156, 158, 161, 165, 167,
 171, 172, 176
 shortages 171–3
Weglein, Resi 118, 121, 179
Weimar 8, 10, 23, 51, 156
 Constitution 8, 10, 52
 Republic 15
welfare 14, 40, 60, 61, 64, 81, 83, 87, 88,
 89, 93, 106, 114, 117, 140, 145,
 147, 154, 169, 170

western Europe 55, 104, 121, 122, 123,
 182
When Biology Became Destiny 25
Wiggershaus, Renate 113
Wilke, Gerhard 135
Winkler, Dörte 51, 57, 66, 92
Winzig 107
Wippermann, Wolfgang 25, 57, 122
Witten 112
Wolters, Rita 115, 126
womanly work/activities 17, 52, 64, 71,
 72, 73, 84, 91, 105
women's magazines
 Deutsche Hauswirtschaft (*German
  Housekeeping*) 92
 Die Deutsche Landfrau (*German Rural
  Woman*) 68
 Die Frau (*Woman*) 85
 Frauenkultur im Deutschen Frauenwerk
  (*Women's Culture in the DFW*) 92
 Mutter und Volk (*Mother and People*) 92
 NS-Frauenwarte (*NS Women's Viewpoint*)
  92, 103
women's organizations 41, 82, 85, 90,
 91, 135, 166
 Baden Women's League 86
 Bund Deutscher Frauenvereine (BDF) xiv,
  82, 83, 85, 181
 Catholic 82, 85, 87
  Women's Union 87
 Christian 83
 churches' 89
 conservative 82, 85, 86, 181
  Bund Königin Luise (BKL) 86, 181
  Ring Nationaler Frauenbünde 86
 Evangelical 82, 87
  Women's Aid 83
 housewives' organization(s) 83, 86, 89,
  92
 JFB – *Jüdischer Frauenbund* xvi, 82, 83,
  87, 117, 182
 nationalist 82, 85, 181
 Newland Movement 82
 SPD 83
 Swabian Women's Union 168
 see also Nazi women's organizations
workforce 68, 155
working class *see* class
Woycke, James 38

Württemberg 12, 76, 78, 81, 86, 91, 99,
100, 107, 108, 123, 132, 169
Heilbronn district 108
Öhringen 91
Swabians 108
see also NSDAP: *Gau* Württemberg-
Hohenzollern

young women 30, 56, 57, 58, 61, 62, 65,
66, 68, 77, 79, 80, 90, 93, 103,
104, 106, 111, 117, 132, 134, 135,
139, 165, 171
youth organization(s) 19, 44, 75, 76, 112

Catholic 76
confessional 76
dissident 77
Edelweiss Pirates 77
Rebels (Meuten) 77
Swing Youth 77
Evangelical 76, 111
see also Nazi Youth organizations:
BDM, Hitler Youth, *Jungmädel*
Yugoslavia 96

Zander, Elsbeth xiii, 83, 84, 85, 181, 186
Zielinski, Senta 124